GHOSTS OVER THE BOILER

GHOSTS OVER THE BOILER

VOICES FROM ALABAMA'S DEATH ROW

Project Hope to Abolish the Death Penalty

Edited by Katie Owens-Murphy

VANDERBILT UNIVERSITY PRESS
NASHVILLE, TENNESSEE

Unless otherwise noted, photographs are courtesy of the University of
North Alabama Archives & Special Collections Alabama Death Row Archive.

Poems by Darrell B. Grayson were previously published in
Against Time: Poems, Birmingham, AL: Mercy Seat Press,
2005. Used with permission.

FRONTISPIECE: "My View of the World," drawing by
PHADP member Kenny Smith, 2002.

LIBRARY OF CONGRESS CONTROL NUMBER: 2022951521
ISBN 978-0-8265-0529-3   (paperback)
ISBN 978-0-8265-0530-9   (EPUB)
ISBN 978-0-8265-0531-6   (PDF)

CONTENTS

INTRODUCTION

Katie Owens-Murphy

How does one begin to tell the story of an organization that routinely outlives its members? One of the astonishing features of Project Hope to Abolish the Death Penalty (PHADP), the nation's only 501c3 non-profit generated and operating from death row, has been its longevity. I first came into contact with this group through one of its only surviving veterans: Gary Drinkard, the nation's ninety-third death row exoneree, whose harrowing account of false conviction and its aftermath is documented in this volume. Though he was exonerated in 2001, Drinkard continues the work he began as a member of PHADP and has been advocating for the abolition of the death penalty for more than twenty years.

Most members of PHADP, however, are executed. Alabama is "unrelenting in the pursuit of the death penalty," as board member Bart Johnson states in our interview, an insight borne out by the numbers: Alabama leads the nation in the number of people sentenced to death per capita.[1] Executions are doubly macabre for surviving members who experience them as personal foreshadowing as well as personal loss. These events are observed, documented, and mourned through rituals that include vigils inside the prison during which PHADP members wear "pressed whites," typically reserved for visitation days, along with a purple ribbon—PHADP's symbol for mourning, which appears in the group's logo.[2] In a showing of solidarity, the men refrain from sports and activities and circle up to share words of remembrance and grief.

Executions are not only traumatic for PHADP, they disrupt the group's organizational structure. PHADP's quarterly newsletter, *On*

Wings of Hope, which provides the most continuous written record of the group's activity, is frequently punctuated by death, especially in the introductory column that frames each issue, "Greetings from the Editor's Desk." Early issues feature editorials written by Brian Baldwin, one of PHADP's chief architects, but in this same column, he is eulogized by Darrell Grayson in the Summer 1999 issue with a grave passing of the torch. "As you know, Brian—we called him 'B'—held this Editor's Desk with distinction," wrote Grayson, "which I shall endeavor to emulate as your next rational voice from the bowels of this man-made hell."[3] Eight years later, Grayson prepares for his own transition in the Spring 2007 edition: "As you should know, the conclusion to my condemnation is to proceed on July 26, which would make this my last editorial for publication. What to say?"[4] Living in such close proximity to death, some PHADP members become despondent. Jeffery Lee laments in our interview that some seem to have "lost focus" while others fall into long periods of depression or even commit suicide.[5] This, too, is reflected in the turnover in the board's structure.

Against all odds, PHADP has not only survived but thrived for more than thirty years on Alabama's death row. This curated collection blends present members' accounts with historical accounts from abolitionist allies on the outside, including Esther Brown, who has served as the group's executive director for more than twenty years. Spanning more than two decades' worth of writings from the group's quarterly newsletter, this book tells a story not only of PHADP and its extraordinary self-advocacy but also of the policy and practice of capital punishment in Alabama and in the nation.

The group's origin story is rooted in a cry for help that became a call to action. Cornelius Singleton (fig. 1), who struggled with a developmental disability, asked his friends on death row for assistance. No physical evidence linked him to the 1977 murder of Sister Ann Hogan, a Catholic nun with whom he had no connection. Unable to read or write, Singleton had been coerced into signing an "X" next to his name on a confession written by police before he was appointed an attorney. The prosecutor in his case had struck nine potential Black jurors from the pool, and Singleton, who was Black, was convicted of

FIGURE 1. Cornelius Singleton

capital murder by an all-white jury. The Alabama Court of Criminal Appeals denied Singleton's requests for a rehearing in 1983 and 1984. Failed by the justice system, Singleton turned to his peers for advice and intervention. Yet even attempts by outside organizations such as the NAACP, Amnesty International, Sisters of Charity, and the Catholic Archbishop of Mobile to intervene on his behalf were unsuccessful. Singleton was electrocuted in 1992. The Supreme Court ruled in *Penry v. Lynaugh* (1989) that executing the mentally handicapped does not qualify as cruel and unusual punishment, a verdict that would not be overturned until 2002 in the *Atkins v. Virginia* ruling.[6]

Unfortunately, the issues at work in Singleton's case are patterns, not outliers, within the history of capital punishment in the US. As the number of death row exonerations would indicate—190 in the modern era, and counting—many capital cases are marked by thin or flawed circumstantial evidence, police and prosecutorial misconduct, inadequate legal counsel for vulnerable defendants, and pervasive racial bias in all stages of the investigation and trial.[7] Tired of feeling hopeless and unprotected by the courts, the men on Alabama's death row decided to take a new approach: to educate the public about the patterns of inequality that shape the practice of capital punishment, and to advocate for an end to the death penalty from death row.

Project Hope to Abolish the Death Penalty (PHADP) is the phoenix that rose from Singleton's ashes. PHADP was founded in 1989 by

FIGURE 2. Jesse Morrison

Wallace Norrell Thomas and Jesse Morrison (fig. 2). Together, they created a name and structure for the organization and began to develop a membership. In December 1989, they held their first meeting in the visitation yard with outside allies. They also launched a newsletter in order to better reach the public. The abolition of the death penalty, they realized, would never happen if the public did not achieve some level of critical consciousness. Their first articles, "From Alabama's Death Row" and "Black America and the Death Penalty," were sent to Black churches, colleges, and newspapers, as well as to friends and family. Realizing that their message would meet many challenges in a red state in the Deep South, the group cemented its mantra to "Be the Other Voice!" (fig. 3).

Yet these founders did not remain in place for long: Thomas was executed in 1990, and Morrison, who secured a new trial, was resentenced and transferred to another facility where he continued to serve as "chairman emeritus" and advisor from afar. These early vacuums set the tone for the challenges inherent in an organization that operates from death row.

Part I, "Beginnings: 1990–2005" chronicles the group's early development as the members rebuilt their leadership structure. Brian Baldwin quickly stepped up, creating an initiative to expand the

Be the Other Voice!

Jesse Morrison, HOPE President

The primary emotions supporting the death penalty are anger
and fear, based on ignorance.
These emotions supply the energy that has turned the argument into a virtually one-sided
affair, giving the impression that
America speaks on this issue with only One Voice.

But we in opposition to state killing are greater in
numbers than the polls indicate. Our battle is to
become an effective voice of opposition, the Other
Voice of reason and compassion. More of us must
speak out to create a true grassroots movement that
will end capital punishment.

State killing not only kills the body of an individual, it kills the spirit of a society. Bringing an end to the
death penalty is therefore not a single, limited objective, but a step toward the elimination of all injustice.
It is the next great social frontier to be conquered. We
believe HOPE can play a vital role in this great work.
Will you help? Your energy and commitment are
needed. Speak out for the right! Be the Other Voice!

FIGURE 3. "Be the Other Voice!" by Jesse Morrison, 1990

organization's newsletter by featuring a range of columns authored by
different people on Alabama's death row; printed and distributed quarterly, it was beginning to reach a wider readership. Baldwin's poignant
piece "Killing the Scapegoat Won't Solve the Problem" established the
strategy behind PHADP's work of building a broad coalition of abolitionists across political, religious, and racial lines for structural change.
Working closely alongside Baldwin was Gary Brown, who helped to
recruit other members on the inside and authored a newsletter column called "The Christian Perspective." Yet the addition of ally and
"outmate" Esther Brown accelerated the group's progress in unprecedented ways. Raised in Germany during the Second World War, her
sensitivity to state power and state-sanctioned murder was rooted in

her own family's history: her uncle by marriage had been part of the plot against Hitler.

Esther Brown initially traveled to Alabama to help investigate Brian Baldwin's case. Unfortunately, her efforts were too late: Baldwin (fig. 4), whose "confession" was coerced through torture and who was sentenced to death by an all-white jury, was executed by the state of Alabama in 1999. Yet her continued devotion to PHADP and its mission enabled the group to establish 501c3 status in 2001 and to secure outside donations and grants that would allow them to distribute their newsletter more widely. She agreed to serve as executive director "for one year," as she recounts; to date, she has served for more than two decades on a strictly volunteer basis. Darrell Grayson (fig. 5) succeeded Brian Baldwin in 1999 and assumed not only the editor's desk but chairman duties, as well. Grayson worked closely with Brown to bring the organization into greater alignment with advocacy groups on the outside.

FIGURE 4. Brian Baldwin

Part II, "Will You Hear Me Now?: 2005–2009," follows the organization as it begins to find its unique voice and reach new audiences through public-facing advocacy and coalition-building. PHADP had already cultivated relationships with the Equal Justice Initiative, the Alabama New South Coalition, and Alabama Arise. During this time, they also initiated a relationship with the Alabama State Conference of the NAACP. Within each organization, Brown worked to ensure that death penalty abolition became a top priority: Alabama's NAACP, for example, became the first state conference with a Death Penalty Moratorium Committee, which she chaired. PHADP continued to develop this initiative with Senator Hank Sanders, a Democratic state representative, culminating in a decades-long push for a statewide moratorium on capital punishment. Individual members of PHADP found their own unique voices in the newsletter, as well. Darrell Grayson published a number of poems related to capital punishment, time, mortality, and hope before his own execution in 2007. Jeffery Rieber, who chaired PHADP from 2007 to 2015, penned a number of important opinion pieces including "Reductive Language," which makes an early contribution to current critical conversations about the labels that plague incarcerated people. During this period, PHADP also conducted advocacy-based research, including a 2005 poll they commissioned with the Capital Survey Research Center to gauge attitudes toward the death penalty in Alabama.

Part III, "The Killing Machine: 2009–2011," depicts a particularly difficult era for PHADP. The state accelerated its execution rate during this three year period, killing six people in 2009, five people in 2010, and six more in 2011. PHADP began to publicize these executions with the help of a website established in 2011 and still maintained by outside ally Brandon Fountain. PHADP celebrated its twentieth anniversary amid this flurry of executions, a celebration that was mixed with pessimism and grief in the addresses delivered from the editor's desk. "We thank each of our supporters for helping us through a difficult landmark year," wrote Jeffery Rieber in December 2009.

FIGURE 5. Darrell Grayson

Yet the worst was yet to come. Part IV, "It's the Southern Way: 2011–2015," displays Alabama's ongoing commitment to capital punishment despite a nationwide decline in executions. The material from this section highlights this growing disparity between state and nation through Alabama's desperation to secure execution drugs in the face of a national shortage. The US Department of Corrections turned to European suppliers, but abolitionist pharmaceutical companies in Italy and Denmark refused to supply drugs for capital punishment. Death penalty states scrambled to create their own lethal cocktails in compound pharmacies; many, including Alabama, began to rely on

FIGURE 6. PHADP's board of directors, photos, years unknown. Group 1, back row, left to right: Willie Smith, Gary Brown, William Snyder, Billy Thomas, Kenny Smith; front row, left to right: Ronald Smith, Jr., Dereck Mason, Richard Gaddy, Anthony Tyson. Group 2, back row, left to right: Matthew Reeves, Dennis McGriff, Trace Duncan, Charles Burton, Mark Jenkins; front row, left to right: Corey Maples, Matt Hyde, Jerry Smith, LaSamuel Gamble. Group 3: photo missing. Group 4, back row, left to right: Larry Dunaway, Anthony Boyd, Jeremiah Jackson, Taurus Carroll; front row, left to right: Tony Barksdale, Jimmy Davis, Nicholas Acklin.

midazolam, a controversial sedative that may actually cause fluid to pool in the lungs and essentially drown those who are being executed. The Supreme Court dismissed this evidence in *Glossip v. Gross* (2015) and allowed lethal injections to proceed, but eyewitness testimony of botched executions continues to tell a story of cruel and unusual punishment.

Part V, "Botched Ruling, Botched Executions: 2016–2020," details the fallout from *Glossip v. Gross*, including failures in lethal injection protocol that impacted PHADP's own leadership. Ronald B. Smith, who chaired PHADP from 2015 until his death in 2016, heaved and coughed for fifteen minutes during his execution, which lasted over a half hour.

According to death penalty scholar Austin Sarat, lethal injection carries the highest rate of failure of all execution methods.[8] Highly publicized botched executions in other death penalty states prompted many to explore alternative methods, with some even reverting to electrocution, hangings, and firing squads. Alabama, following Oklahoma, decided to legislate a new, untested method: asphyxiation through nitrogen gas.

The policy and practice of capital punishment was changing so rapidly that PHADP began to implement law classes. Alabama is the only state that does not provide post-conviction legal representation beyond the direct appeal, and because capital cases are uniquely expensive, demanding, and resource-intensive, good counsel is hard to find. PHADP benefits from its relationship with the Federal Defenders of the Middle District and the Equal Justice Initiative, both based in Montgomery, as well as out-of-state attorneys who work pro bono, but large caseloads and limited resources mean that "your attorney is as good as you make them," as the group likes to say. PHADP therefore insists on staying informed about changes in the law so that they can most effectively advocate for themselves. Under the chairmanship of Anthony Tyson from 2016 to 2019, PHADP began offering two law classes, one of which—the Enlightenment group—is dedicated to contemporary issues and policy shifts that often require people to make difficult decisions within very short time frames. In one instance, people on Alabama's death row had only days to decide whether to opt into the newest approved execution method, nitrogen hypoxia, and struggled to reach their legal counsel before the deadline.[9] The Enlightenment group enables PHADP members to share and disseminate information and strategize among themselves.

Anthony Boyd is the current chairman of PHADP (fig. 7). He sees his role as "mak[ing] sure we stay organized, motivated, and relevant to the fight against injustice and ending capital punishment."[10] In the spirit of maintaining the group's motivation, Boyd has worked with Esther Brown to assist the University of North Alabama in the establishment of a permanent historical archive for the group and its activities.[11] Perhaps most importantly, PHADP continues to cultivate the sense of community that pervades these writings. Studies have shown the dislocation, harm, and isolation the death penalty inflicts on families whose loved ones are sentenced to die.[12] PHADP has nurtured connection and community in a place that is designed to render this impossible. When asked during our interview, "What has PHADP meant to you personally?," Boyd replied, "This is my family."

This collection curates PHADP's work with research notes that contextualize this work within the (d)evolution of the policy and practice of capital punishment in the US. It preserves the chronological ordering of the newsletter to highlight the most important aspects of PHADP, including its perseverance despite the continual executions that disrupt the organization's leadership. This chronology also depicts the tension experienced by PHADP as the direction of Alabama continued to move further away from the direction of the nation, particularly during the Obama administration. The December 2008 newsletter depicts hope and even exuberance: "I so wish that my best friend and mentor Darrell Grayson could have been here to see history made when America elected President Obama! . . . This wonderful event has proven to me that all is not lost and that there is hope of becoming the Nation we claim to already be," writes Jeffery Rieber.[13] Yet in the January 2009 issue, his tone returns to despair: "The state has executed two men already this year. Two more have died from disease and the state is trying to execute a person each month."[14] This sense of doom is heightened during the Trump era. In addition to appointing three conservative justices to the Supreme Court, the Trump administration resumed federal executions for the first time since 2003 with extra zeal: while only three people had been executed at the federal level in the modern era, thirteen were executed under Trump, five of them during the last month of his term.

Chronological sequence is also essential to how PHADP experiences capital punishment. Gary Drinkard composed the poem "Twenty-Six Minutes" while awaiting execution for a crime he did not commit (fig. 8). The poem depicts the final sequence of events that culminate in an electrocution. In the poem's margins, Drinkard annotates each event in the sequence, from the holding cell where people are placed on suicide watch to the moment "when they pack cotton

FIGURE 7. PHADP's board of directors, 2019. Back row, left to right: Randy Lewis, Earl McGahee, Jessie Phillips, Sherman Collins, Nicholas Smith; front row, left to right: Bart Johnson (vice chairman), Anthony Boyd (chairman), Jeffery Lee (secretary/treasurer)

up your rectum"—what he often refers to as the "final indignity"—in anticipation of the body's response to death.

These literary writings, which deliberately turn away from euphemism to name and describe the realities of execution, capture experiential aspects of the death penalty that remain largely unexplored by legal narratives. The courts have focused on the question of proportionality raised in *Furman v. Georgia* (1972) and *Gregg v. Georgia* (1976): what crimes warrant capital punishment?[15] This question has been shaped by cases litigated from the deep South, such as *Coker v. Georgia* (1977), *Beck v. Alabama* (1980), *Godfrey v. Georgia* (1980), and *Kennedy v. Louisiana* (2008), and in other cases that examine aggravating factors that contribute to capital sentencing.[16] The courts are also, however, beginning to take up other questions that examine the consistency of capital punishment with the Eighth Amendment. Cases such as *Ford v. Wainwright* (1986), *Thompson v. Oklahoma* (1988), *Atkins v. Virginia* (2002), and *Roper v. Simmons* (2005) have ruled that executions involving the mentally ill, those with intellectual impairments, and minors under the age of eighteen are unconstitutional, and recent cases such as *Hill v. McDonough* (2006), *Baze v. Rees* (2008), and *Glossip v. Gross* (2015) have begun to explore questions regarding execution methods,

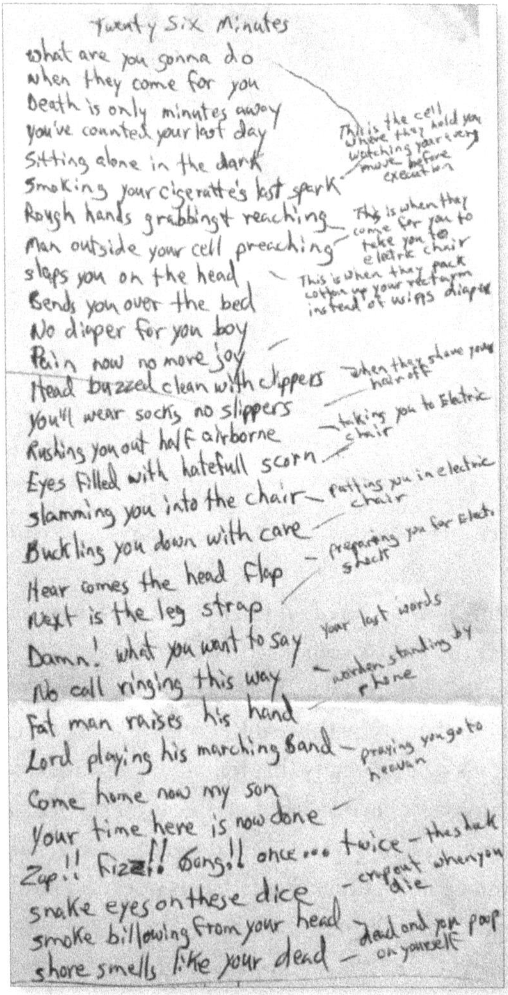

Twenty Six Minutes
what are you gonna do
when they come for you
Death is only minutes away
you've counted your last day
Sitting alone in the dark
Smoking your cigeratte's last spark
Rough hands grabbing & reaching
Man outside your cell preaching
slaps you on the head
Bends you over the bed
No diaper for you boy
Pain now no more joy
Head buzzed clean with clippers
You'll wear socks no slippers
Rushing you out half airborne
Eyes filled with hatefull scorn
slamming you into the chair
Buckling you down with care
Hear comes the head flap
Next is the leg strap
Damn! what you want to say
No call ringing this way
Fat man raises his hand
Lord playing his marching band
Come home now my son
Your time here is now done
Zap!! Fizz!! Bang!! once ... twice
snake eyes on these dice
smoke billowing from your head
shore smells like your dead

This is the cell where they hold you watching your every move before execution
This is when they come for you to take you to electric chair
This is when they pack cotton up your rectum instead of using diaper
when they shave your hair off
taking you to Electric chair
putting you in electric chair
preparing you for electric shock
your last words
warden standing by phone
praying you go to heaven
dead and you poop on yourself

FIGURE 8. Original handwritten manuscript of
"Twenty-Six Minutes" by Gary Drinkard, ca. 1998

as well.[17] Despite these twists and turns, the constitutionality of the death penalty and its methods have been continuously reaffirmed by the Supreme Court in the modern era. Even still, death penalty states such as Alabama do not necessarily follow the federal courts without oversight. As Anthony Tyson wrote in 2016 following the *Hurst v. Florida* ruling, "I am under no delusion that this state will automatically do the right thing."[18] Indeed, the higher courts had to order Alabama's state courts to revise its statutes in light of the ruling. Litigation also spurs legislative backlash that poses new and unpredictable threats: the state legislature developed a bill for nitrogen hypoxia, for example, in response to a lawsuit filed by people on Alabama's death row challenging the use of midazolam during lethal injections.

In contrast to legal "tinkerings," PHADP's writings explore the larger question of *why* we execute over and against the myriad human costs of capital punishment.[19] Some of these pieces consider the state's political motives: Brian Baldwin addresses the governor's manipulation of racial tensions to shore up support for capital punishment through the execution of former KKK member Henry Hays.[20] Other pieces explore economics: Jeffery Rieber details the cost of executions as a talking point for the statewide moratorium, and PHADP has been working with the Alabama Media Group since 2019 to force the state to disclose the cost of executions under the Freedom of Information Act.[21] Still other writings point to what capital punishment costs democracy by exploring the authoritarian power of judges who would often override the recommendations of juries when delivering death sentences and of governors who hold unilateral power to grant or withhold clemency.[22] But the most devastating cost of capital punishment detailed here is the erosion of empathy. The disturbing indifference toward life and death, particularly by correctional staff who work on death row, is depicted through imagined and overhead conversations in poems such as Jesse Phillips's "Do You Remember Where the Line Is S'pose to Go?" and Darrell Grayson's "Ghosts Over the Boiler," which supplies the title for this collection.[23]

Grayson's "Ghosts Over the Boiler" addresses the dehumanization of people on death row through the lens of a suicide (fig. 9). The speaker overhears a conversation between prison staff as they remove the body of the deceased, who had been asking to be relocated to a cell that was "not over the boiler; / He said he couldn't take the heat." As part of their agreement with the state, PHADP does not discuss prison conditions—only capital punishment—but writings such as these provide insight into the sense of helplessness that accompanies long-term isolation.

"What can you do," asks the specter of Darrell Grayson, "When you're a ghost over the boiler?" Still, PHADP continues to meet, print and distribute newsletters, empower one another, and most importantly, strategize about how they can persist, as they put it, in "being the other voice" in the face of a state that continues to organize all of its resources against them.

This collection ends with the ultimate argument against capital punishment by featuring two stories of false conviction: the exoneration of Gary Drinkard and the execution of Nathaniel Woods. Though these stories have very different endings, they both demonstrate the lengths to which Alabama has gone, and will continue to go, to preserve capital punishment. Recently, select death penalty cases have received widespread media attention due to celebrity involvement in cases of false conviction or low culpability. Yet as Keri Blakinger and Maurice Chammah have written, this limited focus on individual cases misses an opportunity to engage the nation in discussions about the systemic inequalities that pervade all capital punishment cases, whether or not defendants are guilty of the crimes for which they have been convicted. "Defense lawyers and prisoner advocates have said that while celebrity involvement can help individuals like [Rodney] Reed and draw attention to the death penalty generally, it can create more disparities in a system already full of them. After all, everyone on death row is appointed a lawyer—not everyone is appointed a Kim Kardashian."[24] Actually, people on Alabama's death row are appointed neither, and in some cases, such as that of Nate Woods, not even Kim Kardashian can save them.[25]

As Jeffery Rieber has written, "The men here are very much aware that working for PHADP will not end the death penalty in Alabama soon enough to save our own lives."[26] Recently, however, there has been renewed reason for hope. On July 1, 2021, President Biden's attorney general Merrick Garland announced a federal moratorium on executions to ensure that "everyone in the federal criminal justice system . . . is treated humanely and fairly."[27] On November 21, 2022, Alabama governor Kay Ivey issued a statewide moratorium on executions, though her reasons were starkly different from Garland's: "For

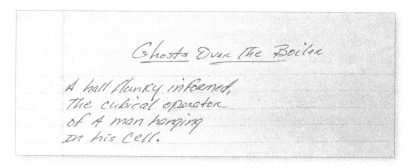

FIGURE 9. Original handwritten manuscript of
"Ghosts Over the Boiler" by Darrell B. Grayson

the sake of the victims and their families, we've got to get this right," she explained.[28] The announcement followed the state's third failed lethal injection over three years, resulting in a singular series of execution survivors: Doyle Hamm, Alan Miller, and Kenny Smith. The moratorium—likely temporary as Alabama perfects its protocol—provides an important opportunity for a statewide reckoning of a system that institutes what Craig Haney has termed "death by design."[29] *Ghosts Over the Boiler: Voices from Alabama's Death Row* contributes to this reckoning by serving as a literary-historical record of execution practices and, most importantly, of the remarkable organized resistance to capital punishment by Project Hope to Abolish the Death Penalty. This book is dedicated to PHADP's members, past and present; to those who seek to interrupt, rather than perpetuate, cycles of violence; and to those who invest in hope as they envision a future built on abolition.

NOTES

1. See "Interview with PHADP," p. 22 of this volume.
2. Ibid, p. 28.
3. See "Greetings from the Editor's Desk," Summer 1999, p. 52 of this volume.
4. See "Greetings from the Editor's Desk," April–June 2007, p. 119 of this volume.
5. See "Interview with PHADP," p. 24 of this volume.
6. *Penry v. Lynaugh* (1989), 492 US 302; *Atkins v. Virginia* (2002), 536 US 304.

7. *Death Penalty Information Center*, https://deathpenaltyinfo.org/policy-issues/innocence.

8. Austin Sarat, *Gruesome Spectacles: Botched Executions and America's Death Penalty* (Redwood City, CA: Stanford University Press, 2016).

9. PHADP and Katie Owens-Murphy, "Choose Your Own Homicide: Tinkering with the Machinery of Death in Alabama." *Mississippi Quarterly* 74, no. 1 (2021): 125–42.

10. "Interview with PHADP," p. 21.

11. The Alabama Death Row Archive can be accessed through the University of North Alabama's Repository of Open Access Research at https://ir.una.edu/collection/1dd9837a-f5a0-4662-a474-4c253b40b49e.

12. Walter C. Long, "Trauma Therapy for Death Row Families," *Journal of Trauma and Dissociation* 12, no. 5 (2011): 482–94.

13. "Season's Greetings from the Editor's Desk," October–December 2008, p. 137.

14. "Greeting from the Editor's Desk," January–March 2009, p. 142.

15. *Furman v. Georgia* (1972), 408 US 238; *Gregg v. Georgia* (1976), 428 US 153.

16. *Coker v. Georgia* (1977), 433 US 584; *Beck v. Alabama* (1980), 477 US 625; *Godfrey v. Georgia* (1980), 446 US 420; *Kennedy v. Louisiana* (2008), 554 US 407.

17. *Ford v. Wainwright* (1986), 477 US 399; *Thompson v. Oklahoma* (1988), 487 US 815; *Atkins v. Virginia* (2002), 536 US 304; *Roper v. Simmons* (2005), 543 US 551; *Hill v. McDonough* (2006), 547 US 573; *Baze v. Rees* (2008), 553 US 35; *Glossip v. Gross* (2015), 576 US 863.

18. "A Christian Perspective," April–June 2016, p. 255 of this volume.

19. Justice Harry Blackmun famously stated that we would no longer "tinker with the machinery of death" by trying to rationalize executions. *Collins v. Collins* (1994), 510 US 1141.

20. "Killing the Scapegoat Won't Solve the Problem," p. 44 of this volume.

21. Rieber, "The Fiscal Distress Caused by Capital Punishment," p. 71 of this volume; see PHADP's letter to the Alabama Media Group on p. 303 of this volume.

22. See Anonymous, "Untitled," January–March 2012, p. 218 of this volume; Arthur Giles, "Mansion of Good and Evil," p. 202 of this volume.

23. Jesse Phillips, "Do You Remember Where the Line Is S'pose to Go?," p. 271; Darrell Grayson, "Ghosts Over the Boiler," p. 93.

24. "Everyone on Death Row Gets a Lawyer. Not Everyone Gets a Kim Kardashian." The Marshall Project, July 16, 2021, https://www.themar shallproject.org/2021/07/16/everyone-on-death-row-gets-a-lawyer-not-everyone-gets-a-kim-kardashian.

25. Kim Kardashian, T.I., and Rhianna were among the celebrities who asked Alabama governor Kay Ivey to stay Woods' execution. See Tamantha Gunn, "Celebrities Ask Alabama's Governor to Put a Stay on Nathaniel Woods' Execution," *Revolt*, March 5, 2020, https://www.revolt.tv/news/2020/3/5/21166989/celebrities-governor-kay-ivey-stay-nathaniel-woods-execution.

26. See "PHADP—On the Inside," p. 185 of this volume.

27. Memorandum, Office of the Attorney General, https://www.justice.gov/opa/page/file/1408636/download.

28. Ivana Hrynkiw, "Gov. Kay Ivey Orders Moratorium on Executions in Alabama," AL.com, November 21, 2022, https://www.al.com/news/2022/11/gov-kay-ivey-orders-moratorium-on-executions-in-alabama.html

29. Craig Haney, *Death by Design: Capital Punishment as a Psychological System* (New York: Oxford University Press, 2005).

EDITOR'S NOTE ON THE TEXT

PHADP's newsletter is typed and formatted on a typewriter at Holman Correctional Facility. I have done light editing to correct obvious typos and errors and have occasionally made small grammatical adjustments to maximize the clarity of a piece. At times, I have edited via excision to help trim and tighten a piece's argument. The format and spacing of the newsletters, which varied widely over the years, have also been standardized for this volume, as have numbers and dates. Otherwise, the following material reflects its original appearance in the group's newsletter. A few pieces were included from sources outside the newsletter, as indicated in the research notes, including final testimonies, interviews, and oral histories with PHADP members as well as poetry from Darrell Grayson's previously published chapbooks. I would like to thank Dale Wisely from Mercy Seat Press for granting permission to reprint Grayson's beautiful poems from *Against Time* here, as well as Pamela Woods for allowing us to print her brother Nate Woods's poem, "The Man He Killed."

Because this project seeks to preserve and amplify the unique voice, tone, and orientation these members have to their work with PHADP, it is minimally curated through the selection of pieces and the addition of contextual research notes. I have regularized capitalization for consistency, with one illuminating exception: the regular column titled "Greetings from the Editor's Desk" frequently ends with the imperative, "Keep Hope alive!" The capitalizations in this phrase vary by editor, which I have preserved to reflect each editor's signature style. That *Hope* is consistently capitalized in this sign-off reveals the group's devotion to what Mariame Kaba calls the "discipline" of hope;

it also reveals the dedication of its members to preserving PHADP as an organization, which they often refer to as "Hope" in shorthand.[1] I have maintained this capitalization to preserve and draw attention to its important double meaning.

Thank you to Gary Drinkard, who first introduced me to this group and has served as a critical advisor on this project, helping to date and contextualize many of the images and writings included in this volume. Thank you to Esther Brown for her tireless work for PHADP, her boundless energy for advocacy, and for her support, communication, and encouragement; this book would not exist without her. I would also like to thank my graduate research assistants Luke Smith and Ashley Massey for their assistance with background research for the preparation of this volume. My greatest thanks goes to PHADP itself—an organization so remarkable that any words I express here will fall short. I can only hope that this volume does justice to PHADP in ways our criminal-legal system has not.

KEEP HOPE ALIVE!

NOTE

1. Mariame Kaba, "Hope Is a Discipline," interview with Kim Wilson and Brian Sonenstein, in *We Do This 'til We Free Us: Abolitionist Organizing and Transforming Justice*, ed. Tamara K. Nopper, 26–28 (Chicago: Haymarket Books, 2021).

PHADP

May 8, 2019

KATIE OWENS-MURPHY: How long has each of you been with PHADP?

JEFFERY LEE: I've been at Holman [Correctional Facility in Atmore, Alabama], this year—October will be nineteen years . . . I've been a part of PHADP since 2002, so seventeen years.

RANDY LEWIS: I've been at Holman since June 26, 2007, and I've been with PHADP since 2008.

ANTHONY BOYD: Oh my goodness. I've been on death row since 1995, and I joined PHADP the same year. You know, we do thirty days on a single walk. That means you had to walk alone in a cage and not with the group. You also had to shower alone, and not in the shower rotation with the group. They pretty much evaluate you to see how you're going to behave or react when you're around everybody else. After my thirty days I was invited out to PHADP and I paid attention, I liked what I heard, and I immediately joined. Really and truly my duties as the chairman of PHADP are dictated by our Articles of Organization, our Constitution, and influenced by the actions of past chairmen and members. I'm driven by the desire, responsibility, and obligation to do what is best for the organization. I speak with our executive director, Esther Brown, daily to organize and coordinate organizational matters at the home office. It is also my job to make sure our quarterly newsletter *On Wings of Hope* has enough meaningful articles and information. I make sure we stay organized, motivated, and relevant in the fight against injustice and ending capital punishment.

BART JOHNSON: I arrived here in June of 2011. I came to a meeting probably in 2012 or '13. I've been six years active in PHADP. My title is vice-chairman—and that is important in that it is a guiding and leadership frame, but it also is trying to find a path that moves us forward so that we don't get stuck. Because when we know we're up against so many barriers, it's really easy just to take the status quo and say, ok, this is where we're at, and this is what we do. But we have to go a step further because Alabama specifically is unrelenting in the pursuit of the death penalty. And this may not be true in some other states. California hasn't executed anybody in many years. The only thing that stops Alabama is the courts. And we know that right now we can change that if we can educate people.

KOM: What is the mission and purpose of PHADP?

JL: When I first joined, the mission was to basically educate not only ourselves but the public about the death penalty and the ins and outs of the death penalty because a lot of us when we first get here— we don't really know much about the death penalty or the law. And so, our family is basically the same way. From my family's standpoint, there really wasn't too much education on the death penalty where I'm from. I think our mission has been a success at times and sometimes it doesn't reach the people in a way that we want it to reach them.

AB: The organization started because the guys felt helpless when another inmate was asking for help—a disabled inmate [Cornelius Singleton] was asking for help. And they didn't know what they could do or how they could help him. Even though they couldn't change the course of that, they wanted to be able to do something to indicate and bring awareness toward the injustices and what was going on with the death penalty: how to educate the families, their families, so they could know what they could do. So that's how it started. And over the years it took shape and form and, because the administration allowed it to happen, we came through the years, we learned. Started a newsletter. Got grant money. As time progressed, we learned more issues, learned how to fight these issues, learned how to cater the arguments to the pro-death penalty circles. You know, you have to be able to stand on the truth. You have to be able to stand on the fact, and not just raw emotion. And that's what we do: we put the facts out there. And no one can debate us on the stuff they say the death penalty does. It's not a deterrent, it doesn't bring closure, it's not financially feasible, and it serves no purpose in our society.

BJ: The purpose [of PHADP] is in the name. We want to end the death penalty. That has changed over time. It started with the need and the desire to meet the need. And that's when things happened. It was obviously a need for support for the individual, and we still try to do that. We try to do it before they set a[n execution] date. We're all in this together. I can't tell you that's universal for everybody on life row. I call death row "life row" because I prefer to think of it that way. I prefer to think that there is life here, and not the other way around. But you know a significant portion of Alabama's death row is at another facility [Donaldson Correctional Facility].[1] And that does make things a little bit harder. Prisoners can't write other prisoners.

KOM: So if you can't write to other people in prison, how do you communicate with folks over there?

BJ: That's the thing. Largely, we don't. It's not impossible, but it's impractical for us to try to maintain anything in two places. We have a tough show of maintaining things here. But there's only one execution chamber, and it's here. And so this next week there is an execution date set and the guy was housed in Donaldson and they took him down here. It gives us a chance to at least meet him and at least offer him the encouragement we can offer. But it doesn't really give us time to build any relationship, you know. If somebody's got to count on you, there's got to be some trust there, and we haven't really had time to build up any kind of trust for him to be able to lean on us for support. But we genuinely want people to know that we're here for them. Not just when we're going to law classes or we have a church service and we get to see them face-to-face or have a PHADP meeting or class. We want them to know that when they go around the corner—that's what we call it when there's an execution date—when they move them to the execution cell, that we're still with them, we're still praying for them, we still have their back. And then when they go to the execution chamber, we would hope that part of what we do as life row is to let people know that, even at the end, we're still with them.

KOM: How else has the organization changed over time?

RL: As far as our supporters: we have gained supporters over the years. Like in the sense that people have even heard of our operations by way of some other source or through Esther, through our Facebook page, so we've gained a lot of supporters over the issues throughout the state as well as the nation.[2] A lot of help gaining those supporters is from the guys who have gotten out there and went home from death row. So, it's gonna allow support in light of those guys being released.

AB: Over the years, we've learned how to get our points across and spread the word and get more people on board, and we've learned how to be more professional . . . because you're talking about guys that are locked up in prison. Nine out of ten people in here —their education stopped in seventh grade, eighth grade. You know, it's very rare to find [that] someone in here actually got a high school diploma. So we had to learn a lot. And when we learned, we progressed. We taught each other some things, and some things we read up on. We didn't know anything about putting a newsletter together, and we were able to learn how to cut it, to format it, and to type it all up, and we got that done. So we kept progressing.

JL: It seems like gradually and over time, as people get here and get steeped in the ins and outs of prison, their focus becomes—not about educating themselves, and educating others about the death penalty—it seems their attention just wavers off of it. Right now, we only have one sub-board meeting, and we have the enlightenment class and the law class. It seems like guys have gotten used to being comfortable with their surroundings and atmosphere. So I think the change is, you have lost focus of those things.

AB: Now we have a structure, including our meetings. We come out here at 8:00 and we start at 9:00, and we go over information that was sent to us by one of our advisory board members, and we discuss legal issues and moral issues and figure out how best to rebut how much stuff is going on out there. Now we have, with the modern stuff—Esther has our Facebook page up, our website is up, so our reach has become great and far and wide. And we have people on the outside in Europe. So we've expanded. We haven't just become a self-contained organization. PHADP consists of the board and there's three sub-groups: we have the Oppose group, which is the working group, where we do a lot of projects in that group, and then we have the Law group, and then we have the Enlightenment group that teaches the guys the basics of staying on top of their lawyers. A lot of the stuff that we know now, if we had known it then . . . we wouldn't be in this situation. Because the lawyers we had. . . . [sighs] Oh my goodness. But then we have the law class to teach guys the basics of what their lawyers are supposed to do, what they are entitled to, what they are supposed to have. Have these documents, ask these questions, stuff you can do like calling your lawyers, writing your lawyers. Because the courts are not going to kill your lawyers; they're going to kill you. And if your lawyer's missing a deadline, it's like you missed the deadline. So this guy went to school for this, so they're supposed to be on top of it, but if you sit by and it happens, you're just as guilty. So we try to teach guys about staying in contact with their lawyers—writing them, calling them, stuff like that.

JL: When you become part of a sub-board, it's taking from the sub-groups—guys we've known are very keen in their writings, and they're focused on the groups, and the attitude and care outside of PHADP, and when they become a member of PHADP—if we have deadlines for articles, they always meet the deadline, always turning in good articles, not slacking doing the work—they potentially become a member of the sub-board, we vote amongst ourselves to allow them to be a part of the sub-board.

KOM: And then do they move up to the board eventually?

JL: Yes, eventually. We now have an election every two years.

AB: That's how we've progressed. We move the meetings along faster, the more information is coming in. The internet is out there. So that's very helpful to us. As I was talking about the classes: we were able to get three classes in, and administration works with us on that. We have the vigils that we have whenever an execution is scheduled. That Wednesday and that Thursday out on the walk yard for vigils to, you know, pray and talk about the guys that are around and what issues they have before the courts. We give the other guys on death row that have [execution] dates what's going on right then.

KOM: How do your law classes work?

BJ: Some guys come in here and they have no idea what a Batson claim is, right? You know—they don't know what Batson is.[3] These are court cases that set precedent in specific areas. And if you don't have that basis, you need a law class for that. You need a law class to build an understanding of basic legal principles and court filings. But when you are facing execution and really up against the law, then you need a different level of understanding in fact, and so that is what created the law classes. Now of course, it has changed over time because the court cases have changed. It's more about keeping everybody who is in that situation up to speed because, unfortunately, your attorney is only as good as you make 'em. Right now we have two law classes. We started the second law class recently because the information that some guys needed for their cases specifically was not being shared with them. And so we wanted to give them an opportunity, the guys who were in jeopardy, the guys who were in danger—those guys, they needed a different level of understanding. They needed to know different things. But we also have to reach out to them if they've maybe given up. Because when it comes down to it, at the very end, they haven't given up: they fight for their lives. They just have lost the drive, and it's easy to lose the drive when they lock you up and put you in a cell for twenty-three hours a day and say, "this is it for the rest of your short life, this is your existence now." It can be very daunting.

KOM: How does PHADP respond when an execution occurs?

JL: I know when I first got here in 2000, they didn't have an execution until two years later. The first execution I went through, they executed a woman. That was the first execution I experienced. And I was a member of PHADP. Back in those days, we was going to exercise yard on the regular—five days a week. And we was told that we had to put on our dress whites and we had to refrain from activities that were outside and sports. And so that week—you could feel a difference. A lot of times, when that's going on, you don't really see people smiling. You see an intense look on guys' faces. Even the officers—they don't really talk and act like they normally do because they know it's a serious situation. Going into that first week, when it happened, that's when executions were happening at twelve o'clock at night, and so I had never experienced one of them kind of like that. And leading up to that, guys would beat on the bars to signal their support for the executed. But now, it's changed where we still go outside and we still oppose and protest the death penalty in that way. Not only do we do it, but we have people on the street that have vigils, as well. So we have vigils . . . and I think that lately, it's been where we talk about the person if somebody had known them, we talk about what's going on in the person's case—we have to educate people when we can educate them. We try to stay together through things like that.

BJ: What we do before an execution is twofold. We are here to support each other. First and foremost, that's what we do at that time. We try to comfort each other. Yes, we want to be there for the person that's going around there, but it's traumatic for all of us when that happens for one person. We all have to go through that, and so we have to be the shoulder to lean on, the person to talk to. And then when that person has . . . maybe it's a legal issue that's the same as yours, and you feel like that's your only hope—that one legal issue, and this person who's going to be executed also has that same legal issue, and he's denied everything in the courts . . . it can be disheartening, and it can be frustrating. So, we try to be there for each other, lift each other up, and that's in here. Of course, out there, we try to put the word out. Esther does execution alerts on the website and Facebook with information. There are different reasons why some executions are more egregious than others, and there are some of these that have legitimate legal issues that, because of the ways the courts work, they were not able to be made. This gives people on the outside the opportunity to contact the governor. You may be asking for clemency, or you may be asking for the state not to kill in your name. If you live in Alabama, and the state kills somebody, you are the state. And so, in effect, you are complicit in that, and so if you don't want to be a part of it, you've got to let the governor know.

KOM: What do your vigils look like?

BJ: Inside and outside, we have vigils —some that we participate in here—and we encourage families to not only reach out to the governor to ask her to stop the execution but also we reach out to our families to attend the vigils that they have in Birmingham, Montgomery, Mobile—they have execution day vigils, and they are opposing the death penalty, but it's also an opportunity for people to get together and pray for the victims as well as the offenders. There are two families in each of these executions that are affected. It's not just the victim's family and it's not just our family. There's healing that needs to go all around. And one of the things that we do in our vigil here, if they allow us to walk on the week of the execution: we will go outside, refrain from yard activity—no basketball game or exercising that we normally would do—pressed whites, purple ribbons in solidarity for the person that has the [execution] date, and we will have a prayer service, praying for everyone involved, even the people having to deal with this as a part of their job. The prison officials—they choose to do this, and that's their choice. But for someone in the media to come down here and cover one of these executions—it's not easy to cover something like this because there's a lot of feelings there. And so we have a prayer vigil and of course, we will talk about the person, and if we knew them personally. Some of the guys I've been really close to. I've been moved to tears. It's an opportunity to grieve. Each time, it's different, and they're always hard. We circle up, and there's usually thirty or more guys out there who are circled up and each one of those take away something different, depending on how close they are with the person and what the relationships are like.

KOM: How do you produce and distribute your newsletter?

AB: I do the cutting and the pasting on the newsletter. Many of the guys write the article up or type them up, and we have another guy who's on one of the tiers that helps—he types up the articles when you bring them out. I crop them down to size, I use Elmer's glue, put it back on the articles, glue them in, glue all of the ornaments and the vines in, glue in the officers' [names]; then, when it's all glued and put together, even down to the little postage thing that's on the back page, we send it to Esther, and she takes it to the printer, and the printer prints it off from there. I've got a ruler and a razor blade, and the back of a legal pad, you know the hard part—the brown part—that I do the cutting on with a little razor blade and a ruler to make sure I'm cutting the line straight, and that's how it's done.

BJ: Esther does [the distribution]—she's outside, so she has access to a computer and printer. But the content is from the guys, and then we don't have a set number of pages, and so we have to fit every- thing together. And that's where there's an editing process, and then there's a formatting process. And all of that kind of happens all at once. With everything typed up, we get all of the stuff together. When I say we, it's really Ant [Anthony Boyd]—he does the work. We basically cut everything out and paste it into blank pages. I like it. I think it comes across very well. So we do that here. Then once the glue dries, we mail it out and there's a prayer and labels and then they get delivered. We have a development officer, Brandon Fountain. He moved to South Carolina but he still puts the news- letter on the website. That's something we greatly appreciate. He's moved away but he's still maintained that role. We appreciate when people are willing to—when they're consistent, when they continue to do it. I've only been on life row since 2011 and he's been with us at least since then. And then of course, once we have stuff up on the website. Usually Esther will make a weekly announcement on the Facebook page.

KOM: What role does writing play in your organization?

AB: There's tons of writing in here. Not only does it help to get the information out, it's therapeutic because you have guys in here that

Codes and Laws

In the spirit of thanking people who have come through the doors here at Holman to share their love and support, I want to say thanks to someone here inside Holman on a regular basis with me. However, we have to take a little trip to get to that point. So please bear with me and stay tuned.

I titled this article as I did, because some of us come from backgrounds where those are instilled in us. Codes and Laws. Both instilled in us, guide us, and on some levels define us. Those of us who are true to them. Codes and Laws can even shape friendships. Friendships, we were foolish enough to tell the other, "I'd die for you." Now, that may seem like some dedicated and loyal friendship, and if each truly would hold up such a pact, it is. However, throughout the years, I've come to realize that it takes a special kind of person to hold such codes and laws. Then, over the years, I came to realize that there's been a part of the "I'd die for you" declaration missing, which is, "don't die for me, live for me!"

Which brings me to this guy, this man of whom I will be so bold as to call, MY FRIEND. I didn't know him when I was out learning my codes and laws. This man doesn't owe me anything. However, he still pushes me to "live for him." To live for my family. To Live! He's never asked me, would I die for him, and I've never told him I'd do so. We are friends, without the codes and laws. We are friends, through God's best intentions. We are friends, because we choose to be, and that friendship is defined by mutual respect, and caring.

My friend has not only passed the asking of would I die for him, but he's never asked me to live for him or anyone else either. He's just stayed determined and steadfast in trying to help me live.

So, I would like to say, thank you to my friend. Thank you, for all you've done and continue to do. Please, know that you and all you do is greatly appreciated. You know! (smile)

Respect,
Maximus Strong

Page 6

FIGURE 10. A page from the January–March 2018 edition of PHADP's newsletter, *On Wings of Hope*. It is typed, illustrated, and formatted by PHADP members at Holman Correctional Facility.

have stuff on their minds and they feel trapped, they feel lonely, they feel thrown away, so writing is an outlet really. I was saying earlier about how many guys—there's nine of us on the board—there's eight in each different group at least, but some of the board will still go sit in on those group meetings—when we consider what PHADP is, everybody that's on Alabama's death row at Holman, Tutwiler [Julia Tutwiler Prison for Women in Wetumpka, Alabama], and Donaldson, and we encourage them to write and send it to us, or send it to Esther and send it to us, and we'll put it in the newsletter, because that newsletter is everybody's newsletter. It's not just for the guys who are here—it's for everybody. Even our supporters—our board of advisors, our friends and family—they write articles and send them in. And as long as they're respectful, informative, we have no problem putting them in the newsletter because it's your way—it's your voice. One of our past chairmen and one of the founders, Jesse Morrison, his favorite thing to say was, "Be the other voice." Be the other voice! Be for those in chains. Speak your mind, speak your voice, and speak from your heart. If you're passionate about something, then you should stand up for it. One of my heroes in life is Dr. Martin Luther King, and one of the things he said is "Injustice anywhere is injustice everywhere." When you know something is wrong and you don't stand up, and you're silent because you're worried about what folks are going to think or what they're going to say, then you're not being real. You're doing yourself a disservice.

JL: Writing—it's raising our voices of how we can speak to the public, speak to other people—that's basically our voice. Because I have a story about one of the guys who became a member of PHADP, and he couldn't even write or read. And that's something that PHADP did, when it first started—it actually taught him how to read and to write, the importance of it. And so, to me, that's our voice and our passion. The way that we share not only how we see what's going on on death row, but we see how we got here, and how we can speak to the people about our experience from the inside because you don't really have that voice from in here. And by us being able to not only read literature and stuff but also put together how we see death row in our writings, which to me is one of the most important things we can do because it's our voice. It lifts our voice—it's the most important thing we have. By being able to share our opinions and our outlook on things.

BJ: One the one hand, it's purpose-driven. The goal of this organization is to convince people that the death penalty is wrong. Right now, the courts are the only thing that stand in the way. I would like for us to one day be where people are standing up and saying, "This is wrong. We should not be doing this locally, here." And for that to happen, we need them to understand not simply that it's wrong—because if your moral compass is leaning more toward vengeance than toward compassion, then we have to convince you in a different way. And I think that way is through logic and knowledge. And so when we can teach people about the injustice that is the death penalty and how unfairly it's applied, then we can convince them—and then we can have another way—something coming between us and death other than the courts. So I think that educating—well, we do that primarily through writing. Some people do that through art, some people do that through poetry—but mostly we are writing to educate. Now there's another side that comes with it: it's cathartic. If you can express yourself, then you're not stymied from expressing yourself. And that—in a situation where you are locked up in a cell and you don't have a lot of ways to express yourself, writing is—it's not just because it's viable, but it's a productive way. It's something positive. There's a lot of ways to express yourself that are not going to get you any good outcomes.

RL: For me, it's a way of expression as well as educating our readers. And I write mostly from the perspective of the legalities of the death penalty and what guys go through legally as far as from arrest to pretrial to the trial, post-trial. So I try to bring as much awareness through my literature to the legal aspects of the death penalty. Cause see—I like history. And that's why my study begins—picks up with the history of the death penalty here in Alabama during the Reconstruction years after the Civil War. Statutes were predominantly against African Americans for whites in the states. They had laws like if you look at a white man or a white woman in the face, then that's the death penalty. Stuff like stealing or picking up fruit out of somebody's yard without permission, that was a death sentence. So a lot of those things—there was a reason why the Supreme Court struck them down nationwide. That was the Furman case: *Furman v. Georgia*.[4] They reinstated the death penalty in *Gregg v. Georgia*. Alabama started out with eight [death-eligible offenses], and now they have twenty and are still trying to add more. A lot of the guys fall under now, including myself, fall under the 1982 statutes, and which, in my opinion, based on my research, is unconstitutional.[5] Right now, I'm up under a 1982 statute that allowed for judicial

Constant Oppression
The black experience in America is marked
by one consistent theme: oppression. In
the early days, treated like property, not people.
After the 13th amendment abolished slavery
a new method of oppression came into view.
Because the amendment made an
exception for slavery as a
SUPREME COURT
punishment for
a crime, a system of
laws were put into place to
criminalize all sorts of behavior.

FIGURE 11. "Constant Oppression" by PHADP, 2019

override—the juror override statute that the Alabama Supreme Court struck down as unconstitutional, where a judge overrides the jury to give a death sentence.[6]

AB: One of the things we try to get the guys to understand: write what you feel; write what you think. Get it out! It helps—it's therapeutic. And that's what the writing does. And it lets the people out there know that we aren't the monsters that society tries—or the people in power tries to portray us to be. They'll paint a pretty picture for a political vote. And it's not like that. People who come in here from churches and different organizations can't believe that this is death row from the things that the politicians say. We want the people to see that some people made mistakes in life. And in life you should be able to recover from your mistakes. Some people are mentally challenged back here, mentally disabled, and they have no control over impulses, so instead of giving them help, you punish them, you banish them, you throw them away. So we try to write to express all that. The death penalty is not a tool for justice. Never has been, never will be. It's a tool for revenge. It's a tool to be able to curry favor with people based on emotion. They make families irate. They make the public irate. And then they get elected. [They say] these are the worst of the worst, and they need to be put down, and there's no way we can keep them in our prisons. There's hundreds and thousands of people charged with raping and murder locked up in prisons with sentences right now. Charged with murder, convicted, and sentenced to prison time. So, there's no excuse for "we can't keep murderers in prison." You have life without [parole]. The only reason the death penalty is used is for revenge and a vote!

KOM: What do you think is the most pressing issue related to the death penalty in the modern era?

AB: There's so many things that's wrong with it. If I have to say what's the most pressing issue: it's the racial issue in the death penalty. We just had a guy [Domineque Ray] who was executed in Alabama. They had an issue about his imam.[7] The United States Supreme Court turned him down. And you had a guy in Texas [Patrick Murphy], he was a Buddhist, and he wanted his Buddhist minister to be with him. Texas allows for a Muslim imam and a Christian minister. But he wants provisions for Buddhism. The courts stopped his execution. The exact same issues. You're killing a Black guy, but you spare the white guy. And then it would be the financial bias—whereas if you had money to afford a competent and diligent lawyer, you wouldn't be in this situation. There's no rich people on death row! There's no rich people on death row. It's not gonna happen. And you have states that are going bankrupt to try capital cases. We have had guys that sit here for ten, fifteen years for a new trial because the county that they were from kept saying they don't have the money right now to retry them. How is that justice? It's not his fault that y'all don't have the money to retry him. Don't just leave this man sitting [on death row] because you don't have the money. You're also taking away money from education. Teachers are having to pay for school supplies out of their own pockets. They're having to take donations. They're not getting paid their worth in educating our future. But you want to spend money on killing individuals. That's asinine to me.

JL: I think it's the disparity in the way cases are being tried from the standpoint of class and race. You're less likely to get the death penalty for killing a Black person. Also, rich people don't come to death row. Like right now up in here, you see it's just that most guys, they didn't really come from much. They couldn't afford to hire an attorney. They had a court-appointed attorney. And some of their attorneys that were court-appointed didn't have the expertise to try a capital case. A lot of the lawyers they had in our trials, they were civil lawyers, and they didn't have the expertise or the time to put in to actually handle a death penalty case. That automatically stacks the odds against you. If you have someone that's not used to arguing a death penalty case going up against a [district attorney] and that's his career, to argue a capital case, the defendant is automatically put at a disadvantage.

RL: Coming out of the gate, the prosecutor is enabled with way more resources than an appointed attorney. They have a leg up. These guys, as far as the racial end of it—a Black individual is more likely to be charged with a capital crime as opposed to a white individual in the state of Alabama. And it also plays a role, the victim. If it's a Black individual that killed a white individual, they are more likely to be charged with a capital offense as opposed to a white individual who kills a Black individual. That is the greatest problem that is wrong with the death penalty in the state of Alabama.

BJ: There were 150 exonerations last year. This isn't just death row; this is 150 exonerations in the United States last year. And of those—over 100 of them—that's two-thirds—they had either police and prosecutorial misconduct, or perjury of testimony. And those problems— whatever the motivation, whether the motivation is racism—they highlight the problem that is systemic. And if we can't put the level of faith in the system that a death sentence would require, then we

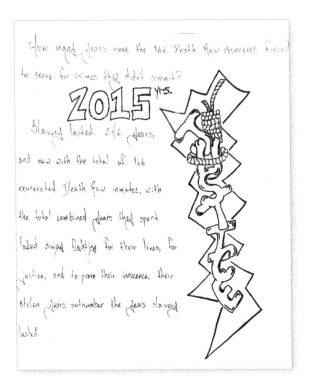

FIGURE 12. "2015 Years" by PHADP, 2019

can't have a death sentence. And so for me—I mean, if you want to look at it in a power dynamic—the problem with the death penalty is we give the state too much power when you give them the power to take a life. Not only should they not have that much power, but it also should not be unchecked. Or, let's say, self-check. That's a basketball term that we use a lot. Somebody needs self-checking. You don't need to defend them; they're just garbage. That's what our system is. It's a broken system that is in charge of itself. So break it down, nuts and bolts: our state should not have that much power, and it definitely should not have that much unchecked power.

KOM: What has PHADP meant to you personally?

BJ: It's family. I never thought I'd be on death row. I never thought I'd be in this situation. I definitely never thought I would have the bonds with these guys that I have. And it's something that you probably wouldn't believe if you hadn't been through it. That's the bedrock of all of this, is the bonds that we make. PHADP stands on top of that. It began because of a broken bond—the state took the life of someone, and we felt that. And so we always, you know, try to keep those bonds intact. You can call it brotherhood, you can call it friendship, you can call it family, but it's the bonds that connect us.

RL: Personally, man, it goes right back to the legal aspect. I've helped to make direction and the guys I associate with take the information provided to them and they can discuss it with their attorneys. So that right there, it means a great deal to me and as far as the spirit of PHADP. Us coming together—the guys—you know, how we conduct ourselves, not just in PHADP but on death row as a unit, so—the reality as far as how we are characterized stands in contrast to what is being publicized to the public. They demonize us. "They don't deserve to live. They're so evil you've got to kill them." But in reality you've got guys looking out for guys here. When any guy gets here, we send them a care package. You've got some guys in PHADP who will look out for the individual until that individual is able to have financial resources to come in. So that's what I would like to add as far as the guys and PHADP as a whole and our roles and what we do.

JL: To me, PHADP as a whole—it's helped me a lot. Because when I first got here, man, hope-wise—I didn't really have that. So when I got here and became a member of PHADP, it's like I changed directions in my life. It allowed me to make a change because not only am I representing myself, I'm representing this organization and the people around me. It gave me a different purpose. The things I used to do—I wouldn't want to do anymore because not only did it look bad on me and myself, it looked bad against the group. You're not only representing yourself, you're representing the entire population back here.

AB: Oh my goodness. Really, PHADP has meant so very much to me personally. It's given me an outlet to do what I like to do. I like to fight. I like to stand up for the less fortunate. I'm in that category, but I've never liked a bully. I never have. And PHADP has given me that avenue to say and do the things that I love to do. And I'm in here with the guys that are intellectually disabled and can't do things for themselves, no matter how hard they try to comprehend. It gives me the opportunity to help people like that. And it's given me the avenues to fight for my life. It taught me the structure of how to better do it instead of just lashing out. It taught me how to better get my point across. I'm so thankful for being accepted—they're my brothers, they're my family. That's what it means to me personally. These are my brothers. This is my family. We can do everything together. But we don't just fight the death penalty together. We don't just try to get reform done in the prison system. We don't just try to educate society about the death penalty. When we're going through stuff with our families, in life, you know, you get depressed. When we're going through stuff like that, we're there for each other, as much as we possibly can. And we give a shoulder. So that's what it means to me. This is more than an organization. It's a family. It has been a family for thirty years. They try to make a circle around you. They try to protect you. That's what they've been doing for thirty years. I'm just a part of it. I'm happy to be a part of it.

KOM: I'm really struck by your organization's focus on hope, which is even in the title that you give to your organization, Project Hope to Abolish the Death Penalty. So my next question is, what hope do you have for the future—either for your organization, or of the death penalty in Alabama, or for yourself personally?

JL: I hope that eventually the death penalty will be abolished. It's not applied fairly, and I don't think killing a person for killing is the answer; that's my belief. That's my hope for the death penalty: that it will be abolished. But my hope for the future of PHADP: that we continue to stay focused and stay committed to fighting this cause from the inside. And that not only does the board and the memories of PHADP continue to stay focused, but the guys who used to be members of PHADP—that they regain a focus and an intent[ion] to come back to be able to enter this fight. Like I said, when I first got here . . . basically, all of us was members of PHADP, and then it just got away from us. But my hope is not only that they come back but that they will become more intent like the board back in those days. And my hope for myself is that I continue to stay focused and maintain my consciousness about what's going on and not lose sight of the bigger picture. To me, the picture is bigger than these bars in front me. The picture is that person that don't know the ins and outs of the legal system. To try to have some kind of educational voice and see where that role can lead you. My hope is to continue to inspire others to look past our mistakes.

RL: As far as the group goes, that I work to bring about a consciousness in the people of the state of Alabama to understand what's going on, what the state is doing in their name, to see how flawed it is, because a lot of people who support the death penalty in Alabama believe it should be carried out fairly. If it's not done fairly, then we should not be executing at all.

BJ: For me, it's reconnecting with my family and getting to get back to life. That's my hope, that's my dream, that's my goal.

AB: Honestly, I hope that PHADP evolves into an organization that no longer fights the death penalty, no longer has to educate the public about the death penalty, and can start to become an organization that has to educate society about the unconstitutionality of life without [parole]—about the injustices of sentencing a person to life in prison. I hope that the abolition of the death penalty in Alabama and nationwide is a thing that comes to pass sooner than later. It is not warranted. It serves no purpose. So I hope PHADP in the future becomes an organization that starts to strictly focus on reform because the abolition of the death penalty will have come to pass. That is my hope.

NOTES

1. There is no longer a death row facility at Donaldson Correctional Facility.
2. Esther Brown also sends updates about PHADP and capital punishment in her "Weekly Notes" to the organization's email list and posts them to the Facebook page.

3. A Batson challenge is a party's objection during jury selection that the other party has used a preemptory challenge to strike a potential juror from the pool based on race, ethnicity, or sex. A Batson challenge may result in a new trial. *Batson v. Kentucky* (1986), 476 US 79.

4. The Supreme Court's verdict in *Furman v. Georgia* (1972) marked the beginning of a nationwide moratorium on the death penalty that would end with *Gregg v. Georgia* (1976). Randy Lewis is describing here the legal and historical shift to what scholars call the "modern era" of capital punishment.

5. "By the end of 1982, 37 states and the Federal government provided for the death penalty. . . . For the first time since the *Furman* ruling, no state's death penalty law had been overturned." "Capital Punishment 1982," *Bureau of Justice Statistics Bulletin*, July 1983, https://www.ncjrs. gov/pdffiles1/Digitization/89395NCJRS.pdf.

6. The authority of a judge to override a jury's recommendation of life imprisonment was abolished by Alabama in 2017 by SB 16 but was not made retroactive. Many people currently on death row were sentenced to die via judicial override.

7. The Alabama Department of Corrections (ADOC) does not allow for anyone except ADOC staff to be present in the execution chamber; only Christian chaplains are on staff. Ray was African American and Muslim and his request for his imam's presence was denied. See Maximus Strong, "A Divided People" on p. 291 of this volume.

PART I

Beginnings

1990–2004

From the Editor's Desk

Brian Baldwin • 1990

On Wings of Hope is a publication of Project Hope to Abolish the Death Penalty. We are hoping that you, the reader, will try to find an understanding of the death penalty in America today.

I, as well as most of the writers in this publication, are on death row. I don't think you will find another publication that is more meaningful, sincere and straight from the heart of the writers than the articles you will read in this newsletter.

This will be an open publication for all who want to be heard. Only in this way will two sides be able to come together and express their views in a rational and fair way.

To better help you understand our writers, it would be helpful to put concentration on finding the message that our writers are trying to share with you. We ask you to see them as writers, not as people of fault.

The writers were asked to express themselves about anything they wanted to talk about. You may find some of the articles to be opinionated to the extent of being offensive; however, we hope to show that inmates on death row have the ability to think, make decisions, and care about other people.

The death penalty is a big concern of ours, but it is not our only concern. We think the loss of life should concern everybody, no matter what the circumstances are. The death penalty in America reduces the value of life. It is vengeance, to stay the least.

What would this country be if everybody sought revenge? Would there be an America?

In closing, I want to say once again, please read the articles to get the message and remember revenge is like a black hole in space. It consumes everything. There is no fulfilling it, but forgiving is like an education. It is forever fulfilling.

Please feel free to send in your comments concerning this newsletter. We want to hear from you, if you agree or disagree.

Killing the Scapegoat Won't Solve the Problem

Brian Baldwin • Spring 1997

In a high-profile case that garnered national attention, Ku Klux Klan member Henry Hays was sentenced to death by an Alabama jury for the 1981 lynching of nineteen-year-old Michael Donald. He was the first white person in Alabama to be executed for a crime against a Black victim since 1913. Governor Fob James refused to grant clemency and Hays' execution was widely heralded as a triumph for racial justice.

Brian Baldwin's piece cautions that Hays' death does nothing to alleviate or rectify the long history of state violence against African Americans in Alabama—including Baldwin himself. Tortured into making a confession through beatings and shocks from an electric cattle prod, Baldwin, who maintained his innocence, was sentenced to die by an all-white jury. Though the only piece of evidence tying him to the crime was his coerced confession, Baldwin would be executed in 1999.

As Remembrance Day approaches, we are sad to say we have lost *HOPE* board member Henry Hays to the electric chair, adding one more to the long list of brothers across the US murdered by the states. On the row here, most of the talk has been about how the state of Alabama was trying to get a badge of courage for killing Henry because he was a white former Klansman accused of killing a Black teenager, as if killing Henry was going to appease all the wrongs the state of Alabama had done toward Blacks over the centuries.

Henry Hays was a poor white who didn't have much of a chance, so he chose to join a group that would find another group to abuse and look down upon to make themselves look better. And now the state of Alabama makes Henry a scapegoat, when the governor of Alabama has said if it was up to him the confederate flag would still be flying

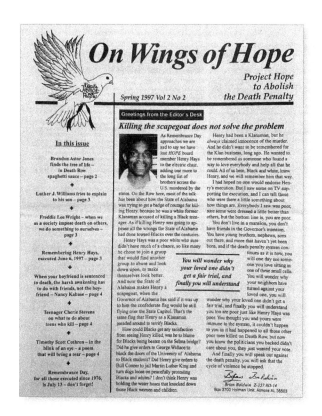

FIGURE 13. "Killing the Scapegoat Won't Solve the Problem," by Brian Baldwin, 1997

over the state capitol. That's the same flag that Henry as a Klansman paraded around to terrify Blacks.

How could Blacks get any satisfaction from seeing Henry killed—was he to blame for Blacks being beaten on the Selma bridge? Did he give orders to George Wallace to block the doors of the University of Alabama to Black students? Did Henry give orders to Bull Connor to jail Martin Luther King and turn dogs loose on peacefully protesting Blacks and whites? I don't think Henry was holding the water hoses that knocked down those Black women and children.

Henry had been a Klansman, but he *always* claimed innocence of the murder. And he didn't want to be remembered for the Klan business, long ago. He wanted to be remembered as someone who found a way to love everybody and help all that he could. All of us here, Black and white, knew Henry, and we will remember him that way.

I had hoped no one would endorse Henry's execution. But I saw some on TV supporting the execution, and I can tell those who were there a little something about how things are. Everybody I saw was poor—sure, some were dressed a little better than others, but the bottom line is, you are poor.

You don't live in a mansion, you don't have friends in the governor's mansion. You have young brothers, nephews, sons out there, and more that haven't yet been born, and if the death penalty system continues as it is now, you will one day see someone you love sitting in one of these small cells. You will wonder why your neighbors have turned against your loved one, you will wonder why your loved one didn't get a fair trial, and finally you will understand you too are poor just like Henry Hays was poor. You thought you and yours were immune to the system, it couldn't happen to you as it had happened to all those other poor men killed on death row, but now you know the politicians you backed didn't care about you: they just wanted your vote.

And finally you will speak out against the death penalty; you will ask that the cycle of violence be stopped.

Will I Be Remembered?

Henry Hays • Spring 1997

On the evening of his arrival at Holman, Henry Hays was greeted by Jesse Morrison and Norrell Thomas, both founding members of PHADP and both African American. Hays came to repudiate his white-supremacist ideology thanks to his involvement with PHADP, a predominantly Black organization. In his recent memoir, African American death row–exoneree Anthony Ray Hinton also recollects his unlikely friendship with Hays, who told him: "Everything my mom and dad taught me was a lie, Ray. Everything they taught me against Blacks, it was a lie."* Hays was a PHADP board member and remained active in the organization until his execution in 1997.

HOPE board member Henry Hays – shown here with one of many long-term pen-friends, Mrs. Judith Moore, of England – was executed on June 6, 1997. We reprint here an essay he wrote a year ago – a message especially relevant as we approach Remembrance Day.

Hank maintained his innocence to the end, despite the outrageous claim of a stranger who visited him the day before the execution, that he had "confessed." Hank told friends just before he was led away this was untrue, and we believe Hank. One friend said "Hank's last day was filled with his ever consistent compassion, as he worried more about how we were holding up than about his inevitable fate." Hank's last words, from the chair, were "I love you." We love you, Hank. And we remember.

Henry F. Hays
Alabama Death Row

Will I be remembered?

July 13th has been established by *Hope* as a Remembrance Day for those executed, plus all victims of crimes. My name could be added to this list, and so I wonder, important "How will I be remembered?"

During the recent primary elections, Alabama Attorney General Jeff Sessions, running for the U.S. Senate, remembered how his diligent efforts and investigative skills sent me to Death Row. Every time Judge Galanos puts on his robe, he looks at his career built on the convictions of me and others. One man even looks on his failures in memory of me: losing an election, he doesn't say, "Maybe my opponent was more qualified." No, he says, "My last name was associated by too many with that convicted killer." It's useless pointing out that although sounding alike,

"Haas" has no connection with "Hays." I was friends for years with Walter McMillan, then saw him leave Death Row after being found not guilty. Does he remember me? In a lifetime, a person has many chances to touch others, either briefly or continuing over the years. We hope the memory is good, but unfortunately sometimes it's bad. The family of the young man I'm accused of killing no doubt will remember me, and not fondly.

My correspondence with many over the years has given me the chance to leave memories of a good nature, hopefully. My daughter will tell my grandchildren about me, and the son I met for the first time just three years ago will remember me, too. I hope their memories will be good! Execution of a person doesn't leave good memories for anyone. It only adds to the bad ones already remembered. For future generations, we need to stop the legal killing by our country.

---

* Anthony Ray Hinton and Lara Love Hardin, *The Sun Does Shine: How I Found Life and Freedom on Death Row* (New York: St. Martin's, 2018), 135.

To Remember Is to Act!

Arthur Giles • Spring 1998

PHADP memorialized those who were executed by the state during "Remembrance Day" ceremonies. They also turned these events into opportunities for direct action. Below, Arthur Giles urges supporters to contact international authorities in order to place moral and economic pressure on Alabama's practice of capital punishment.

Dear families, friends, and people of great and moral heart here and abroad!

Please join us in an International Letter Writing Campaign to our world leaders, especially to members of the United Nations Human Rights Commission, who voted in favor of a resolution calling for a moratorium on and eventual end of the use of the death penalty in the US and other countries.

We feel an earnest show of support and solidarity by the people will go a long way in helping our world leaders who support our cause to stop the executions by our government of its citizens, sooner than later. Because the courage and strength of our leaders is the strength and power of you, the people!

We earnestly ask you on behalf of all the men and women on death row to participate in this effort. We ask that you commit yourself and encourage your friends, family, and church members to write a letter once each month to UN Secretary-General Kofi Annan and to heads of governments supporting our cause, especially those belonging to the European Union (see suggestions [fig. 14]). EU members are bound by treaty to eliminate capital punishment and there is a movement in the European Parliament to persuade member states to discourage business investment in American states with the death penalty.

Your letters should explain your feelings about the issue but should be brief, clearly asking these international leaders to use whatever influence they have to place sanctions on the US to bring an end to the death penalty. Your letters can make a difference! Remember some of the world's greatest feats over evil were accomplished by people who did not believe it was possible. Until victory.

Please help us—Put the pressure on. Ask heads of governments and the UN to do all they can to prevent companies from doing business in states with the death penalty. Remember, international sanctions were a major force in ending apartheid in South Africa, where the first act of the new democratic government was to abolish capital punishment!

Please make your commitment to write at least one letter each month to at least one of the following international leaders (look for further suggestions in the next *On Wings of Hope*):

United Nations:
Secretary-General Kofi Annan
United Nations Plaza
New York NY 10017

Germany:
Chancellor Dr. Helmut Kohl
c/o Ambassador Juergen Chrobog,
4645 Reservoir Rd NW,
Washington DC 20007

United Kingdom:
Prime Minister Tony Blair
c/o Ambassador Sir John Kerr,
3100 Massachusetts Avenue NW,
Washington DC 20008

France:
President Jacques Chirac
c/o Ambassador Francois V. Bujon
de L'estang, 4101 Reservoir Rd NW,
Washington DC 20007

Please remember too that
HOPE is an all-volunteer non-profit
organization with no paid staff.
We depend on your generous
support to continue the struggle.

FIGURE 14. "To Remember is to Act!,"
by Arthur Giles, 1998

Thankful Season's Greetings

Brian Baldwin • Fall 1998

Until the so-called "Fair Justice Act" of 2017 consolidated the appeals process, people on Alabama's death row had opportunities to appeal their capital convictions at distinct times and stages through the Alabama Court of Criminal Appeals, the Alabama Supreme Court, and the US Supreme Court.* The first stage involves an automatic or "direct" appeal related to issues at trial. The second stage, the post-conviction appeal, may involve claims of new evidence in the case, ineffective assistance of counsel, or prosecutorial or juror misconduct. Defendants whose appeals are denied may also petition the court for a writ of certiorari at both stages in order to examine possible constitutional violations. The third and final stage is the federal habeas corpus appeal, which is limited to federal issues raised during appeal in the state courts. Once these appeals are exhausted, people on death row are unable to challenge their convictions any further.

As the song goes, "This is the time of year to be with the ones you love." How we all wish we could be surrounded by family and friends.

This year has not exactly been what I had hoped for—I lost my appeal in the Eleventh Circuit Court, and now I'm preparing to appeal to the US Supreme Court.

I thank God for blessing me with life each day, and for blessing me with the greatest friends in the world.

Losing an appeal in the Eleventh Circuit is alarming. The reality of the electric chair comes forth, demanding attention. But my friends have kept me thinking positive. The guys here on the row are really true friends. They understand my situation in the courts, but they still treat me the same, offering legal assistance as always, and keeping a

---

* See "Greetings from the Editor's Desk," Jeffery Rieber, January–March 2014, p. 236, and "Rush to Kill: Troubling Way to Die" by Randy Lewis, April-June 2017, p. 270 of this volume for PHADP's account of the Fair Justice Act legislation.

positive attitude. Nobody treats me as if I'm doomed. I don't want the sad faces; I prefer the smiles and a handshake.

I am thankful for the members of Murder Victims' Families for Reconciliation. Please remember them in your prayers, as well as all other victims and their families.

I refuse to be bitter. I refuse to hold grudges, because so many wonderful people have offered me love and friendship. All PHADP supporters have shared their love with us simply by reading our message. We are thankful for your support.

Remember, the holiday season is not about how much money you spend on family and friends; it's about reflecting on the love you have shared over the years, and rekindling that love.

the Editor's Desk

Darrell B. Grayson • Summer 1999

For the past four months our hearts have been as leaden with grief and sadness as on any occasion I can recall; and there are quite a few that spring to mind. In due course we've had one stay and two executions, those being Victor Kennedy and Brian Baldwin. As you know, Brian—we called him "B"—held this Editor's Desk with distinction which I shall endeavor to emulate as your next rational voice from the bowels of this man-made hell. Together we'll seek that light which casts out darkness and brings forth clarity.

Many will recall my admonition on conduct when some were televised cheering at the murder-by-execution of ex-Klansman and PHADP member Henry Hays. I said this behavior would come back to haunt us, because the treatment that Henry received from the courts, unjust as it was, served the purpose to solidify the state's posture to murder more "mothers' brown babies," not to give justice for the victim's family. I hate to say I told you so, but here you have it in the murders of Victor and Brian, and the same will hold true for more of us to come.

Let's just consider the outrageous handling of Brian's last court hearing and his appeal for justice to the governor. The circumstances surrounding this deadly farce exemplifies the monumental need for a moratorium on capital punishment in Alabama. You have serious racist Robes that put up the blockade to the defense's full disclosure of information, newly discovered evidence, etc. One judge was cited for racism, only to hand it off to his brother. Then we have Wilcox County's historic and understandably fearful Deputy Manzie who, after a private meeting with Governor Siegelman, recanted his testimony pointing to a confession extracted by torture. We would be remiss if we overlooked the governor's lack of forthrightness as to what took place in that meeting. Calling the deputy "courageous," the governor said he was distressed about issues raised in Brian's case, but he was not distressed enough to stay his execution. The list of injustices goes on. A moratorium would show the system for what it is: biased, racist, vengeful, sadistic.

Let's heed B's last editorial, let's "do as family does"—let us turn toward each other for strength in these difficult times, for more are coming! And in the spirit of keeping "Hope" alive, we search ourselves, teach each other, recognize our shortcomings, and then do the right thing!

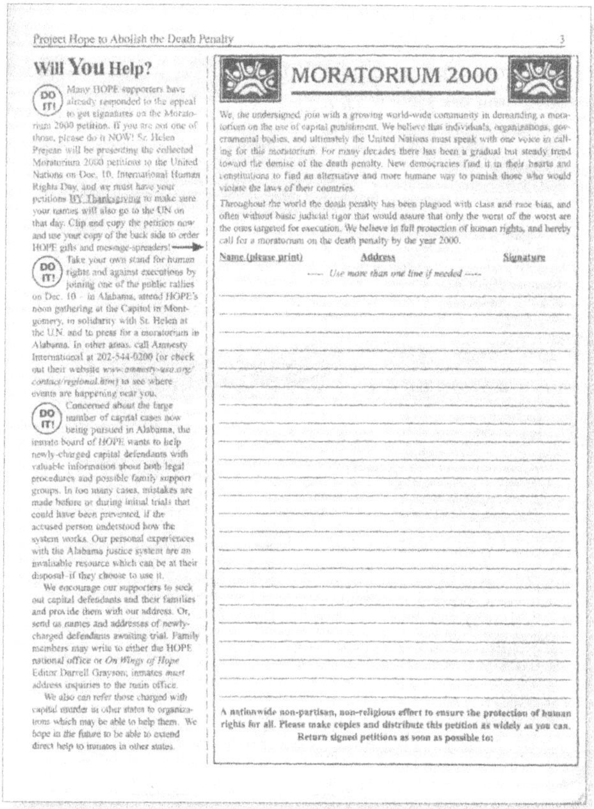

Project Hope to Abolish the Death Penalty 3

Will You Help?

DO IT! Many HOPE supporters have already responded to the appeal to get signatures on the Moratorium 2000 petition. If you are not one of those, please do it NOW! Sr. Helen Prejean will be presenting the collected Moratorium 2000 petitions to the United Nations on Dec. 10, International Human Rights Day, and we must have your petitions BY Thanksgiving to make sure your names will also go to the UN on that day. Clip and copy the petition now and use your copy of the back side to order HOPE gifts and message-spreaders! →

DO IT! Take your own stand for human rights and against executions by joining one of the public rallies on Dec. 10 – in Alabama, attend HOPE's noon gathering at the Capitol in Montgomery, in solidarity with Sr. Helen at the U.N. and to press for a moratorium in Alabama. In other areas, call Amnesty International at 202-544-0200 (or check out their website *www.amnesty-usa.org/contact/regional.html*) to see where events are happening near you.

DO IT! Concerned about the large number of capital cases now being pursued in Alabama, the inmate board of *HOPE* wants to help newly-charged capital defendants with valuable information about both legal procedures and possible family support groups. In too many cases, mistakes are made before or during initial trials that could have been prevented, if the accused person understood how the system works. Our personal experiences with the Alabama justice system are an invaluable resource which can be at their disposal–if they choose to use it.

We encourage our supporters to seek out capital defendants and their families and provide them with our address. Or, send us names and addresses of newly-charged defendants awaiting trial. Family members may write to either the HOPE national office or *On Wings of Hope* Editor Darrell Grayson; inmates *must* address inquiries to the main office.

We also can refer those charged with capital murder in other states to organizations which may be able to help them. We hope in the future to be able to extend direct help to inmates in other states.

MORATORIUM 2000

We, the undersigned, join with a growing world-wide community in demanding a moratorium on the use of capital punishment. We believe that individuals, organizations, governmental bodies, and ultimately the United Nations must speak with one voice in calling for this moratorium. For many decades there has been a gradual but steady trend toward the demise of the death penalty. New democracies find it in their hearts and constitutions to find an alternative and more humane way to punish those who would violate the laws of their countries.

Throughout the world the death penalty has been plagued with class and race bias, and often without basic judicial rigor that would assure that only the worst of the worst are the ones targeted for execution. We believe in full protection of human rights, and hereby call for a moratorium on the death penalty by the year 2000.

Name (please print)	Address	Signature

—— *Use more than one line if needed* ——

A nationwide non-partisan, non-religious effort to ensure the protection of human rights for all. Please make copies and distribute this petition as widely as you can. Return signed petitions as soon as possible to:

FIGURE 15. Moratorium flyer, 2000

An Execution Feast?

Leroy White • Summer 1999

PHADP executive director Esther Brown bore witness to Brian Baldwin's execution as well as the "execution feast" that was prepared for state officials. She recalls:

> *In those days they used to wine and dine important people beforehand and I remember waiters rushing back and forth with dishes from where Brian and I were in the visiting room. After they took him back (and I was his only witness—he did not want others), I just sat in an anteroom and waited. Actually, I was taken to the warden and DOC head and told that I could still get out of being the witness. I said "no." Finally I was taken by car by two guards (I recall loud blaring music and laughter) and I think I was the last to arrive where Brian sat strapped in the electric chair. I was behind glass maybe six feet away. There was a delay and it was because they needed the okay from the governor who apparently was doing better things. I pointed to the phone to explain the delay to Brian who was wondering. Then the warden came in for his last words and Brian said something and looked at me. Then the blind was lowered and when it came back up he had a hood on . . . he could see me, but I could not see him. He had prepared me for this. I know he was also muzzled. After the first shock, his whole body jerked and his hand crumpled and then another shock . . . as the undertaker said to me in North Carolina, it is very difficult to prepare a body for viewing after that. When I came out of the room I had to approach the warden to ask what Brian had said. He would not have told me otherwise. His last words were "Tell Esther I am alright."*

In addition to the high cost of carrying out an execution, some states have added on the expenditure of feeding invited guests with the finest foods taxpayers' money can buy.

Attorney Michael Mears, director of the Georgia Indigent Defense

Council, in a recent article points out that this has long been a common practice in Georgia. Mears was able to obtain records showing menus and costs for Georgia execution "banquets" in the 1980s. For one execution "luncheon," for example, the state provided invited guests with an elaborate meal including 225 pounds of chicken, 20 pounds of turkey pastrami, and 10 pounds each of turkey ham and turkey salami—at a cost of $821.

That is certainly a small sum compared to the millions spent in legal fees to support the prosecution's charge, conviction, and sentence. But it is definitely an enormous sum compared to the $212 that state and county governments combined allocated each year per case for defense of poor people accused of criminal offenses, according to a 1997 American Bar Association report.

The poor funding of indigent defenses helps to explain why so many totally innocent people spend decades on death row before limited outside help rescues them, and many others get executed that are guilty of felony murder but not necessarily of capital murder. Believe it or not, money is power, and too often all the money is on the side of the prosecution. Without a good enough lawyer with enough funding to conduct a real investigation, a poor person has no chance for a fair trial or fair sentence.

In an effort not to seem insensitive to the pain of families and friends of murdered victims, I will rule out saying it is ludicrous to go feasting at the site of someone being killed. But I do want to point out how states are persuading guests to overlook the bad that is really being done by providing them with such elaborate meals. The focus is taken away from the actual killing and any possible forethought of whether it is wrong or right, or even necessary, to kill the prisoner.

The true nature of these events is clear from another execution lunch menu Mears published. In addition to the basics of twenty pounds of roast beef, four cases of chicken, thirty pounds of lunch meats and cheeses, and cases of chicken, tuna, and macaroni salad, the menu includes "1 pan of cheese straws, 2 trays of hors d'oeuvres, and 3 trays of party sandwiches."

Friends and family of the inmate being killed, it goes without saying, are not often included with the invited guests.

Show the utmost respect for life by example—and get rid of the death penalty. Teach people to love one another, regardless of the faults found in others. What good is it to kill for killing, when the youth see it as an example to solve problems, and more lives are lost in the end? Feast on efforts to save life, and not to end it!

Prosecuting Children for Murder Is Barbaric

Trace Duncan • April–June 2000

The US Supreme Court would rule in Roper v. Simmons (2004) that it is uncon-stitutional to impose capital punishment on anyone under the age of eighteen.

I turned twenty-three last year (November 1999). The death penalty was reinstated the year I was born (1976). I am still young, but the ideals behind capital punishment are old and primitive. I was seventeen at the time of my arrest. According to the law, I was restricted from certain activities. I could not vote, could not sign a contract or join the armed forces (without parental consent), and I could not buy tobacco or alcohol. These restrictions were designed to protect me—by legal definition of a child—from the harm of others and the harm of myself.

Yet, when a child commits a heinous act, he or she is automatically beyond redemption, subject to the toughest laws of the land.

How outrageously barbaric have we become as a society that we execute our children?! Communist China, renowned for its human rights violations, has stopped executing people below the age of eighteen. If one of the most oppressive countries in the world can do this, why is it that we cannot? Why are children expected to take on complete responsibility for their crimes, like adults, when they cannot fully understand that kind of responsibility?

It is absolutely counterproductive to throw young lives away this way. Proponents of capital punishment often make statements such as, "You were tried and convicted by a jury of your peers, accept your punishment." However, a person below the age of eighteen cannot serve on a jury, so how then can a minor be tried by a jury of his/her peers? They can't. If the state wishes to deter kids from violent crime, they need to lead by example. Don't show kids that you should kill the people you don't know how to forgive.

I am not trying to belittle the victims of violent crimes or their families. Nor am I trying to minimize the crimes themselves. Children who kill deserve to be punished, and their victims deserve justice. Real justice would be ten or twenty years of life spent learning their lesson and contributing back to society, not sticking them in a cell for fifteen years while their minds rot away in the fear of death, then executing them.

Prosecutors Manipulate Victim Families to Hate

Gary Drinkard • April-June 2000

Gary Drinkard, whose false conviction involved prosecutorial misconduct, was exonerated in 2001. His full story, "Surviving Death Row," appears at the end of this volume.

It always amazes me to see how far politicians and prosecutors for the state will go to further their careers. They take good, intelligent people and use their grief over a loved one's death to breed hatred in them. The more a politician can control your emotions, the more he can control your vote. They can lie to your face with the most sincere of looks and then beg for forgiveness down the road when they get caught.

If I were jerked around each year with a reminder from the prosecutor and made to feel guilty if I didn't appear at each trial and motion procedure, I would start to hate, also. Even if, after many years, the person is proved to be innocent, some of the victims' families will still hate that person because the politicians and prosecutors misused their power to further their careers.

If a person's grief is treated with love, they can get on with their lives and become whole again. The constant reminders and guilt trips fuel the hatred and leave so many empty and lost. In order to hold onto that old feeling, you lash out at everyone around you and, odds are, your family has suffered from and because of your hatred.

How in the world do good, intelligent men and women allow their emotions to be manipulated by mortal men? If God chose to manipulate your emotions, there would be no room for free choice. Do the politicians not believe in your ability to know right from wrong without attempting to control you? Aren't they elected to speak for you, not to use and destroy you as a loving, caring person? There are even organizations that provide free counseling for victims of violent crime. But

I would bet any amount of money that the prosecutors fail to mention that fact because they would rather have control of your emotions in order to use you to their ends.

It sounds like wolves in sheep's clothing to me, someone that would use your grief and turn it into hatred so they could take another soul for their master. In fact, they end up taking your soul as well. "The only thing necessary for the triumph of evil is for good men and women to do nothing" (Edmund Burke). "Loyalty to petrified opinion, never yet broke a chain or freed a human soul" (Mark Twain).

For all those who have been executed

Remembrance Day

July 13, 2000

PROJECT HOPE TO ABOLISH THE DEATH PENALTY has declared July 13 as a day of remembrance for all those who have been executed throughout the United States since the reinstatement of the death penalty in 1976. The *HOPE* board of directors, on Alabama's Death Row, invite all Death Row Inmates and all our supporters to join us on this date at 12 noon (CDT) in a moment of silence or prayer. Group observances may be scheduled at another time. We see capital punishment itself as killing and as a cause of further killing, creating a cycle of violence which must be broken. The ultimate aim of *HOPE* is to end ALL killing, and on July 13 we mourn ALL victims, whether of individual or state-sanctioned killing. On this day we especially lift up the names of those executed because these are the outcast ones whose humanity has been denied by the media and the government. As citizens, we all bear responsibility for taking these lives. We do not say that individuals who kill should not be punished – far from it. But killing is not a punishment, it is disrespect for the sanctity of human life. More killing does no honor to the victims of murder, and most victims' families find no healing in it. Executions breed more killing by their celebration of vengeance and violence as acceptable social values.

Our suggestions for this day include but are not limited to: Holding services, vigils, etc., displaying purple ribbons on clothing, mailboxes, car antennae, etc., speaking to others about the injustice of the death penalty, and writing letters to the editor and/or elected representatives concerning the death penalty. On the Alabama Death Row, we are asking that inmates wear pressed whites and purple ribbons and refrain from sports activities. The following have been executed on Alabama's Death Row:

John Evans	Arthur Julius	Edward Horsley, Jr.	Victor Kennedy
Arthur Jones	Wallace Norrell Thomas	Billy Waldrop	David Ray Duren
Wayne Ritter	Larry Gene Heath	Walter Hill	Freddie Lee Wright
Michael Lindsey	Cornelius Singleton	Henry Francis Hays	Robert Lee Tarver
Horace Dunkins	Willie Clisby	Steven Thompson	Pernell Ford
Herbert Richardson	Varnell Weeks	Brian Keith Baldwin	

The following have died while awaiting execution in Alabama:

Sammy Felder	Tommy Stains	Kenneth Magwood	Edward Evans
Patrick Carr	John Daniels	Eddie Harrell	William David Scott
Samuel Ivory	Patricia Ann Thomas	William Gregory	James W. Smith

Join us in spirit wherever you are at noon on July 13 –
and if at all possible in person in Mobile, Montgomery (July 15) or Birmingham –

MOBILE – July 13, at Bienville Square (downtown Mobile) – come at any time during the day for a few minutes, a few hours, or all day – display will include posters and photos of innocents released, and of those executed in Alabama – an Alabama Death Row information brochure, church statements on capital punishment, and more.

MONTGOMERY – July 15, Saturday, 3:00 p.m. – Remembrance Day will be observed on the State House steps (11 S. Union St., behind the Capitol) as part of the national Prison Reform Unity Project rally – Bo Cochran, *HOPE* board member released as innocent after 19 years, will speak, and eulogies of those executed will be read.

BIRMINGHAM – July 13, 12 noon to 1:00 p.m. – Remembrance Day observed at Kelly Ingram Park (between 5th and 6th Avenue North and 16th and 17th Street North, downtown, across the street from the Civil Rights Institution and 16th Street Baptist Church).

– SHOW UP TO SHOW YOU CARE! –

Closure
Reality or a Catch Phrase?

Timothy Scott Cothren • Christmas issue, 2001

A 2007 study found that only 2.5 percent of co-victims (family of murder victims) reported achieving closure as a result of capital punishment; 20.1 percent said the execution did not help them heal. *

I am constantly hearing politicians say the death penalty proves closure for victims' families. The family members of victims of violent crime, without a doubt, are forced to endure the most traumatic experience I can imagine. I can understand how justice would help in the healing process. But how does the violent death of another human being, which in most cases the victim's family will witness, bring about closure?

Vengeance is a very temporary "fix" for a long term problem. When a loved one is lost, that person will be greatly missed . . . Always! Closure is a business or real estate term. It has absolutely nothing to do with healing a broken heart. That type of healing must come from within.

The best way I've heard it expressed was in the final words of a man in Texas just before he drew his last breath. Lying there strapped to the execution gurney after saying goodbye to his family, he turned to the victims and quietly said, "You will still hate me tomorrow."

Some people will disagree as to exactly what his intentions were when he said that, but the truth of the matter is that those few words sum up the absolute futility of state-sanctioned murder for any reason . . . especially "closure."

There is a prime example of what I'm saying right here in Alabama. This person lost a loved one to violent crime many years ago. The person accused, convicted, and sentenced to death for murder was

---

* Scott Vollum and Dennis R. Longmire, "Covictims of Capital Murder: Statements of Victims' Family Members and Friends Made at the Time of Execution." *Violence and Victims* 22, no. 5 (2007): 601–19.

executed in July of 1990. Still today, this person is making television appearances to defend the death penalty and attempting to have various death penalty statutes changed to limit the appellate process. This person rallies in front of the prison at every execution and it is quite obvious that this person is still very bitter. Does that sound like "closure?"

In no way do I wish to tread upon the very real feelings of these families. My best friend was brutally beaten to death over a two dollar game of pool. I know exactly what it feels like to stand in the midst of the storm of hurt, confusion, anger, the sense of helplessness, and the multitude of emotions that wreck a home when a loved one is lost in such a senseless fashion.

What I do "tread upon" is a state prosecutor's "right" to exploit a family's grief, then perpetuate that suffering by preaching "closure" to them, offering them hope of relief which will never come in the way they are encouraged to seek it. It just sounds good on television. Stay true to the struggle!

Reflections

Torrey McNabb • Christmas issue, 2001

I reflect the streets, I reflect pain,
I reflect the struggle, I reflect anger,
I reflect poverty and starvation for knowledge,
The dreams of a generation
That's been reduced to rubbish
I reflect
No dreams, pipe dreams, dope fiends,
Crime scenes of burglaries, homicides and suicides
I reflect
A mother's tears, a mother's fears, a mother's cheers
The sole corruption of her hard taught wisdom
Her blood, sweat, and tears
I'm the reflection of realness
Warriors, soldiers, and hustlers
Street life, thug life
Ghettos and gutters
Drug dealers, addicts, alcoholics and downfalls
A generation of young men that's last
It's storming, yet the rain's still pouring down
I reflect tomorrows
Brightness and promise
Its troubles, its problems
Stress and drama
I reflect me
Strong, righteous, honest, a fighter, stunning
And charming.
These are my reflections
Reflections of me.

Paradise

Vernon L. Yancey • Christmas issue, 2001

Paradise would be a life free of strife
And vice and devices of destruction
With subtle seduction from the beauty
Of living and giving your all and the
Hope that you'd not fall from the good
Graces of kind faces in loving places,
Because you'd be perfect, without flaw
Held steadfast in awe.
Paradise would be knowing that you
Have the freedom of growing whilst
Free flowing like an apparition through
The trees with no need
To feed on the mundane or those things
Less important in paradise
Which is actually a paradox.
So incredibly impossible that the
Possibility of it gives calm to your
Dreams, and it seems
Within reach within your mind.
And to yourself, there, you are so kind
Ignoring ignorance and substance:
Those things which cause other beings
To bleed from the soul because of greed—
It's so new but yet so old.
Be bold!
In paradise, your paradox, your
Politically incorrect and unorthodox
Hope, that a world full of only beauty is
The personal duty of all mankind and
Subject one to another, brother to sister,

Sister to brother.
Life in a perfect world in your mind—
You, my dear dreamer, are one of a kind
The kind who sees his fellow human
Without hate, without great distaste,
Prejudgment or prejudice.
Each resident not hesitant to fulfill
Those needs of his neighbor as a favor.
The flavor of a life so nice, bittersweet
Perfect and neat so why not speak?
Speak it and believe it. Dream no more
About it but cause it.
Paradise lost, what's the cost?
Gather its reality back to yourself.
Wake and see it on the lowest shelf.
Reach out for that hope inside.
Paradise, a paradox? Politically
Incorrect? And unorthodox?
Utopia, free of lies and division and derision
They say it's not possible, but who are "they" to speak for you?
Did you give them your permission?

To the Contrary

Jeffery Rieber • October-December 2001

Death row inmates are perceived by many as people without the right to express anger. To speak frankly and openly about the failings of the US justice system, the political manipulation of voters, and the public's apparent willingness to believe what politicians tell them, in the face of overwhelming evidence to the contrary, tends to be viewed as "complaining" or "whining" if spoken by death row inmates.

I understand this tendency. The reasons are twofold: (1) the justice system and all its political influences directly affect death row inmates, so when an inmate calls attention to him or herself by pointing out the faults of the system, it's naturally received as self-serving, and (2) it is perceived as disrespectful and audacious for a person who has been convicted of capital murder to object to *anything* concerning what is happening to them as a result.

The gravity of the crime leads many citizens to disregard the legal and human rights violations endured by death row inmates, thinking that "whatever happens to them is too good by half" or "they deserve whatever they get."

Personally, I thought the same way until I found myself learning about the system from the inside.

Death row inmates are human beings and we have all the emotions that everyone else has. I'm a death row inmate and the more research I do into capital punishment, the sadder and angrier I get.

Project Hope to Abolish the Death Penalty is run by death row inmates. Our task is to tell the public all of the little-known facts concerning the death penalty in hopes that they will make more informed judgments. If revealing systematic flaws and injustices in the system is "complaining," then we will continue to "complain" until everyone has heard the truth.

Feelings from Death Row

Willie Smith • October-December 2001

On September 11, one of the most unthinkable and horrific tragedies ever took place in the USA. As the events were unfolding, an awesome fear came over me. I thought about my mother and her safety. I thought about the fate of the families and others.

How could such a tragedy happen to the most powerful country on earth? Why is there so much anger in the hearts of those who did this? What will happen next? Are our families and friends still in harm's way?

Something I often think about now is the pain on the faces of those who lost loved ones in the attacks and those who risked their lives to help. My sympathy goes out to all of those involved.

Many may read this and wonder how or why a death row inmate would care about such things. To so many, I'm not considered an American citizen. I'm considered the scum of the earth. Many feel I should be executed. Many don't realize that I think and feel just like anyone else.

Many would think I don't support this country or care anything about it, but I do. This country has done me no wrong. I strongly disagree with the leadership and biased ways I see working within our government, but I still love and respect my country.

However, I can't support or agree with those who believe the death penalty is justice. I believe it teaches that there is no better way than death to solve the worst problems. Those who support the death penalty think that we can't be rehabilitated but many of us have put away the old things and become new. Many of us have grown into men and women who have now learned the values of responsibility. We have learned about respect and learned to be content with what we have. We have learned to be conquerors through Jesus Christ. I pray that in the midst of this tragic loss of life, some will realize that capital punishment is killing, too, and that it always leaves behind grieving families.

Closure

Anthony Tyson • August–October 2002

"We want to make sure you and the family have closure in this situation. We are doing this for you."

That is the voice of a prosecutor talking to family members about seeking the death penalty. The sad part is that families believe them. But it is never all about the victim's family. It is about the political aims the prosecutors achieve. Once the US Supreme Court said no to executing juveniles, prosecutors had to change their tunes as to what closure is. Once the death penalty is abolished, what will you do?

Prosecutors do not care about closure. Have prosecutors ever sought the death penalty against the victim's family's wishes? Of course they have. How do you think the victim's family feels about those who have been proven innocent or exonerated—cases in which the prosecutors were wrong?

Soon, prosecutors will not be able to prosecute capital murder cases. The high court has said no to executing the developmentally disabled. Then no to those who did not have competent lawyers. Lack of competent lawyers is how many of us end up on death row.

We cannot afford to give up hope. We must remain optimistic that, in time, the "evolving sense of decency" will mean a complete "closure" of capital punishment.

Alabama Death Row Fact Sheet

August-October 2002

ALABAMA DEATH ROW

Total on Death Row   186

Black (85) White (98) Latino (2)   Asian (1)   Women (2) Juveniles (14)

Executions Since 1976   **24**   Men (23)   Female (1 in 2002)

Executions by Region Since 1976: South (**636**) West (59) Midwest (85) Northeast (3)

Alabama does *NOT* forbid the execution of the mentally retarded or juvenile offenders.

Sentencing is decided by a Judge who can override the jury's recommendation.

COSTS OF THE DEATH PENALTY
IS IT WORTH IT?

The most comprehensive study in the country found that the death penalty costs North Carolina $2.16 million per execution *over* the cost of a non-death penalty murder case with a life sentence. (Duke University, May 1993)

Florida spent an estimated $57 million on the death penalty from 1973 to 1988 to achieve 18 executions – that is an average of $3.2 million per execution.

While we have been unable to find numbers for Alabama specifically, it is fair to assume that we are spending a great deal of money *over* what it would cost to keep someone in prison for life. Alabama's justice system is bankrupt and yet, they are pushing ahead to spend $250,000 on the lethal injection chamber and untold amounts to fight the new ruling from the United States Supreme Court against executing the mentally retarded and the role of Judges in the sentencing process. How might this money be better spent?

ALABAMA is 44th in the nation on per pupil expenditures. The states that spent less are Arizona, Arkansas, Idaho, Mississippi, South Dakota and Tennessee. (National Center for Education Statistics) Spending in 2002: *Alabama $5,937 Georgia $7,633 Louisiana $6,270*

From 1992 – 2000, **ALABAMA** was *below* the national average in every tested area in grades 4 and 8. The areas tested are Math, Reading, Science and Writing. In 2001 the ACT-tested graduates in Alabama scored *below* the national average.

Fact: Elected Judges in Alabama are among the highest paid in the nation. In the year 2000, $13.3 million was raised for 13 candidates running for bench seats, compared to the closet contender, Illinois, with $7 million for 11 candidates.

Fact: This year Bob Riley and George W. Bush broke records by raising $3.8 million in B'ham for his race for Governor.

The Fiscal Distress Caused by Capital Punishment

Jeffery Rieber • ca. 2003

Recent documents from the ACLU reveal that the Federal Bureau of Prisons spent nearly $4.7 million on the first five executions carried out by the Trump administration.[*]

On June 26, 2002, New York became the largest of the eighty-one municipalities so far to adopt a resolution in favor of a moratorium on executions.

In every instance where a city council adopted such a resolution, the economic ramifications of funding capital punishment were major considerations in the decision making process.

USA Today recently reported that Alabama will have a shortfall of over $500 million in its two major budgets for the coming year. Already this year, Alabama could not afford to pay out the citizens' tax return in a timely manner. It has paid out $100 million but can not pay the rest unless it borrows from other departments.

As in years past, there is talk of prorating school budgets which means possibly taking away extracurricular activities. Alabama is already forty-fourth in the nation on per-pupil expenditures and Alabama students test below the national average in math, reading, science and writing, as well as in the overall ACT scores.

Alabama courts were recently forced to suspend jury trials due to a lack of funds, and there is talk of the need to do so again.

Municipalities in Alabama, and other states, are extremely vulnerable to fiscal distress imposed by capital trials, which bring large and

---

[*] "Records Disclose Taxpayers Picked Up a Nearly Million Dollar Price Tag for Each Federal Execution," Death Penalty Information Center, February 23, 2021, https://deathpenaltyinfo.org/news/records-disclose-taxpayers-picked-up-a-nearly-million-dollar-price-tag-for-each-federal-execution.

unexpected negative shocks to state and local budgets. They affect the distribution of public funds because the cost of death penalty cases are borne in part by reducing expenditures on highways, police, etc., and in large part by increasing taxes.

The *Savannah Morning News* reported that some counties in Georgia are going broke prosecuting death penalty cases, and that at least one county (Long County) had to rely on emergency state grants in order to keep checks from bouncing.

Georgia's Fulton County Superior Judge Stephanie Mania was led to question the value of expensive capital trials, saying, "The death penalty has great popular appeal, but I don't think the tax payers have looked at the bottom line. The death penalty is damn expensive."

The most comprehensive study in the country found that the death penalty costs North Carolina $2.16 million per execution OVER the costs of a non-death penalty murder case with a sentence of imprisonment for life. The majority of those costs occur at the trial level (Duke University, May 1993).

Enforcing the death penalty costs Florida $51 million a year above and beyond what it would cost to punish all first-degree murderers with life in prison without the possibility of parole. Based on the forty-four executions Florida has carried out since 1976, that amounts to a cost of $24 million for each execution (*Palm Beach Post*, January 4, 2000).

In Texas, a death penalty case costs an average of $2.3 million, about three times the cost of imprisoning someone in a single cell at the highest security level for forty years (*Dallas Morning News*, March 8, 1992).

The death penalty costs California $90 million annually beyond the ordinary costs of the justice system. $78 million of that total is incurred at the trial level (*Sacramento Bee*, March 28, 1998).

States are spending untold millions (above and beyond what it costs for life without parole) on giving people the death penalty, yet mistakes and misconduct throughout the system lead to a high reversal rate in the appeals process. This in turn leads to even more money spent on retrying those cases or pleading them out to life without the possibility of parole. Millions upon millions could be saved by just eliminating the death penalty and sentencing offenders to life without parole in

Project Hope to Abolish the Death Penalty
Inmates, Families and Friends Working to End All Killing
P.O. Box 1362, Lanett, AL 36863
Phone (334) 499-0003
E-mail: beesther@earthlink.net Website: www.phadp.org

Execute Justice not People

THE FISCAL DISTRESS CAUSED BY CAPITAL PUNISHMENT

On June 26, 2002 New York became the largest of the 73 municipalities, so far, to adopt a resolution in favor of a moratorium on executions.

In every instance where a city council adopted such a resolution, the economic ramifications of funding capital punishment were major considerations in the decision making process.

U.S.A. Today recently reported that Alabama will have a short-fall of over $500 million in its' 2 major budgets for the coming year. Already this year, Alabama could not afford to pay out the citizen's tax returns on a timely basis. They have payed out $100 million but can't pay the rest unless they borrow from other departments.

As in years past, there is talk of prorating school budgets which means possibly taking away their extra-curricular activities. Alabama is already 44th in the nation on per-pupil expenditures and Alabama students consistently test below the national average in math, reading, science, and writing, as well as the over-all A.C.T. scores.

Alabama courts were recently forced to suspend jury trials due to a lack of funds, and there is talk of the need to do so again.

Municipalities in Alabama, and other states, are extremely vulnerable to fiscal distress imposed by the presence of capital trials, which bring large and unexpected negative shocks to state and local budgets. They affect the distribution of public funds because the costs of death penalty cases are born in part by reducing expenditures on high ways, police etc. and in large part by increasing taxes.

The Savannah Morning News reported that some counties in Georgia are going broke prosecuting death penalty cases, and that at least one county (Long County) had to rely on emergency state grants in order to keep pay checks from bouncing.

Georgia's Fulton County Superior Court Judge Stephanie Manis was led to question the value of expensive capital trials saying, "The death penalty has great popular appeal, but I don't think the tax payers have looked at the bottom line," "The death penalty is damn expensive."

The most comprehensive study in the country found that the death penalty costs North Carolina $2.16 million per execution OVER the costs of a non-death penalty murder case with a sentence of imprisonment for life. The majority of those costs occur at the trial level. (Duke University, May, 1993).

Enforcing the death penalty costs Florida $51 million a year above and beyond what it would cost to punish all first-degree murderers with life in prison without the possibility of parole.

FIGURE 16. "The Fiscal Distress Caused by Capital Punishment," by Jeffery Rieber, ca. 2003 the first place. The vast majority of capital defendants end up with life without parole anyway.

The Alabama Department of Corrections is more than 400 correctional officers short of the authorized number. The DOC houses a daily average of 25,155 inmates in facilities designed to house only 12,387. On average, there are 275 new inmates going into the Kilby Prison Processing Center DAILY. Alabama DOC officials say they need a more than $100 million increase in next year's budget, an amount NOT likely to be found.

The Alabama House of Representatives recently voted on $4.55 million in emergency funding for the prison system. Another $25 million emergency bill is being sought.

CONSIDER THIS: Alabama has the largest per capita death row population in the nation. There are 192 men and women on death row now, with 300 in county jails awaiting trial. If Alabama spends approximately $2 million per inmate, above and beyond what it would cost to give them a life without parole sentence, Alabama COULD save well over a half billion dollars by eliminating the death penalty in favor of life without parole. That half billion would be saved on the inmates awaiting trial and additional money could be saved by commuting existing death penalty sentences. Factor in the amounts savable on future death penalty cases and the boon to Alabama's economy becomes truly astounding.

In closing, I would like to mention the war in Iraq and the national concern for lives lost and costs incurred. War is more personal to society physically and psychologically because our young men and women are dying in service to our nation; however, economically the death penalty is worse because war is expensive for a finite amount of time while capital punishment drains budgets every single year.

Will You Hear Me Now?

Michael Thompson • April–June 2003

Executed by the State of Alabama March 13, 2003

This piece was published following the author's execution.

Judicial prejudice and malice; prosecutorial misconduct; ineffective assistance of counsel; involuntary confessions forced by promises, threats and trickery; the failure of investigators to produce favorable evidence while creating unfavorable, false evidence—these are the components that not only violate the rights of the guilty, but also conflict the innocent. Components of a system of justice which has run amok for far too long under the guise of being "tough on crime" from the circuit courts to the US Supreme Court. When our highest judiciary fails to enforce the rights guaranteed to *every individual* under the United States Constitution, society as a whole inherits a corrupt system of justice that functions not to protect, but to prosecute, and only fools would believe that the innocent are not convicted and even put to death. A corrupt, zealous justice system can make the most innocent among us appear to be guilty monsters, especially with the assistance of the "spin-doctors" media who graduate from the Jerry Springer school of "shock TV."

Today, the state of Alabama has put to death an innocent man. Since I'm already dead, and have *nothing* to gain, perhaps society will finally listen. My blood is on your hands, but I've prayed that God will forgive you all, for you don't realize what you are doing. You are kept in ignorance of the truth and made to believe that our justice system is perfect and that it's hard at work protecting you from people like me. I spent eighteen years behind bars for a crime that I did not commit and now I've been put to death. You should fear the system that did this to me.

On December 10, 1984, I found myself caught up in something that resembled a segment from the TV series *The Twilight Zone*, and it chewed me up like a lion devouring fresh kill. Every twist and turn only sunk me deeper and deeper until, had I not known better, even I would have thought myself to be guilty. The justice system devoured me. It took an innocent man and ripped him to shreds and devoured him. I was that man.

My only reason for leaving you this last statement is to beg you to please put an end to this madness. Stop the killing! At least a live person stands a chance of one day proving his innocence. Don't ever murder an innocent person again. Let my execution be the end of the death penalty in Alabama. I love this state. I love the people in this state. Please love yourselves enough to rise above this evil and be a Godly people, and a just people, for today, as I was executed, you were the only ones present who were guilty of murder.

I am a Christian—a born again Child of God, and all I feel is love and forgiveness. I choose to see my execution as a sacrifice. A wake up call to you. You have executed an innocent man! I'm with God, but you are not, and I pray that you will be one day, for Jesus died for your sins also. But you must repent and ask yourself, "What would Jesus do?"

Please stop the killing. It's not God's will—it's man's will.

God love you all.

Now I'm Gone

Timothy Scott Cothren
January-March 2004

_____

The rain falls, an even mist
The wind blows, a gentle hiss
Two bodies, soul as one
In the blink of an eye, one is gone.
Just two kids, talking about life
He timidly asks, "Will you be my wife?"
Time won't stop, it marches on
In the blink of an eye, one is gone.
A little reckless, a little wild
All is lost, and he's just a child
His time is up, he's all alone
The blink of an eye, now I'm gone.

Homicide? Suicide? Euthanasia? Volunteer

Jeffery Rieber • July–September 2004

Approximately 10 percent of those sentenced to die have willingly given up their appeals through a practice known as "volunteerism."* Volunteers exhibit high rates of substance abuse and mental illness, which raises questions of competency and consent. The first execution in the modern era was an act of volunteerism. Gary Gilmore, the subject of Norman Mailer's The Executioner's Song, waived all of his appeals and was scheduled to die just five months following the commission of his crime. As John H. Blume has written, "by the time Gilmore's case reached the Supreme Court, his motivation was transparently suicidal: he had attempted to kill himself six days after he personally told the Utah Supreme Court that he wished to withdraw an appeal previously filed without his consent."†

The following piece by Jeffery Rieber is responding to the execution of Alabama "volunteer" David Hocker in 2004. It reflects the tension between PHADP's collective advocacy and its commitment to respecting the independent will and autonomy of each person on death row. Rieber remains on death row after the Alabama Supreme Court refused to review his petition for a writ of certiorari. He is one of many people in Alabama sentenced to die via judicial override, a practice that is now illegal.‡

I recently experienced a very strange moment in time. An event that I hope to never endure again. I told a human being exactly what day he was going to die. It was not something I had planned to do. Our office

---

* For a list of volunteers, see the Death Penalty Information Center, Executions Overview: Execution Volunteers, https://deathpenaltyinfo.org/executions/executions-overview/execution-volunteers.

† John H. Blume, "Killing the Willing: 'Volunteers,' Suicide, and Competency," *Michigan Law Review* 103, no. 5 (2005): 944.

‡ The jury's 7–5 recommendation for life in prison without parole was overridden by the judge. A 2017 law has banned the practice of judicial override but has not made the ban retroactive.

manager checks the Alabama Supreme Court's website daily for important rulings and execution dates. PHADP's chairman of the board, who lives in the cell next to me, told me that the court had set a date for a man but he didn't recognize the first name. I recognized the last name but not the first name. This person lives upstairs from me on the same tier. Without giving it much thought, I called up to him and asked what his whole name is. He told me. It was him. Since he and I do not usually associate with one another he was justifiably curious and asked, "Why?" That caught me flat-footed. I stuttered and hesitated, then told him that he was going to die in one month's time.

The only thing worse that I could think of doing was giving that information to a person who didn't want to die. You see, this man is a volunteer.

The word *volunteer*, in almost any other context, is usually a good thing, but if you're a death row inmate it means that you are asking the government to kill you. It's a shame to put that noble word to such a use.

As I am also a death row inmate and cannot begin to imagine ever being a "volunteer" myself, I asked myself what would motivate a person to give up his or her appeals and actually seek execution. Do they do it because they're tired of the fight for life, terminally ill, mentally ill, cowards, maybe out of spite? I don't know, but I do know that it is *state-assisted suicide.*

It is *homicide.* (Homicide is listed as the cause of death on the death certificate of people who the state executes.) And since the executed, in volunteer cases, is a willing participant, it can be correctly labeled *euthanasia.*

All three of these practices are illegal for you and me, but I guess it's ok when the government practices them.

Most death row inmates view volunteerism as a form of disrespect and an act of weakness. It evokes anger and disgust from us because we are trying to move heaven and earth to keep from being executed.

For an abolitionist organization, volunteerism presents further difficulties. When an execution date is set, PHADP and other orgs ask people to write to the governor for clemency and orchestrate vigils. We usually work with the inmates on what issues to use when requesting clemency. How do we respect a volunteer's wishes and still stay true to our cause and the belief that executions are wrong? What message does volunteerism send to those in the abolition movement and to other death row inmates? What do the people who value all life do in a situation like this? Do they write the governor? Not write the governor? Do people of faith pray for a stay or commutation? Do we hold vigils for a person who asked for and received their own death? Does it make the activists who spend so much time, effort, and emotion on trying to stop executions rethink their positions? I don't know.

The argument can be made that a person has the right to kill themselves. If so they should do just that—kill themselves. They shouldn't help to legitimize state-sponsored murder just because they have decided to die but don't possess the strength or purpose to do it themselves. State execution is never right, and that is what I hold on to in these situations. If it's not ok for Jack Kevorkian to help someone commit suicide, it's not ok for the state to do so. I will protest *every* execution, no matter if the person volunteers or not. It matters not what the inmate's action may be; I know that the state's action is wrong in either case.

Jeff Rieber
Alabama Death Row

Our goal: ABOLITION!

Project Hope to Abolish the Death Penalty has been striving towards its goal for over 11 years now. This type of work is fraught with heartache, disappointment, and crushing setbacks that sap the will of the abolitionist. Victories are few and far between. In fact, *HOPE* will not achieve true victory unless and until capital punishment is abolished.

Having said that, I would like to point out that there are "little victories," or steps along the path to abolition that can be attained, such as a moratorium or certain changes in legislation. *HOPE* has supported some of these causes even though they may not be strictly abolitionist in nature. These causes are important, not only because they may bring us closer to our desired goal, but because winning these little victories brings about a much needed boost to morale.

HOPE is in this fight until the end. We will utilize whatever methods that we can, in order to bring about an end to capital punishment. Be assured, we always have been, and will remain, an abolitionist organization.

FIGURE 17. "Our Goal: Abolition!,"
by Jeffery Rieber, 2000

Season's Greetings

Christmas issue, 2004

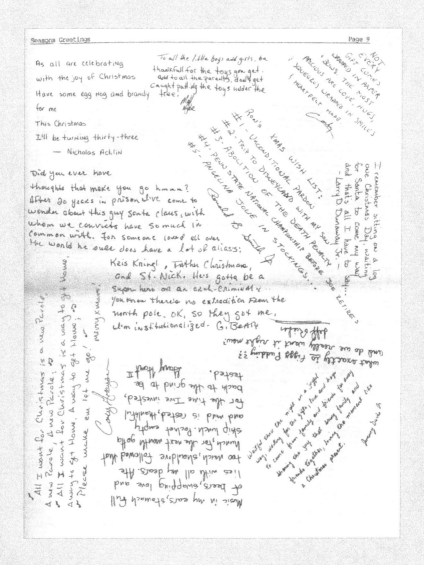

As all are celebrating
with the joy of Christmas
Have some egg nog and brandy
for me
This Christmas
I'll be turning thirty-three

— Nicholas Achlin

Did you ever have
thoughts that make you go hmmm?
After 20 years in prison alive come to
wonder about this guy santa claus, with
whom we convicts have so much in
common with. For someone loved all over
the world he sure does have a lot of aliases:
Keis Kringl, Father Christmas,
and St. Nick. He's gotta be a
super hero or an arch-criminal &
you know there's no extradition from the
north pole. OK, so they got me,
I'm institutionalized. G. Beatz

To all the little boys and girls, be
thankful for the toys you get.
And to all the parents, don't get
caught patting the toys under the
tree!

Ron's XMAS WISH LIST:
#1 - Unconditional pardon with my son
#2 - Trip to Disneyland
#3 - Abolition of the death penalty
#4 - Penn State National championship before Joe retires
#5 - Receuna Joue in stockings.
Ronald F. Smith

NOT every gift comes wrapped in paper & bows. The most precious are love, hugs, squeezes wrapped in smiles & heartfelt hope.
Cathy

I remember sitting on a lap
one Christmas Day, waiting
for Santa to come, my how
and that's all I have to say...
— Larry D. Dunavey Jr.

All I want for Christmas is a new Parole.
A new Parole, A new Parole,
All I want for Christmas is a way to get Home.
A way to get Home. A way to get Home.
Please uncle em let me go!
Cory Berger

Music in my ears, stomach full
of beers, swapping love and
lies with all my dears. Ate
too much should've followed that
lunch, for the next month gotta
ship lunch. Pocket empty
and mind is rested. Thankful
for the time I've invested,
Back to the grind to be
tested.

Merry Xmas!

What exactly do we really want right now?
Figgy Pudding??
Jeff Butler

We wish you this might be a joyful time; wishing for the gifts, love and hope to come from family and friends for many to enjoy the joy that bring family and friends together, having the moment like a Christmas planet.
Jimmy Brown

PART II

Will You Hear Me Now?

2005–2008

True Romance

Darrell B. Grayson • 2005

In an enchanting place,
In a mellow-colored room
The occupant's heart is placed
On his sleeve. Sparkling bracelets
Adorn his wrists. With the muted
Roar of a wounded panther he
Leaps into the pack. Grasping
The collar of his warden's
Riotous-black robes he draws
Near and releases a plaintive wail.
Afterwards he pants out a mournful
Declaration, "I'm innocent, you
Murdering sons-o-bitches."

Of course his natural abilities
Can't compare with Cagney's performance
In Angels with Dirty Faces

Originally published in *Against Time* (2005) by Mercy Seat Press.

FIGURE 18. Protest and press conference calling for DNA testing in
Darrell Grayson's case at the state capitol in 2007

Faulty Logic

Jeffery Rieber • January–February 2005

According to the Innocence Project, 375 people have been exonerated through DNA testing, twenty-one of whom were on death row. *Some states set a very high bar for post-conviction DNA testing, effectively placing the burden on the accused to solve the crime before DNA testing is approved. Many states do not adequately preserve DNA evidence at all.*† *DNA testing was not available when some PHADP members, including Darrell Grayson, were convicted and sentenced. Though Grayson would repeatedly request testing post-conviction, his requests were denied.*

Justice is the noble goal sought by prosecutors and all other law enforcement officials working within the system. That is a fact. Justice cannot be had without the truth. That is a fact. DNA testing is a remarkable technology which can be used to help exonerate the innocent and convict the guilty in many cases.

With those simple, basic truths in mind, one would think that DNA testing would be applied in every case in which DNA evidence is available—not only in new cases, but also in old cases that were tried before this technology was in use. If the justice system seeks truth, this MUST BE DONE. It is not, however, being done. DNA testing for inmates is actively and aggressively fought by prosecutors in many jurisdictions throughout America. Less than half of the states with the death penalty allow inmates, to differing extents, the right to DNA testing. Many prosecutors who oppose this testing argue that it would reopen too many old cases. It is shocking that these seekers of truth and justice would rather let innocent men and women rot in prison and die than

---

* "Exonerate the Innocent," Innocence Project, https://innocenceproject.org/exonerate.

† "Post-Conviction DNA Testing," Innocence Project, https://innocenceproject.org/causes/access-post-conviction-dna-testing.

increase their workload. What is unbelievable is that they admit this is the reason why they oppose it.

I think part of the reason there is such strong opposition to DNA testing for inmates is the fear that uncovering wrongful convictions would highlight the many "mistakes" of the criminal justice system, adding weight to the argument in favor of a moratorium on executions. Further, I came to the realization that there is another reason, a reason that is as shameful as it is sad. The thought of an innocent person on death row does not bestow the fear of imminent danger upon prosecutors or, indeed, the public. The consequences of the justice system "not getting it right" are not widely felt or feared. How many people, on their drive to work, say, "I sure hope there are no wrongfully convicted people in prison."

Consider the massive recall of Firestone tires that occurred a number of years ago. The Department of Transportation, a government agency, forced Firestone and the automakers to recall millions or cars and trucks in order to replace tires that "could be faulty, causing injury or death." The people who owned the vehicles with the questionable tires were, understandably, terrified to drive until the tires were replaced. They feared for their lives and the lives of their loved ones. The recall cost an astronomical amount of time and money, but the government forced the recall because there was a demonstrable clear and present danger to the public. Not all of the tires were faulty; many would have performed exactly as they were supposed to.

There are lives at stake here, but because they are not the lives of justice system officials or their loved ones, they do not feel a clear and present danger of imminent death. Do any of us believe that Alabama senator Jeff Sessions (who opposes DNA testing) would not move heaven and earth to spare a loved one?

It is reprehensible that they are being allowed to shirk their duty and responsibility to those citizens who have been wrongly condemned simply because inmates are deemed less worthy and there is no public outcry and outrage at the thought of a "few" innocents on death row.

We are shaming ourselves and the American ideals of truth, justice, and equality. If the statue of liberty could cry, she would.

Against Time

Darrell B. Grayson • 2005

Always pushed, pressed and molded
By these ageless stones, this
Ancient Indian burial ground, this imperial
Ant-hill,
Holding pens in death's domicile
And we its domain.

Here, aging souls grow increasingly sour,
And these mature spirits are sadly
Reverting to juvenile states, congregating
With youths also condemned to objectification
And social apathy.

And mothers (always mothers) are crying
In their coming in and going out,
In their restless sleeping and awakenings
They too are slammed about in the ever
Unending sounds that echo within the
Illusion of having time.
Bang, bang, bang against time and
The newest mother's startled wail,
The soul wrenching cry of disbelief is heard
As some jump and shout against time,
Before and after the killing game has ended.

Originally published in *Against Time* (2005) by Mercy Seat Press.

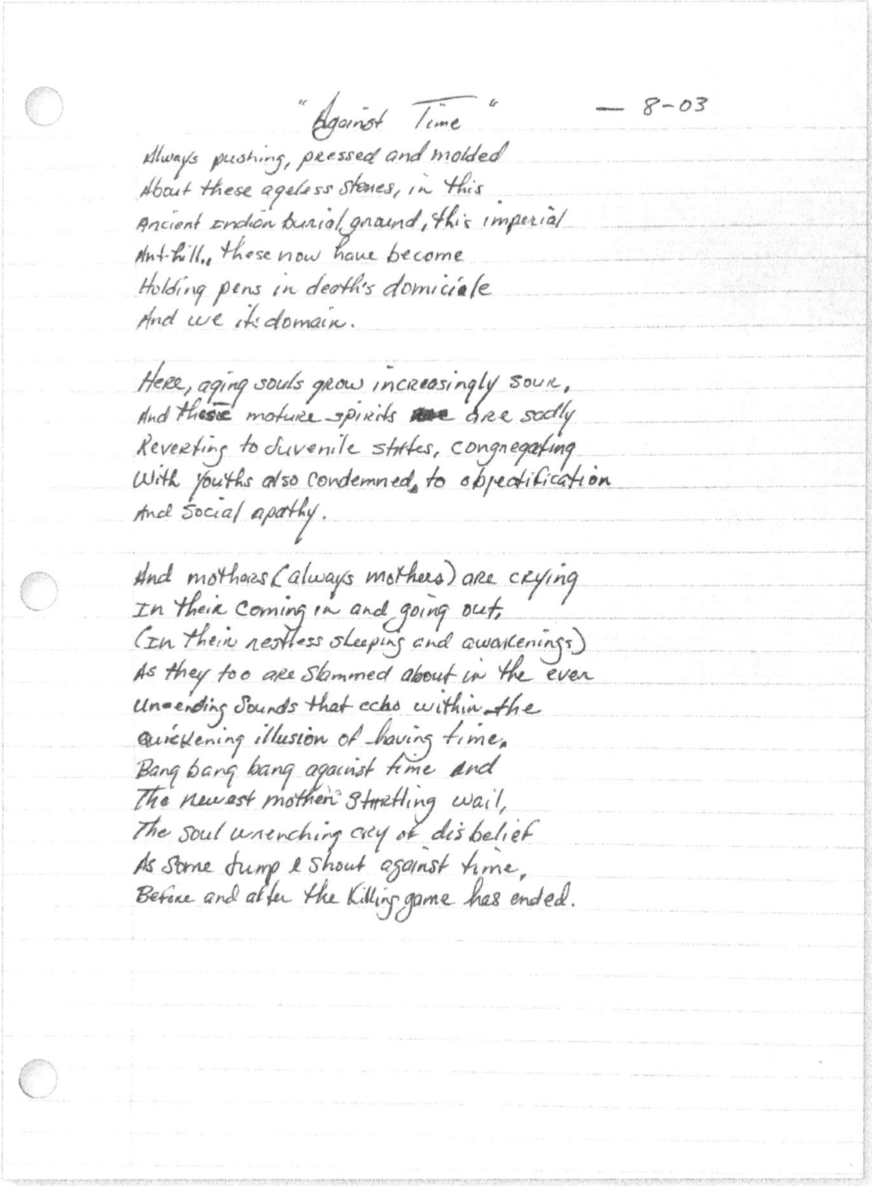

"Against Time"   — 8-03

Always pushing, pressed and molded
About these ageless stones, in this
Ancient Indian burial ground, this imperial
Ant-hill, these now have become
Holding pens in death's domicile
And we its domain.

Here, aging souls grow increasingly sour,
And these mature spirits are are sadly
Reverting to Juvenile states, congregating
With youths also condemned, to objectification
And social apathy.

And mothers (always mothers) are crying
In their coming in and going out,
(In their restless sleeping and awakenings)
As they too are slammed about in the ever
Un-ending Sounds that echo within the
Quickening illusion of having time,
Bang bang bang against time and
The newest mother's startling wail,
The soul wrenching cry of disbelief
As some Jump & Shout against time,
Before and after the Killing game has ended.

FIGURE 19. Original handwritten manuscript of "Against Time," by Darrell B. Grayson

Reductive Language

Jeffery Rieber • April–June 2005

In 2006, Eddie Ellis, formerly incarcerated activist and founder of Center for Nuleadership on Urban Solutions, famously penned an "open letter" to allies insisting on people-first language that does not reproduce the institutional labels of the criminal-legal system.[*] Rieber's 2005 piece makes a similar case, reflecting on the ways in which his own use of language reveals the labels he has internalized.

As an abolitionist and a man on death row, I have been known to refer to myself and others in similar situations as "inmate." I had never given it much thought but it was recently brought to my attention that the term "inmate" reduces an entire life down to the lowest possible denominator, thereby allowing death penalty proponents to think of me as nothing more than the perpetrator of a crime. By helping people to discount the entirety of who I am, I have been doing myself and others a great disservice in that it is easier for society to kill an "inmate" than it is to kill a complete, complex and precious human being who had a childhood, teenage and adult years that had nothing to do with a crime. It is easier and quicker to say "inmate" than it is to say "man or woman in prison," but I pledge to erase this convenient, reductionist term from my vocabulary and ask that our supporters try to do the same.

---

[*] Eddie Ellis, "An Open Letter to Our Friends on the Question of Language," (New York: Center for NuLeadership on Urban Solutions, 2003), https://cmjcenter.org/wp-content/uploads/2017/07/CNUS-AppropriateLanguage.pdf.

Souls, Souls, Souls

Greg Hunt • July–August 2005

---

*A 2018 poll conducted by the Pew Research Center found that 73 percent of
white Evangelical Christians support the death penalty.[*]*

> Lost soul sentenced to die.
> Christian's raised fist
> Hand high, shaking.
> And saying:
> Die, Devil!
>   Die, killer!
> Let the sinner die!
> Converted soul, still on death row
> Christian yet to lower hand,
> Or ire, to caress me.
> And say:
>   Live, Brother!
>   Live, friend!
>   Let the forgiven live!

---

[*] "Death Penalty Support Ticks Up in 2018 after Years of Decline." Pew Research Center, June 8, 2018, https://www.pewresearch.org/fact-tank/2018/06/11/us-support-for-death-penalty-ticks-up-2018.

Ghosts Over the Boiler

Darrell B. Grayson • 2005

A hall flunky informed
The cubical operator
Of a man hanging in his cell.

I lifted my head,
As I was one at the time.
Eventually, a guard walked
To that part of the Row.

Preacher's death was like the others.
Nope, wasn't the first time:
It started with a complaint,
The fixable kind.

The guard manages every step.
He takes out his key,
Opens the outer door,
Walks to the cell door.

He sees Preacher hanging,
Walks to the cubical,
Calls the operator and mumbles something,
Lights a cigarette, then leans.

Originally published in *Against Time* (2005) by Mercy Seat Press; this poem was also published in *POETRY Magazine* (February 2021).

Eventually,
A fat nurse climbs the stairs,
Another guard passes her,
I continue to mop.

Eventually, they come out with Preacher
On a stretcher with a sheet.
I know he is dead.
It is on his face.

Like ghosts they walk.
The guard and nurse,
They were talking about buying a truck.
Didn't hear what kind.

Well, I told a few guys.
They said:
He was a strange old fellow,
Tried to change cells.

One not over the boiler,
He said he couldn't take the heat.
I said, yeah,
Those other guys were fed up too.

It was bound to happen again,
But what can you do
When you're a ghost over the boiler?

Ghosts Over the Boiler

A hall flunky informed,
The cubical operator
of a man hanging
In his cell.

I lifted my head,
As I was one at the time.
Eventually, a guard walked
To that part of the Row.

Preachers death was like the others.
nope, wasn't the first time:
It started with a complaint,
the kind fixable.

The guard manages every step,
He takes out his key,
opens the outer door
walks to the cell door.

He sees preacher hanging,
walks to the cubical,
call the operator and mumbles something
lights a cigarett then leans.

Eventually,
A fat nurse climbs the stairs

FIGURES 20A AND 20B. Original handwritten manuscript of
"Ghosts Over the Boiler," by Darrell B. Grayson

Another guard passes her,
I continue to mop.

Eventually, they come out with preaching,
on a stretcher with a sheet.
I know he is dead.
It is on his Face.

Like ghosts They walk.
~~They walk~~ The guard and nurse,
They were talking about buying a truck
Didn't hear what kind.

well I told A few guys,
They said:
He was a strange old fellow,
Tried to change cells.

One not over the boiler,
He said he couldn't ~~take~~ take the heat.
I said yea,
~~One of those~~ Those other guys were fed up too

It was bound to happen again,
But what can you do?
When you're a ghost over the boiler

Poll Data

Dececmber 2005

In 2005, PHADP commissioned a poll about Alabama voters' attitudes toward the death penalty. The survey was conducted by the Capital Survey Research Center from July 12–14 and 18–21, 2005, and 863 registered voters participated. While 70.8 percent of people polled said they "support the death penalty," 79.6 percent also said that they believe "an innocent person may be convicted and executed." As PHADP writes, "Aren't we forced to conclude here that those who favor the death penalty favor it so strongly that they are willing to accept the execution of innocent people?"

We thank the Capital Survey Research Center for so graciously responding to our request for a death penalty survey in Alabama and we thank all who contributed to this survey. It confirms that a solid majority of the people of Alabama believe that the time has come for a moratorium on executions while an independent study is conducted into the fairness of the application of the death penalty. It also confirms that

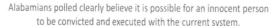

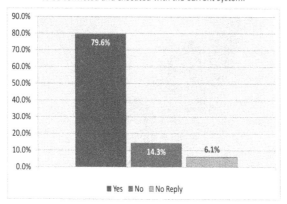

FIGURE 20. "Do you believe an innocent person may be convicted and executed?" All the charts in this section are from a survey by Capital Survey Research Center for Project Hope to Abolish the Death Penalty. To see the full survey results visit www.phadp.org/2005_poll

most Alabamians do believe in justice and that candidates running for election can embrace it and win. Looking at the numbers, it is obvious that Alabamians are uneasy about the application of capital punishment in their state. We hope that the candidates are listening as they develop their platform!

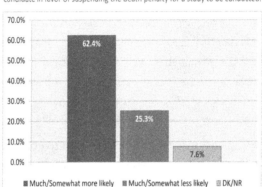

FIGURE 21. "There have been cases in which someone sentenced to be executed was found not guilty based on new evidence, usually DNA testing. How do you feel about suspending the death penalty in Alabama until questions about the fairness and accuracy of the death penalty have been studied and confirmed?"

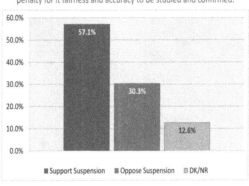

FIGURE 22. "Would you be more or less likely to support a candidate for public office who supports a suspension of the death penalty until questions about the use of DNA testing have been answered?"

Education remains the key and so we look to you to help spread the word. When I wrote last week three hundred organizations, churches, businesses, etc. had come out in support of a moratorium. We now stand at 340! Does that not tell you that the time for a moratorium is NOW? Please share this survey widely!

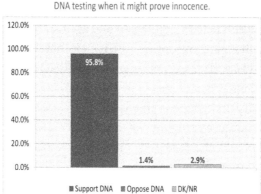

FIGURE 23. "How do you feel about the use of DNA testing in cases where it might prove a person's innocence or guilt?"

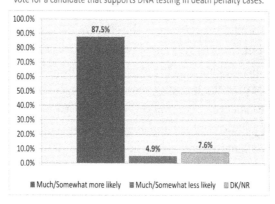

FIGURE 24. "Would you be more or less likely to support a candidate for public office who supports the use of DNA testing in cases that involve the death penalty?"

The Killing Machine

Nicholas Acklin • January–March 2006

Since the reinstatement of the death penalty in the US in 1976, over one thousand condemned have been executed. The debate over the death penalty continues, with pro-death penalty supporters and opponents of the death penalty arguing for and against the nation's "killing machine." Public support for the death penalty has decreased over the past twenty-five years. Death penalty opponents argue that the system is being used unfairly, and the possibility of innocent lives being taken is high. Death penalty supporters continue to argue that the death penalty deters crime, even pointing out that murder rates have dropped in the past years. Will the debates go on with no resolution?

Recent statistics have shown that our nation's use of the "killing machine" has decreased. A recent Gallup Poll taken in October 2005 shows that national support of the death penalty has dropped from 80 percent in 1994 to 64 percent. With 122 exonerations over the past twenty-five years, the use of the death penalty has to be in question. The October 2005 Gallup Poll also shows that support dips to 56 percent if the alternative is life without parole. The number of executions has dropped from ninety-eight in 1999 to fifty-nine in 2004. Death penalty supporters would say this is due to the effect of the death penalty being a deterrent, but couldn't this also mean that our citizens are realizing the flaws in our system, and the fears of executing the innocent?

In the past year, the haunting fear of wrongful executions has been raised by the *Chicago Tribune* and the *Houston Chronicle*. Opponents of the death penalty will say the appeals process afforded to the condemned is too lengthy, and delays justice to the victims and their families. This does not show fear of executing the innocent on the part of death penalty supporters. Should not a condemned person be afforded every avenue to prove innocence, as well as the time needed? DNA has been a key tool in exonerating many who were once condemned.

This raises another question: what about those who are innocent, but those cases did not involve DNA? Recently, a bill has been submitted to Congress that will drastically shorten the appeals process at the Federal stage. If this bill passes, not only will it eliminate an important stage in the death penalty appeals process, it will also put innocent lives in high risk of being executed. Can we truly fix a broken system when we continue to create flaws by eliminating the structure that was obviously put in place for good reason?

The debate over the death penalty will continue, and sadly at the cost of innocent lives possibly falling through the cracks. Why not put a nationwide moratorium on the death penalty while we debate and seek to fix a "beast" that has become rabid? It could possibly be that death penalty supporters fear it leading to abolition. If so, more questions must be raised. Has revenge taken the place of justice? Have we as a people grown "bloodthirsty"? How much do we truly value life? It's time that we as a free nation do some much needed soul searching and stop killing to show that killing is wrong.

Dispute Resolution

DBA A Person • January–March 2006

---

*In his State of the Union address from the White House on January 31, 2006, George W. Bush asked Congress to pass legislation banning research involving stem cells: "Human life is a gift from our Creator, and that gift should never be discarded, devalued, or put up for sale."**

I held off writing until the State of the Union address. I wanted to address how we continue to fill our killing machines and vent about the condition, health, and capacity of those being murdered by the state, but I waited. It doesn't matter that a person is placed in a wheelchair, pushed into a death chamber, lifted up and strapped onto a gurney, and murdered. It doesn't matter that there is no national standard for mental incapacity, though any common sense leaves one wondering how it is possible for anyone to be mentally incapacitated in Kansas and yet be competent in Texas? It really doesn't matter that society is not one bit safer because a sick, elderly, disabled, or mentally incompetent person is executed. It only matters that programs continue, death chambers remain filled, and society remains tricked into believing that no one intends for this circus of slaughter and immorality to be used as revenge. Now, that is what I wanted to write about, but I waited.

Somehow I just knew that quizzical George [W. Bush] would give me a nugget to hold on to. For all the subjects he discussed, my nugget came in stem cell research. Our President, leader of the democracy, made the statement that life is a gift from our Creator and we should never discard that gift.

I wonder if George W. would mind coming to sit with me for a few days in my little 5×7 and feel the discard? Sit with me through the struggle of emotion and reality in what amounts to a concrete and steel

---

* "January 31, 2006: State of the Union Address," Miller Center, January 31, 2006, https://millercenter.org/the-presidency/presidential-speeches/january-31-2006-state-union-address.

closet for twenty-three hours a day? Feel the frustration of one court saying you've brought this issue up before, therefore you can't bring it up again, while the next court says you've never brought this up before, therefore you can't bring it up now.

"Never discard" is a tough pill to swallow when you watch people who can't read or write sit and wait to be executed. Is it "discarded" that I'm feeling as I feel like a complete burden to my family and loved ones who wish there was something they could do? Is it "discarded" I am experiencing when my mom falls and I can't speak to her because the hospital won't accept collect calls? Am I being discarded when visitors are turned away because they wore the wrong color shirt, there are too many people on the yard, or my special visit allowance list is already filled up? Am I being discarded when I am subjected to cavity searches and I ain't even flying anywhere?

It came from our president: "never discard the gift of life." He mentioned violent crime and how statistics are down. He went over our need for educational advances to secure our future freedom and leadership. He discussed fighting terror abroad as opposed to within our borders. He throws out words like "prosperity," "opportunity," "advancement," "security," "freedom," "agenda," "initiative," and "every American." Meanwhile, our country continues to fill execution chambers and kill our own citizens.

Somewhere in all of that, our moral compass has been misplaced. Our courts are not about truth and justice! They merely represent dispute resolution regardless of validity. Facts based on theory and imagination are nothing more than fiction! Do I feel discarded? A thousand times over! Would President Bush consider me to be a gift from our creator?

Welcome to My World

Jimmy Davis Jr. • April–June 2006

Welcome to my world, where people are compassionate about others, about life, and how politics is shaping America right in front of our eyes. Although the people in my world have been cut from society, they do not give up on helping society to understand capital punishment and to help bring change in a system that many Americans support. In my world, no death row brother is left behind. Welcome to this world called death row, where people still believe that one day America will have a change of heart and value life.

Welcome to my world where there are kids without a father or mother due to this system. Welcome to my world where people have reached out to guide lost cousins, brothers, sisters, daughters and sons to the right path in life. Welcome to my world where we come together for each other in crises. Where friendship means a lot to us. Where communication and understanding means something. It's not about what valuables you have in your cell, or what shoes or watch you have on. Those things mean nothing in my world. What matters is the heart we have. Welcome to my world where brothers and sisters show love to each other at their weakest moments. Welcome to my world, where September 11 and Hurricane Katrina affect us and brought anger and tears.

My world has people who have done wrong in their lives but have changed for the better. My world has been badly affected by the brothers and sisters who have been killed by the state, or died of natural causes. We miss them dearly! A lot of people in my world are still working on bettering themselves and have made a 180 degree turn-around with their lives. This is the world that society has turned its back on. For the families and friends that have been in our lives before, thank you for the support and understanding. The difference in my world is, we wish all people the best, but a lot of people in society wish us death.

Change

Darrell B. Grayson • April–June 2006

If we embrace the power to change, we can transform our lives. In order to participate in this conversion one has to be removed from one's comfort zone, as the decision to change is a frightening one. Letting go of the status quo helps one to grow and expands one's horizon. All men are condemned to death. This being true, each of us has to come to terms with this knowledge in our own way. Most people do not have to wrestle with the day and hour of their death, as do those of us on death row, but we are all chained to the quality of life we choose. Whether we see our life as a glass half empty or half full depends on our choices and the changes these bring about.

As someone condemned to death, one would assume that I view my life as a glass half empty. Once, this was true! For the first eight years on death row, I was on a roller coaster headed toward the dark underbelly of what was left of my life. I wallowed for years in self-pity and ignorance until my mother's death became the catalyst for positive changes in my life. My perspective on life and personal accountability changed. A new belief system came into being in which ignorance and discord became repellent. I no longer felt helpless or indifferent toward my environment and my brothers on the row. I began to use my time wisely on socially productive endeavors and personal growth.

During one of my quiet, lucid moments, I was shocked to realize the depth of loss and deprivation that is endured here on death row. This insight created an urgency for action in me. I understood that each of us, in our own way, chooses to open doors that can limit or increase the possibilities in our lives. Some doors open only onto the miseries of the world, overwhelm us, and make us lose our focus. We see the world as an awful place: violence, fear, and loathing. But there are other doors we can open that lead to spiritual growth and positive action.

Change comes when we open our minds and hearts. For me, it brought the realization of just how impoverished our lives are in here, while at the same time understanding not only that the lives of many in the free world are no better, but that the lack of insight into ourselves will not shield any of us from the harsh realities of life. I have accepted that change is in my best interest and crucial to my survival.

The Continuing Journey

Derrick Mason • April–June 2006

The judge presiding over the trial of Derrick Mason asked Governor Bentley to commute his sentence to life in prison. He admitted that Mason's was his first capital trial and that he was overly zealous in his sentencing due to inexperience. Mason would be executed on September 22, 2011.*

In my last article in *Wings of Hope*, I discussed the topics of redemption and change. I now desire that you become aware of the awesome work that is being done by people that society has discarded as worthy of death. It is my heart's desire that folks who are in favor of the death penalty will come to appreciate the uniqueness of human beings in contrast to all other created things, being that we are more than just the worse act we have committed. It would be hypocritical to admire the transformation of the caterpillar into a beautiful butterfly and yet deny these possibilities in humans. Human growth and development are far more amazing than that of the butterfly. The first step toward change can be the next step taken. And I am seeing the fruits of this decision in my life and in many of the lives of my comrades who are incarcerated with me.

But for the grace of God go I.

---

* "State of Alabama Executes Derrick Mason Even though Sentencing Judge Admits His Death Sentence Was a Mistake," Equal Justice Initiative, September 22, 2011, https://eji.org/news/alabama-executes-derrick-mason.

Thoughts in Time

Nicholas Acklin • April–June 2006

Beyond these walls
Life goes timeless
The shuffling of feet
In a fast pace to the unknown.

While inside
Concrete and steel stand guard
Life is determined by time
Each second, minute, hour
A reminder of what life is

Teeth chatter in its wake
One being hopeful and clinging
Surrounded by negative images
Of hate and hope lost

Thoughts of what lies beyond the walls
Sleepless nights of what could be
To live again free
Bondage no more
Peace with life
In unison with time until death

Nobility's True Badge

DBA A Person • April–June 2006

Nobility's true badge: that is what Shakespeare called mercy. Of course, to comprehend nobility, one would have to understand terms such as honor, virtue, character, and moral fiber. These elements are quickly becoming absent from our society. Mercy is undeserved and yet time after time you hear pro-death penalty advocates say the person [executed] did not deserve mercy. No one deserves mercy! It is presented by the aforementioned traits of the giver.

Recently, Supreme Court justice Scalia said that when we hung someone, it wasn't painless.* Seems to me that Justice Scalia needs to have someone explain evolving standards of decency. As we have evolved as a people, the threshold of acceptance has changed—in theory, anyway. In a discussion of the death penalty and lethal injection, Justice Kennedy seemed to rebuke several other justices as they chuckled over what kind of execution lawyers would come up with for clients facing this organized process of murder. I think that speaks volumes as to the mindset of those considered noble.

While the US is quick to lead the world toward democracy, we remain the only Western nation in the world to cling to its archaic practice of killing its own citizens. You may think I have a vested interest, but you're incorrect. If I have to spend the last day of my life in prison, I wish it were sooner rather than later; but for the greater good of society and for the lives of the men that surround me, I fight the fight the only way I can. I fight with words.

---

* In hearing arguments during *Hill v. McDonough* (2006), Justice Scalia remarked that lethal injection is less painful than hanging, which can result in strangulation or decapitation. See Bill Mears, "Justices: Does Lethal Injection Hurt?," CNN Law Center, April 26, 2006, http://edition.cnn.com/2006/LAW/04/26/scotus.injection.

I beg for mercy. I scream for enlightenment. I plead with citizens to speak out against the decomposition of our social values. I ask Alabamians and Americans to please stop killing in the name of justice.

Nobility's true badge: do more than pin it on your shirt. Live it by being merciful, compassionate, kind, and tolerant to all people.

the Editor's Desk
Darrell B. Grayson • July–September 2006

Project Hope to Abolish the Death Penalty has initiated a project to address the disparate treatment of family members of victims of violent crime (fig. 25). Family members fall into three groups: those who do not want to be reminded of their loss; those who support legalized killing and are supported by the state; and finally, those who find no solace in creating other victims.

Those who support legalized killing have a powerful lobbying voice in the body politic of capital punishment. They are represented by the majority of legislators who support the death penalty and the state's leading victims' advocacy group, Victims of Crime and Leniency (VOCAL). This group is headed by an individual who experienced violence in her close family and who subsequently became a staunch advocate for state-sponsored killing. This group, which is supported by the governor's and attorney general's offices, is a consistent source of lobbying for the status quo on capital punishment. As a citizens' group, they are the main voice speaking against a moratorium at the legislative hearings and we respect their right to do so.

When we spoke about disparate treatment, we were talking about those family members who have also lost loved ones but who receive little support from the state because they do not see the death penalty as giving them closure. Their voices have not been given much of an opportunity to be heard so that if one is not careful it is all too easy to get the impression that VOCAL represents all who have lost someone to violence in Alabama. If so far they have not had much of a voice in Alabama, it is perhaps because it is not easy for us on death row to reach out to those who have been traumatized by us. And yet, do we not perpetuate the injustice by presuming that all think alike? We know the state has no interest in hearing them and so we have begun to reach out to them by letter and by one-on-one contact to allow them to speak on this matter of life and death. Answers are beginning to trickle in—answers that touch us, humble us by their generosity and understanding, answers that make us deeply grateful to those who stand with us for fairness and justice for all.

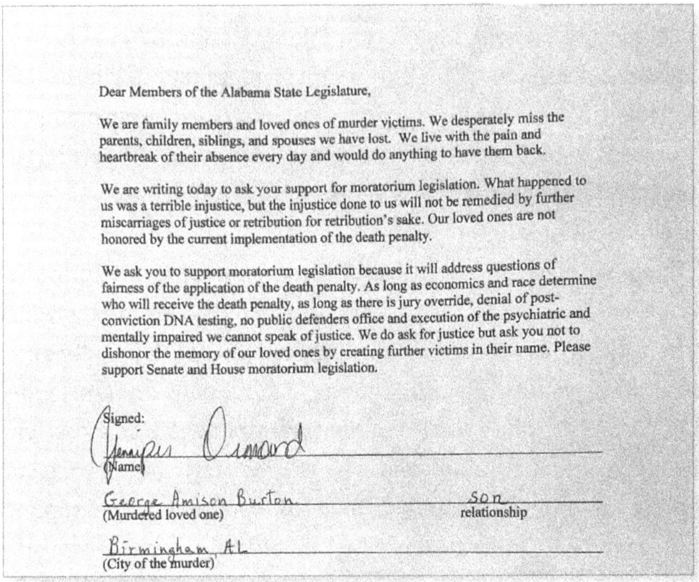

Dear Members of the Alabama State Legislature,

We are family members and loved ones of murder victims. We desperately miss the parents, children, siblings, and spouses we have lost. We live with the pain and heartbreak of their absence every day and would do anything to have them back.

We are writing today to ask your support for moratorium legislation. What happened to us was a terrible injustice, but the injustice done to us will not be remedied by further miscarriages of justice or retribution for retribution's sake. Our loved ones are not honored by the current implementation of the death penalty.

We ask you to support moratorium legislation because it will address questions of fairness of the application of the death penalty. As long as economics and race determine who will receive the death penalty, as long as there is jury override, denial of post-conviction DNA testing, no public defenders office and execution of the psychiatric and mentally impaired we cannot speak of justice. We do ask for justice but ask you not to dishonor the memory of our loved ones by creating further victims in their name. Please support Senate and House moratorium legislation.

Signed:

Jennifer Dinnard
(Name)

George Amison Burton _____ _son_
(Murdered loved one)   relationship

Birmingham, AL
(City of the murder)

FIGURE 25. PHADP's moratorium campaign included
signed letters from murder co-victims

A Time of Remembrance

Jeffery Rieber • July-September 2006

At this time of year toward the end of the summer, we here on death row turn our minds and thoughts to the remembrance of those men and women we have lost over the years to execution and natural causes.

Those men and women were our brothers and sisters in this fight to end state-sanctioned murder and each one is missed dearly.

Some were well known by all and some were not, but all are counted as equally deserving of our thoughts and respect.

This is a time of reflection for us still here on the row. We reminisce with each other about old friends and old times, events that occurred in days gone by. We keep their memories alive because we loved them yet were unable to keep their bodies alive.

They remain vividly animated in our minds, their personalities unique and precious. Each one special and worth keeping. We do this for them because we also do it for ourselves because none of us knows when or if we will be added to the list. No one wants to be forgotten.

Everyone wants to believe that others will remember them fondly after they are gone.

In addition to those of us on death row, there are others who keep these memories alive. Those other people are the friends and families of men and women who are, or were, on death row. They too are victims of the capital punishment system. We keep the friends and families in our hearts, as well, because it is a unique kind of pain they feel due to the fact that the population as a whole feels little or no sympathy for them or their loved ones.

We will do these things as long as we are alive, and hope that others will remember us once we are gone.

the Editor's Desk

Darrell B. Grayson • January-March 2007

The big news, in this our first issue of 2007 of *On Wings of Hope*, is that there have continued to be numerous death penalty studies on such weighty issues as the prevalence of ineffective assistance of counsel for death row prisoners. The irony is that Alabama was prominently mentioned in the McClatchy report but continues to forge ahead with its usual vengeful ferocity. Sadly, the state has set an April 5th execution date for Aaron Jones, and this while he and other prisoners on death row are challenging Alabama's lethal injection methods and protocol.

The setting of this date is one more illustration of our state's head-in-the-sand mentality when it comes to judicial fairness or standards of decency. And so while our state ignores these important issues, the following states are considering legislation to repeal capital punishment or to impose a moratorium on executions: CO, DE, KS, MD, MO, MT, NE, NJ, NM, SD and WA.

The lethal injection concerns continue in these states: AR, CA, DE, FL, MD, MO, NJ, NC, OH, SD and TN, [which] have effectively halted executions until these issues are resolved. In NY the existing death penalty has been declared unconstitutional by its high court.

On the downside, states like TX, UT and VA are attempting to expand existing capital punishment statutes. Closer to home, GA has asked its legislature to eliminate the provision that requires a unanimous vote to impose a death sentence. All of these issues affect Alabama's capital punishment system, but nothing is being done by the state.

In the midst of this silence, PHADP will continue to work on a moratorium and support Sen. Hank Sanders (D, Selma), when he again introduces the moratorium bill in the senate this year. We also expect Rep. Merika Coleman (D, Birmingham) to reintroduce her bill in the house.

To those of you who have signed on your businesses, churches and organizations in support of the moratorium, thank you! We invite others to join with us in this struggle. Please see the talking points inside this newsletter for further information.

And as always, thank you for helping us help ourselves!

Keep Hope Alive,

Darrell B. Grayson

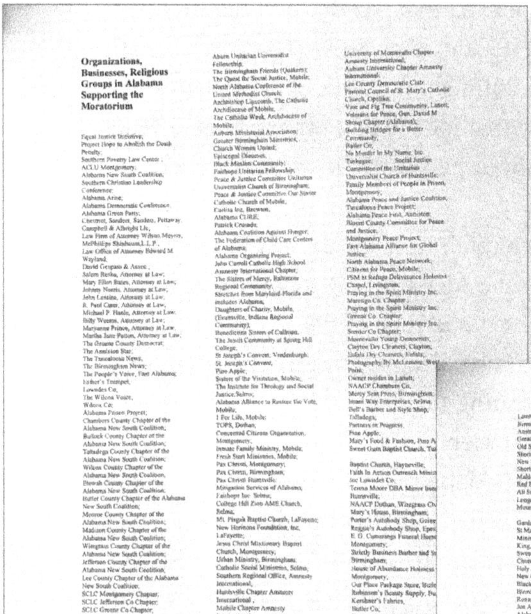

Organizations, Businesses, Religious Groups in Alabama Supporting the Moratorium

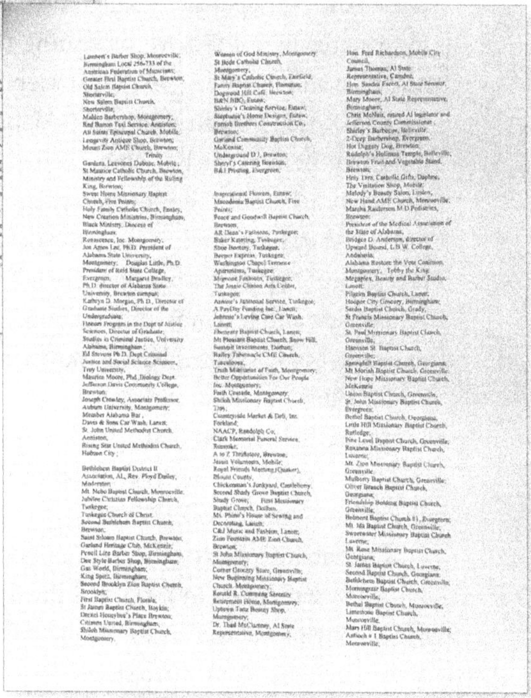

FIGURES 26 AND 27. Organizations, businesses, and religious groups in Alabama supporting the moratorium, ca. 2007

Alabama Alone in Denying National Trend

Jeffery Rieber • January-March 2007

Across our nation, this past year, fewer men and women were sentenced to death. Yet Alabama bucked that trend according to capital punishment watchdogs and state statistics. This reduction in death sentences is said to reflect the diminishing public support for capital punishment. Gallup polls show that for the first time in twenty years, more people preferred life without parole (48 percent) to the death penalty (47 percent).

Alabama, as usual, is slow to catch up with the rest of the nation. A survey conducted in 2005 by the Alabama Education Association's Capital Survey Research Center stated that 71 percent strongly supported the death penalty. That number dropped by three points in 2006 to 68 percent, but the overwhelming majority of registered voters in Alabama still favor capital punishment.

This doesn't mean that more Alabamians trust or believe in the judicial system. It can be demonstrated that the opposite is true. When people don't trust the judicial system to keep killers off the streets forever, they then tend to favor the death penalty as a sure-fire way to take care of murderers once and for all. The problem with that mindset is that, first and foremost, innocent people will unquestionably be put to death. Many say this has already happened. Another reason is that capital punishment diminishes us as a people and country.

In the '90s, about 300 people were condemned each year. Since 2000, the nation has averaged 150 death sentences, with the number dropping annually to 114 in 2006.

In Alabama, thirteen defendants were sentenced to die in 2006. Ten were sentenced in 2005 and the total for 2002–2004 was twenty-three. One of the factors for Alabama's higher sentencing rate is that Alabama is one of only two states that allow a judge to override a jury's sentencing recommendation. It is the only state that allows this without any guidelines or standards governing the practice of overrides. By overriding life without parole sentence recommendations, elected judges can appear to be tough on crime in order to get reelected but they deny and disregard the will of the people every time they do it.

Alabama has executed twenty-eight men and women since 1990. It carried out four executions in 2000 and 2005, and one in 2006. The Alabama attorney general has asked for one date to be set already this year, and that man still has appeals pending.

"I am firmly convinced that the passionate will for justice and truth has done more to improve (the human condition) than calculating political shrewdness which in the long run only breeds general distrust." —Albert Einstein, "Moral Decay" (1937)

A Christian Perspective

Ronald B. Smith • January–March 2007

DEAR FAMILY AND FRIENDS,

The year 2007 is off and racing in more ways than one. Project Hope to Abolish the Death Penalty has gathered more than eight hundred signatures for a moratorium resolution. Forty-two city/county legislatures have signed moratorium resolutions. And we have twenty-five family of victims support letters (these are letters from family members of murder victims who support a moratorium.) A lot has been done in the last few years and there is still much more left to do.

So many people in this country stand strong in their belief that capital punishment is justified. Others disregard the issue altogether in the apathetic belief that they can do little to change how justice in the United States of America is being carried out. That is, until they become involved in the system they have ignored for years.

We here at Holman recently received a visit from the Browder Prison Ministry. I was given a daily meditation calendar and at the bottom of the calendar is the verse of scripture from Psalms 119:17: "I shall not die, but live and declare the works of the Lord." What a mighty sentiment! Something I myself need to put into practice more often. Speaking life, appreciating the blessings I receive, and declaring them to others. This is something we can all do on a daily basis.

As societies develop, so do their laws.

Certain practices become unconscionable relics and are cast aside as inhumane. After a generation of often reckless expansion of the death penalty, the pendulum is starting to swing back. The change did not start in 2007. But it sure looks like it is picking up the pace.

the Editor's Desk
Darrell B. Grayson • April–June 2007

Once again the PHADP / death row family offers its heartfelt condolences to the other family and friends of one of our own. This time we mourn Aaron Jones who was executed by the state of Alabama on May third. We feel your pain.

As you should know the conclusion to my condemnation is to proceed on July 26, which would make this my last editorial for this publication. What to say?

I believe there's a time and place for every eventuality, and at this point, the work I've dedicated myself to should continue to be our focus. No final statements here, just outrage at the blatant disregard for justice and at the ignorance and apathy that continue to support the most egregious system in our society, the criminal justice system.

But all is not as it seems in Alabama. There are considerable forces at work, for the benefit of all citizens, helping to bring what's done in the dark into the light. The eyes of the nation are on the request before the country's highest court to hear the case of Alabama death row inmates who lack adequate legal representation. Our state is the only one in the nation that doesn't provide attorneys for post-conviction appeals. Three former Alabama Supreme Court justices, a former appellate judge and three former presidents of the Alabama state bar filed a friend of the court brief in support of this claim. Who better than they to know!

Also, the lethal injection issue is before several courts and addresses more than just who is qualified to stick a needle in the veins of the condemned but also the chemicals used and their unique effect on people of differing physical characteristics.

My current status not withstanding, I intend to remain focused on PHADP's mission to educate the public about capital punishment and to maintain the gains we have made over the last six years. Together

with other conscientious individuals and organizations we will continue to speak out against the injustices of Alabama's judicial system.

Much could be said about the failure of Alabama's elected officials
to get much accomplished during this session. The bills which never
made it to the floor included several death penalty bills. Maybe you,
the voter, will voice your displeasure at the polls.

And so I ask you to remain at your post, ever vigilant with your
feet firmly planted on integrity. In this way you will help us to help
ourselves. Peace!

Never Fails to Amaze

Jeffery Rieber • April–June 2007

Alabama never fails to amaze me with the things it does. I don't mean all of its citizens, because a growing number of citizens are coming to see that the death penalty is wrong. I'm talking about the illusive "Them." Some would say "the powers that be." They always seem to be up to something that makes you just shake your head when you see it on the news.

Here's the thing, all over America more and more states that have the death penalty are stopping their executions until the higher courts figure out this problem with lethal injection. But Alabama, in all its wisdom, has decided to execute as many as possible before the court hears the issue.

If you haven't yet heard what's wrong with lethal injection, here it is in a nutshell. There are three drugs. The first one is an ultra-short-acting barbiturate that begins wearing off as soon as it is administered. It is supposed to put you to sleep and keep you unconscious, but it wears off and the person wakes up. The second drug paralyzes you so that you can't even blink an eye. It also paralyzes your diaphragm so that you cannot breathe. This drug, by the way, has been banned from use by veterinarians when euthanizing animals because it masks pain and is therefore cruel and unusual to use on animals. The third drug stops your heart. It is very caustic and burns like acid as it courses through your veins.

Taken together, as the protocols now stand, this is a recipe for torture plain and simple. The courts have even agreed to hear the issue and have set a date to hear it. You would think that Alabama would do the prudent thing, the same thing so many other states have done, and halt executions until this is settled. They are scared the courts will leave them without a viable method of execution so they are getting as many as possible done before that happens. It's always something in Alabama.

A Christian Perspective

Ronald B. Smith • April–June 2007

DEAR FRIENDS AND FAMILY,

In the midst of all the trials and tribulations the world is facing
we can take comfort in knowing we serve a mighty God. Though
poverty, war, famine, and disease have besieged certain parts of the
globe, God has not forgotten us and still hears our prayers. Even
when they are made from death row (Psalm 102:17–20).

The past few months have been tense here, especially when word
got out that the state of Alabama is seeking execution dates for several death row inmates, even though there are very important hearings on the horizon that could bring about some changes regarding
the administration of capital punishment and the method of execution in Alabama. Among all of the problems and shortcomings in
Alabama's criminal justice system, one of the worst is that we are the
only state in the nation that does not provide condemned inmates
with attorneys for appeals. The fact that three former Alabama
Supreme Court justices, a former appellate judge and three former
presidents of the state bar weighed in on the side of the inmates in
a friend of the court brief is a compelling development that should
weigh heavily against the state. Also, the research recently released
by Miami University concluding that lethal injection, as currently
administered, is painful and cruel, and that the condemned suffers
and could suffocate during the execution, has caused several states
to pause, but not Alabama.

What is Alabama's leadership afraid of?

How could a study of the current administration of capital punishment in Alabama so frighten Alabama's legislature? It seems a
practical concern as well as a moral one. The state of Alabama
cannot justify its willingness to let condemned inmates go to their
deaths without an attorney and with overwhelming evidence that

the method of execution employed in Alabama constitutes cruel and unusual punishment. Its current policy is wrong. Dead wrong.

Change is coming and so is Jesus. And I am looking forward to both.

the Editor's Desk

Jeffery Rieber • July–September 2007

This is a sad time for PHADP and a sad time for Alabama as well. This issue is dedicated to our fallen brother, Mr. Darrell B. Grayson. As you all know, the state of Alabama executed him on July 26. What you may or may not know is the caliber of man he was. He was not only my best friend, he was the model of the kind of man that I hope to be one day. Everyone on the row who knew him admired and looked up to him. No man is perfect in this world, but Darrell was kindness personified. He was a poet, he was smart, and yet he was never the kind to think he was better than someone else. He shared his wisdom with the young men here at Holman in order to help them deal with life and death on the row. He was gentle and kind, and his accomplishments for PHADP are too many to list here. He led PHADP into a new age of effectiveness and renown. Our job now is to keep up the momentum that has been generated over the last seven years. His execution has created a fervor of activity that needs to be capitalized on. It's what he would want. I promise to do my very best as the new chairman of PHADP. I have a board full of dedicated men who will all do their best. I have the utmost confidence in them all. We have an executive director [Esther Brown] who has no equal in any organization. With dedicated people like this, along with our wonderful supporters, "Hope" will survive and prosper. I grieve with all of you who knew Darrell and those of you who knew of him. Let us do what he would want and stay focused on our objective of abolition. My brother, you will be remembered and honored always. I can't improve upon his customary benediction at the end of his editorials, so I will copy him unashamedly and say simply this: PEACE

MEMORY OF A MENTOR:

On July 26, we lost our dear brother Darrell Grayson to the executioner. It was a sad day for all of us, especially as we were taught to keep hope and were hopeful for a positive outcome. Darrell, even while drawing closer to his execution, continued to encourage us all to keep our focus. Darrell was and will always be a shining example for us all.

Darrell was a positive influence in my life and the lives of others. He had the ability to see in others what they didn't see in themselves. Before prison I never took time to pick up a book and read. I never concerned myself with politics, or even envisioned that I would one day be able to hold the position of editor of a newsletter. Darrell challenged me to do better myself and push myself to do things I felt I was incapable of doing. I learned first that I have a voice and should take advantage of that voice. Since then, I have encouraged others to do the same, while stressing its importance. All this I owe to my brother, friend and mentor, Darrell Grayson.

The shining example has passed on through the PHADP family of insiders and outsiders. Each and every one of us has a reflection of Darrell within us. It shows through in all that we do and focus on. The words Keep Hope Alive will forever be in my memory as Darrell instilled that in us. His positive reflection will continue to shine, as the memory of his ideas continue to mentor. So to the family of PHADP, our supporters and sister organizations, we must continue in the direction Darrell has set for us, and in all things, KEEP HOPE ALIVE!

IN LOVE AND PEACE,
Nicholas Acklin, Sec./Treas. PHADP

MY BROTHER:

How do you say goodbye to someone you love and care for? How can you look into someone's eyes knowing that he is about to be killed? Those questions have haunted me for over thirteen years. Every execution gets harder and harder for me. Brothers that are fathers, uncles, counselors, mentors who changed me! Brothers with big voices that have never been heard! Why are all these brothers getting murdered?

My brother, I want to let you know how much you mean to me. I want you to know how you have been the reason I thirst for knowledge. My brother, I will never let anyone shame your name or character. I want you to know that I won't let their actions toward you turn my mission into one of anger and revenge but into one of truth and justice. I know you want me to be strong, keep fighting and keep carrying the torch on. My brother, the state killing you has brought so much hurt to my soul, but I will never show them my tears and I promise my voice will be bolder.

My brother, a lot of people don't even know your life, past or present. They don't even know how talented you are. They don't know how you took lost men and women that society not only gave up on but threw into a cage called prison and forgot about, and you made them see the power in themselves that has scared powerful people all across the nation. My brother, I want you to know that you have shown me things about myself no college could have brought out in me. The sad part about this article is I'm saying all of this after they've taken you from us all. I love you, brother, and you will always be in my heart.

Jimmy Davis

DEAR FAMILY AND FRIENDS:

We have just recently suffered a terrific blow to our organization in the loss of our chairman, Darrell B. Grayson. But many of us suffered a far greater loss as Darrell was also our brother, friend and neighbor. G Bear was one of the strangest characters I've met on this journey called life. We share little in the way of past experiences as he was born Black in the oppressive and racist South, while I was born white as an Army brat with what most would consider a traditional education. So what do you suppose would happen if these two diametrically different individuals met and became neighbors? (At the time, all we had in common, as far as we knew, was the fact that we had both been sentenced to death by the state of Alabama.) The first time we met was during my orientation to PHADP. And in the mid-nineties we often played basketball against each other. (The Bear could rebound and shoot the short jumper on me like few of our peers even though I had the height and weight advantage.) But our relationship really came together after Darrell became my next-door neighbor. We were both on the board of PHADP and he was soon to become our chairman. We were allies but we really became friends shortly after he moved next door to me.

You can really get to know a person after sharing mutual pains and suffering together. But we also shared laughs and good times. We had late night talks about family, religion, literature, music and sports. We also shared stories of our childhoods and our hopes for the future. No topic of conversation was off limits (including race relations). He could be trusted to get your mind off whatever distraction was stealing your energy and focus from what is really important: leaving the world a better place than it was. He was successful. And I am grateful to have called him friend. He made this place easier to stand and challenged me to be better myself. Brother, you will be missed. May the Good Lord send someone across your path that will benefit your life and lead you to become a better person. Keep us in your prayers in these trying times. God bless you all.

Ronald B. Smith

DEAR READERS,

We lost a very good man, Darrell Grayson, who was executed by the state of Alabama. A system that is slowly drifting toward despotism. The governor turned down Darrell's clemency, ignoring the idea that he could very well be killing an innocent man. All he could see was blood as he went after Darrell's life. Darrell Grayson fought for true justice. What happened to him was not justice. Anything that is loved is never lost or forgotten. When I spoke to Darrell he had such a true, sincere hospitality and an overwhelming spirit of true brotherhood. The loss of such a good person left me utterly speechless. As his friend, brother, and fellow member of PHADP, I will do my best to end state-sanctioned murders. The death penalty is a plague that is running through the justice system like an incurable cancer. It is a tool that is used for revenge and not justice. The writings are on the wall and shouldn't be ignored or overlooked. The people that are running this country don't want to admit how arbitrary and capricious this legal system really is. Although America is a Christian nation they don't seem to understand that murder of any kind is wrong! I am honored to say I was able to get to know Darrell. And if you readers would have known him, then you too would call him brother just as I did.

If Governor Riley had taken the time to get to know Darrell, then he would have seen him in a different light because that is what kind of person Darrell was. Although Darrell Grayson is no longer with us, he will be immortalized in the hearts and minds of all the people he touched.

D. L. de'Bruce

I MISS MY NEIGHBORS:

Darrell Grayson has only been gone a little while but I miss him already. He was executed by the state of Alabama as scheduled for a crime of which he had no knowledge because he was passed out in a state of intoxication at time the crime occurred. Darrell will be forever missed like all the rest taken from my neighborhood here on the row, especially those like Darrell whom I knew well and shared a daily sociable relationship. Then there are those I never got to know as close friends but certainly acquaintances whose faces, voices, gabs, quietness or something else made deep enough impressions to be forever remembered and greatly missed. Never again able to ask, What do you think of this or that? Never again able to share ideas as death penalty opponents in the midst of memorable smiles or critical laughter so desperately needed by the souls of this dark place. Hardly, if at all, are we ever sent here fastened securely in handcuffs and leg irons under armed guard already knowing each other; but once we are here, this place becomes our neighborhood, our residence, and our everyday livelihood. Therefore, we all share the commonality of a community where everyone shares another's pain and suffering. Some may share more of another's pain and suffering than others, depending on the closeness, friendship, etc. When one of us is placed back into the restraints of hand and leg irons under armed guard and taken away by force, if necessary, to never gasp another breath, it is felt by the whole neighborhood. It is no different than on the outside, so we all share the grief and the pain. Neighborhood is still neighborhood, and when one falls, everyone stumbles until strengthened to walk again without the limp. We are presently facing even darker days with so many appointed to be executed soon. So not only do we cry out for your sincerest prayers but also for every possible echo of our cries to be heard in hopes of creating enough compassion to stop the madness.

Leroy White

HOW CAN I?

Ever since the day it happened, July twenty-sixth, I've been asking myself how I can best remember our beloved brother, friend, and leader Darrell B. Grayson? To this day (a few weeks later), I'm still struggling to come up with the best solution. It's hard to come up with one when you can't seem to accept the fact that Darrell is no longer with us in the flesh and you still want him here with you doing things you always did together. It's hard to come up with the right format when you still have a lot of (beep) anger looming over you and inside of you because of a few (beep) politicians who are more concerned with a damn vote than doing what's (beep) right. They could have granted him a DNA test, but they didn't.

No matter what I come up with, when I'm able to think clearly, I feel as if it's not enough. The last thing I want to do is cheat Darrell out of his glory because then I'll have to answer to a lot of people, among other things. Darrell truly meant a lot to each and every one of us, and I can see how people will be quick to let me know that I left too many things out. Yes, Darrell was a very bright man, loving, dedicated, giving, athletic, as well as a leader, a poet, and the list goes on.

But how can I best remember him?

So as I'm struggling to come up with the best solution I must turn the table. How will you best remember Darrell B. Grayson? Will you remember him by continuing the fight against injustices that he was so very passionate about to the very end? Yes, that is part of how I will remember Darrell, but I still feel that I can do more.

ALWAYS,
Omar

the Editor's Desk

I hope the new year is treating you all well. The first quarter of 2008 is almost over and people across the nation are talking about the *Baze v. Rees* case, involving lethal injection protocols. However, there is something as or more important going on in Alabama right now and that is what I need to talk to you about.

As you read this, our legislators are in session and there are several bill proposals that are extremely important to our cause. Sen. Hank Sanders and Rep. Marika Coleman have both introduced bills calling for a moratorium on executions while a study is done to find and correct the flaws in the system. Sen. Sanders has introduced several others concerning capital punishment which also need our support. In order to be voted upon, the bills first have to make it out of the House and Senate Judiciary Committees. I can't stress enough how important it is that everyone reading this take action and contact the members of the Judiciary Committees in support of these bills. Also, we ask that you contact the legislators from your district asking them to support these bills.

Without your individual support and action, these bills stand very little chance of passing. Legislators can be contacted by phone, mail or online. In an effort to help you help us, we will list as much of the contact information as possible. Please, please, take the time out of your busy day to help make history in Alabama. Thank you all.

Death Row Artwork

BOO • January-March 2008

For years now there has been a movement to stop the sale of artwork from death row. A movement that has found its way to the highest authorities in the land.

In the last Alabama legislative session, a bill to prevent the sale of art, essays and memorabilia was introduced into the House of Representatives. This bill passed unanimously in the House and was sent to the Senate with hopes of the same.

Were it not for the political maneuvering of state sen. Phil Poole of Tuscaloosa, this bill would have passed the senate into law with no opposition. State rep. Cam Ward of Alabaster created and introduced this bill to stop the sale of inmate art that depicts victims and the crimes that were perpetrated against them.

Even as a death row inmate and artist, I see both the need and desire for such legislation. I have never felt the need to glorify my greatest regret, nor have I ever condoned that behavior in others.

I do, however, condone the sale of inmate artwork on the net, or otherwise. You see, I often use the net to sell my own artwork. I do not do so in order to strike at the families of the victim in my case, nor to promote such behavior. There are only two reasons I sell my art in any medium. The first is the most obvious. I do not believe my own friends and family should have to be burdened with my support. While the money I generate from the sale of my art doesn't alleviate the financial burden placed upon them, it does ease it. And have no doubt, for those who love us, that burden is substantial.

The second is more personal, though equally important. I simply don't want to be remembered solely for the actions of a single night. I want to be remembered for more than the person I was that night. Someone better. I am not that person, and will never be that person again. The artwork I sell reflects that fact. My legacy will never be great, but perhaps I can show the world that I am not the monster I was believed to be.

You may be asking why I would be concerned about this bill if the artwork I sell is positive. Why would this affect me or others of like mind? That's simple as well. You see, this bill will not only affect the one or two who abuse this right. As with all things that make the lives of death row inmates and their families harder, the DOC will see this as an opportunity to punish us all. With the passing of this bill, wardens across the state will stop the art from leaving death row, an action that would place a massive burden on some families.

I am not the only one here who uses his talent to assist in his care. There are men here whose only income is from their artwork, which is not the sinister depictions the bill targets, but beautifully positive art.

They do not rely on their crime to sell their work, nor do they attempt to cause harm to anyone with that work. They sell positive depictions for positive reasons. Depictions and reasons that are greatly threatened by the ambiguous nature of this bill.

Please do not misunderstand my intent. I agree that there should be a filter to ensure that harmful, deplorable art does not leave the prisons. I only wish to point out the harm that would come from not protecting the rights of those who wish only to assist their loved ones and improve themselves through their art. To ask that you take care, Rep. Ward, that you don't cause more harm than good with your bill.

Not everyone here is evil.

SEBO

Carey Grayson • April–June 2008

For the past few weeks I've wracked my brain for the words to express my feelings on the loss of my best friend. Time and time again I have failed to put those feelings in ink and I am still failing. I just don't know what to say. How do you put a decade of friendship into a few paragraphs? Better yet, how do you talk to strangers about friends? I don't know what to say but I know I have to try.

My friend's name is Danny Siebert and on April twenty-second he died of cancer. I can't help but think that if he wasn't in prison he may have lived, or at least held on a little longer and been cared for better. You see, at the end, the pain was so great that death was a blessing. I can't explain to you how it felt to see a man I admired and trusted writhe on his bunk trying to ease a pain that could not be eased. I can't explain how it felt to hear him tell me he wished he would just die, understand that wish and agree with it.

The only consolation I can find in his death is that he escaped the state and is finally free of this prison. Free of the pain that plagued his last days.

Sebo and I had very little in common, truth to tell. Other than a love of art and solitude, we were at opposite ends of the spectrum. He was a driven man, always working or debating some point or another. I'm lazy and have little patience for debates. We would spend months without speaking to each other, both nursing some imagined wound inflicted by the other. Then one day, one of us would speak, the other responded, and all was well until the next bout of stupidity hit and another few months would pass in mutual hatred.

It was an odd relationship, to say the least, but it was one we were both comfortable with. Most of the time we disagreed; sometimes we were in full accord. The disagreements were of little matter in truth, the passing of time, you could say. It was the times we agreed that we remembered.

I suppose the reason we were such good friends is that we both understood the basics of true friendship. Friends are not the people who tell you what you want to hear or show you what you want to see. They are not the people who ask for perfection or demand you change to fit their mold. Real friends are the people who see you for what you are, know you for who you are. They know your secrets and refuse to use them against you. They tell you in no uncertain terms when you're being an ass, and defend your stupidities to the world while naming you an idiot to your face. They are the ones that accept your flaws as readily as your assets.

Sebo was my friend and all who know me know that I choose those to whom I attach carefully. There is no secret I would not trust him with, no help I would not offer him. He was my best friend and I miss him more than I can say.

You Have a Right to Know

D. D. III • April–June 2008

Alabama ranks at the bottom of the fifty states when it comes to education and income. Schools are being closed due to a lack of funding.

Alabama attorney general Troy King is the second-highest-paid attorney general in the nation at $163,744 per year. That's four times the annual earnings of a typical Alabama tax payer.

Troy King had the temerity to say that if judicial salaries fall too low, the quality of Alabama justice could suffer. Pay should have little to do with taking the job of attorney general. Would King admit that lesser pay equals lesser quality when it comes to court appointed attorneys, who are paid less money to take capital cases in Alabama than in any other state in America?

Why does King pay his paralegal $94,000 annually? A man who is not only NOT a paralegal, but is basically nothing more than a neophyte who has since been promoted to chief of staff at $104,000?

Troy King should run his office scandal free and be scrupulous in dealing with those in his employ. He can't do that by promoting a young man from unpaid student intern to executive assistant at $57,504 annually.

Although none of this is illegal, certainly it smacks of the good ole boy system. King's hiring and promoting practices should be raising troubling questions from a state whose income ranks as low as Alabama's.

Alabama's judges are some of the highest paid judges in the nation. Maybe that's why they fight so hard to be reelected. Overriding juries' life-without-parole sentences, imposing death instead of life-without-parole sentences is an effective tool in helping judges look tough on crime, thereby making them re-electable.

During election years, there are marked increases in override cases. That fact alone should illustrate to any thinking person that the death penalty is politically influenced, and as such, should be abolished.

Justice in America is supposed to be blind, that's why the statue wears a blindfold. We are dealing with human lives here but the justice system has been co-opted by highly paid politicians, i.e., our overpaid attorney general and overpaid elected judges. The corruption of true American ideals, of which blind justice is of one of the originals, will lead to the collapse of our society. Like the Romans, we will be nothing more than a memory if we are not careful.

the Editor's Desk

Jeffery Rieber • October-December 2008

2008 is coming to a close, and above all, I am thankful that there have been no executions in Alabama this year. Of course, thinking about that brings to mind all of my friends who, over the years, have been executed and are no longer with us. I have gotten to know, and become friends with, over twenty men who were intentionally killed by the society that I grew up in. The society that claims to be the best in the world. I still believe very strongly in the idea of a democratic society and I love what America could be. I just think that our collective arrogance and the "might makes right" mentality have blinded us into thinking that we are a fully formed, complete society that is at the pinnacle of maturity when it comes to civilization, governance and morality. I would imagine that many of the societies around the world that are much older than America look at us like the strong, young teenage boy who thinks he knows it all. Just because we can beat up our dad doesn't mean that we have more wisdom than he does. Please pay special attention to the quotes in this issue and give them some real thought!

I so wish that my best friend and mentor Darrell Grayson could have been here to see history made when America elected President Obama! He would have been so proud of his country. This wonderful event has proven to me that all is not lost and that there is hope of becoming the nation we claim to already be. Racism, however, is not gone and we have a very long way to go. We are not going to crawl out of this hole overnight and I hope we, as a people, give our idealistic new president enough time to effect real change without expecting too much too soon.

Project Hope to Abolish the Death Penalty and all of our supporters in this struggle have already accomplished a lot in the last several years. I thank you all for all you do to help us. Without you, there would be no PHADP. On a personal level, without you I would not be able to do this meaningful work of which I am proud. You give me the chance to do something positive with my life and I can not express how much that means to me. Thank you, thank you! Thank you for allowing me a shot at some small measure of redemption and peace of mind in what is left of my life.

Over the years I've heard many little adages such as, "It's not the quantity of friends, but the quality that is important." I don't have a lot of friends anymore, maybe I never did. I do have a small circle of true friends that have become my family since I lost the ones related to me by blood. I have come to realize that family is what is in your heart, not what is in your DNA. I am extremely thankful for my small band of new family and I wish them all a very happy holiday season and an even better year to come. You know who you are and you are all tasked with the job of eating wonderful holiday foods and shamefully rich desserts in my stead. You know me, so you know how much food means to me. You'll know that I'm very serious about this and I expect to hear all about it after the holidays are over.

To my PHADP family: I wish you joy, happiness and contentment throughout the holidays and the year to come. May you appreciate your loved ones, and be appreciated in turn. May the fallout from the Bush Doctrine not affect you too adversely, and may you be filled with hope for the future . . . and eggnog and pumpkin pie!!

It falls to me to remind you that without your support we cannot continue this fight for truth and common sense in our justice system. Please help us to keep Hope alive. Thank you.

PEACE

Faith vs. Fear

Derrick Mason • October–December 2008

As I pen this article, I have cause to pause for a bit of quiet reflection on the state of things in our country. We are in a very fearful and uncertain time full of possibilities. Our country decided to go the way of faith and hope rather than fear in its election of Barack Obama. But with the economy doing a roller coaster ride, fear and uncertainty are ever present in the hearts of the people. So . . . what to do?

It is certain that these two, faith and fear, cannot occupy the same vessel. Crime is on the rise in many of our cities and this quite naturally gives rise to fear. Fear that is manipulated by dishonest politicians gives birth to draconian laws that do more harm than good. What we need in this country is more of what we have just witnessed in this recent election . . . people stepping out in faith.

For the past few years we have been a people besieged by fear and as it turns out we haven't made very good decisions in terms of our leadership, and I'm talking about both parties. The scriptures say in one place that "perfect love casts out fear." And in another place the scriptures say that what matters in Christ is "faith working through love." This is the key to all of the emotional bitterness that has come to the surface during the election cycle. This, of course, is the key that society has missed with regard to the question of capital punishment. Sure, I understand the despair at the constant incidents of crime! I'm in prison, and I watch the news and hang my head at some of the stories I hear. It sickens many of us who are incarcerated to see the crime rates. But at the same time, we know that a knee-jerk reaction out of fear will only apply a band-aid where surgery is required. We must change our methods, America! Change is in the air. Change the philosophy behind our corrections policy.

Step out in faith and try a new thing! After all, where has our current way of thinking gotten us? Where has "locking 'em up and throwing away the key" gotten us? "Kill 'em all and let God sort 'em out."

Where has this fearful line of thinking gotten us? It certainly has not made us any safer! Surely, there has not arisen a deterrent from any of these lines of thinking. It does not work on an international level. It has not yielded fruit on the national level, and as we all know, it has not changed a thing on the local level. There must be a balanced approach to solve the problems that we face on a global scale. You can't just go to war with every perceived offender. And you can't win every conflict with bombs from the sky. We need thinking, reasoning, fluid leadership. And this type is not weak as we have painfully learned. Likewise, we need this kind of leadership on a statewide level. Obviously not giving crime a tap on the hand, but at the same time not being fearful of a different approach. It takes faith to take the road less traveled.

Faith vs. fear: what will we take, America?

PART III

The Killing Machine

2009–2010

the Editor's Desk

Jeffery Rieber • January-March 2009

The state has executed two men already this year. Two more have died from disease and the state is trying to execute a person each month.

While Alabama has started this year off fast, and last year sentenced more people to death than anyone else, Alabama seems to be slow in acknowledging rulings of law by our United States Supreme Court [USSC].

For example, it was years ago when the USSC ruled in *Atkins* that it is unconstitutional to execute the mentally retarded.* Yet Alabama still does not have a law on the books which sets parameters and defines "mentally retarded" for legal purposes. The USSC made the hard decision and asked the states only to come up with a standard definition, but Alabama can't be bothered. Plus, as long as there is no set standard, the state can continue to claim that no one on death row meets the legal definition of mentally retarded.

Also, years ago, the USSC ruled it unconstitutional to execute those who were minors at the time of their crime, yet Alabama still has no law reflecting that ruling even though Senator Hank Sanders routinely introduces bills that would bring Alabama in line with the Supreme Court.

Now, to top it all off, there is a proposed bill in the Alabama House of Representatives to execute pedophiles for crimes in which no murder occurred. It seems as though some of our lawmakers don't even read the paper because the USSC just ruled this idea to be unconstitutional in a Louisiana case. If they won't let Louisiana do it, they won't let Alabama do it. I wonder how much money and billable hours went into this bill that Rep. Hurst is proposing? Doesn't it seem that the money could be better spent, in these trying times?

---

* *Atkins v. Virginia* (2002), 536 US 304.

These are indeed trying times. With the executions, deaths and even more executions scheduled, it's hard to find a happy thought to write about and hold on to but our friend and co-founder of PHADP, Jesse Morrison, came through for us when he reminded us that it was during trying times like these that PHADP was born. Good things do come from strife and struggle. We just have to remember that and keep fighting. Please help us to keep Hope alive. Thank you.

Time in a Box

Carey Grayson • January–March 2009

The longer I spend in prison, the more it seems as if the DOC has man-aged to find a way to trap time in a box. From my cell I look out on a world that I am no longer a part of and realize that it has passed me by with a speed I find astounding. Although I understand that it moves no faster than when I was a part of its current, my incarceration has allowed me a rare view of just how fast that current flows.

Throughout my tenure on death row, I have watched the computer age blossom from the isolated obsolete islands of my youth into the hub that the world revolves around. I have seen the toys of the rich grow into the cell phones and Blackberrys that have become the lifeblood of a nation.

I have seen the TV shows of my youth come to life through technol-ogy that allows a man to replace whole limbs with working replacements, and contacts that allow you to see the Internet float in the air before you.

I have watched the birth of an age of conservation and preservation where the very wind is trapped and used to fuel our energy needs. And oil, the staple of my youthful world, hears the first tolling of its death knell.

I have seen a nation of institutional racism put aside its antiquated hatred and elect its first Black president. A nation where women have thrown off the image of support staff to become a true force in their own right through a refusal to be anything less.

In my decade plus in this cell, I have watched the world explode and grow as only outside that world can. And I wonder, having truly been excluded from that growth, if I can find a place in this new world should I be released. I wonder if it has in truth passed beyond my reach as I sit in this time warp called prison. Questions I am most eager to have answered should the chance arrive. It is indeed a brave new world. The question is, can I escape my time in this box and become a brave new man?

School vs. Death

E. Mason • January-March 2009

What do we do? We've elected a new president . . . the people have spoken and the people have resoundingly spoken for change. But isn't that easy to say? How do we manage this change, and furthermore, to what do we change? Our economy is on a desperate downward path and we have half of Congress who would rather argue than to get with the president and pass this stimulus bill so we can try to right this ship.

Down here in good old Alabama the economic pressures are beginning to show. The state is having to tighten its fiscal belt and the local municipalities are scrambling, trying to figure out creative ways to stretch a dollar. Many of our school boards don't know what to do.

They're having to make the decision to fire certain teachers and some are even wrestling with the idea of closing some schools. These are heavy decisions that have to be made in dire circumstances. Yet, in the midst of all of this, Alabama is still churning away with their machinery of death. The millions that the state is having to shell out in order to pursue capital punishment is simply mind boggling when you consider the present situation.

College grants are down, teachers are getting laid off, schools are closing, the health care system is far below where it ought to be. So many Alabamians aren't covered and we are making it on a wing and a prayer. I wonder, dear reader, when will it dawn on all those heavy thinkers in Montgomery that they have a choice to make? They can begin to vote for schools or continue with playing on the people's fears and frustrations and casting their voices for death.

Let's run capital punishment up out of our state . . . that's one good thing I can see coming from this economic crisis.

A Newcomer's Perspective on Holman's Death Row

Demetrius Jackson • January-March 2009

These words are not directed at our PHADP supporters, but at my peers of the row. Please don't let the content discourage you or sway your determination to fight the injustices of the death penalty. I am writing this only in the hope of opening the closed eyes of those who have fallen asleep or lost focus of what is truly important.

I'm still a fairly new addition to death row here at Holman. I was sentenced to death in March of 2008. Before coming to the row, I had fixed opinions of how it would be. I thought it would be a serious, dangerous, violent and intense environment. I was so wrong!

One would think men facing the ultimate sentence would be very focused. You wanna believe ALL or at least the majority would support PHADP. Not so! I am frustrated with the things you dwell on! What is the problem? A house divided among itself cannot and will not stand. Yes, we are all different. From different cities, races, cultures etc. but we are now one family. Why? Because we're all we got. Yeah, you may have people you can call, receive mail from, etc., but we are the ones who you live with and are facing the same fate if change doesn't come. You wonder why the administration does not respect us. Simple: we don't respect ourselves or each other!

What would you think of a man sentenced to death who is petty and small minded? I have seen men curse and wish ill on each other over a single thirty-eight-cent bag of chips. Some of you only focus your all on store items, TV shows, and frankly, gossiping about each other. There are men here without lawyers, some who don't even communicate with the lawyers they have and sadly, those who don't even know what the appeals process is.

We all, or most of us, have a common goal and that is to help in the fight to abolish the death penalty. Just think of how much we could gain, accomplish if we could work together on this common goal. How can we expect others to take us seriously or listen when we don't take ourselves seriously or listen to one another?

Men, there is strength in numbers, two heads are better than one. Let's stand for something or you can keep falling for foolishness. To my brothers of PHADP: thanks for all the insight, help and love. I could only imagine how I would carry on without you. PHADP is what I thought the whole row would be. Men fighting for justice. But sadly, PHADP is only about 30 or 40 percent of a two-hundred-plus death row population.

Twenty Years of Hope
1989–2009

Jesse Morrison and Esther Brown

January–March 2009

As we gratefully celebrate twenty years of Hope it is appropriate to remember our history and those who made it happen, our founding brothers. There is none better to guide us in this than Jesse Morrison, co-founder of our organization, and so I asked him to help us to remember and here are his notes:

> "In May of 1989 Jesse Morrison and Wallace Norrell Thomas got together a committee of five, which included Johnny Harris (Danny Siebert after Harris was transferred), James "Bo" Cochran and Joe Duncan. This committee worked for four or five months getting the structure together.
>
> Around September, we had the structure in place, along with the name Project Hope to Abolish the Death Penalty, and began open membership, setting up study groups, classes, and different committees.
>
> Around December, the officers of the organizations held the first meeting on the visiting yard with potential members of an outside board of advisors and supporters.
>
> The very first initiative was Wallace and I writing two articles, "From Alabama's Death Row" and "Black America and the Death Penalty." We sent out over three hundred copies to Black churches, Black colleges, Black newspapers nationwide, death penalty organizations and friends and families.
>
> As our membership grew, we expanded the committee, and had to replace some. The new members were Brian Baldwin, Gary Brown, Leroy White and Ward Gentry."

I asked Jesse to say a little something about our founding brothers, and here it is:

Wallace Norrell Thomas, executed 1990: "the political and legal mind of the group. On death row, he was the constant voice for change in conditions as well as the legal system."

Johnny Harris: "mentor/advisor, knew Alabama prison system officials and had outside contacts and support system but was transferred soon after the beginning."

Bo Cochran, exonerated in 1997 and still supportive of PHADP: "solid supporter who had the respect of all death row inmates."

Joe Duncan: "solid supporter, willing to take a stand against the system, eager to get involved."

Danny Siebert, died in 2008: "knowledgeable about organizational structure and running a campaign. Got involved only at my request."

Gary Brown, executed 2003: "was asked to come aboard to help recruit whites and Christian inmates. Proved to be a very hardworking and totally committed member."

Brian Baldwin, executed in 1999: "my most valued co-worker; took on the job of building our newsletter; acted as my confidant and advisor on all the important decisions I had to make; brought a lot of outside members into the organization. Brian was very popular, fun-loving, outgoing but also had a quick, intelligent mind, which allowed him to not only grasp an issue but to see it from all sides."

Jesse Morrison gave me the task to write about him. We have been close friends for the last ten years, ever since my dear friend Brian Baldwin's execution. In recalling the birth of PHADP, he wrote: "I was only doing what I thought was right and necessary at the time, and I was mad as hell." If ever there was an example of channeling anger into positive action, our organization was it. 1989 was the year of four executions—a record which we are unfortunately likely to break this year.

In writing about Jesse, I could talk about his natural charisma, his leadership qualities, his fighting spirit, but all of those would mean nothing if they were not about what was right and necessary. Jesse sees a problem and wants to address it for the sake of those around him. After his sentence was commuted to life without the possibility of parole, he tried to found the Lifer's group, and when that was denied, start a NAACP chapter in the prison, all ways to bring hope and meaning to a place where there is little of either. It is the loss of the Department of Corrections that it denied permission for both.

Jesse is famous for his admonition to be the other voice. He lives that and is at his very best when he can inspire, motivate, work hard and bring people together for the common good. He wants to make a difference and he has in so many of our lives, even in the lives of some who do not know him because they came to death row after his re-sentencing.

I know I have repeatedly attempted to explain the spirit of Project Hope to Abolish the Death Penalty, which still endures now that we are twenty years old. When I read Bo what Jesse had written over the phone, there was silence and then I heard sobs and the words, "We were family." Yes, you were and we still are and we thank our dear friend Jesse Morrison and all who were part of the beginning for this vision. We thank you for daring to dream a bold dream and for not counting the cost. We do not forget and we love you!

These are the names of some of the Hope members who, for one reason or another, are no longer on Holman's death row. Each man was integral to Hope in his own way and we honor them for what they gave of themselves.

Jesse Morrison
Wallace Norrell Thomas
Danny Siebert
Johnny Harris
Brian Baldwin
Edward Horsley
Gary Brown
James Bo Cochran
Joe Duncan
Ward Gentry
Henry Hayes
James Martin
Gary Hart III
Darrell B. Grayson

the Editor's Desk

Jeffery Rieber • January–March 2009

PHADP was founded in the spring of 1989. It is now spring of 2009 and the struggle to end capital punishment in Alabama continues. While it is a shame that there is still reason and need for Hope's existence, I can't help but take great satisfaction and pride from the fact that Hope has survived and flourished for two decades. Considering where it was started and where it has been run from all of those twenty years, I think I can say, without hubris, that this is an achievement of some note. Make no mistake: this is not something that I accomplished. I am merely the current chairman trying to do right by this amazing organization and its amazing members and supporters. I would never have had the vision, nerve and audacity to think that I could launch a lasting anti-death penalty organization WHILE ON DEATH ROW. I am truly in awe of Mr. Jesse Morrison and the other men who founded Hope. That said, Hope would never have lasted without YOU, the dedicated and caring believers who have kept us afloat and bolstered our strength and purpose with your own determination and desire for social change. Thank you for everything.

Sadly, I must end this with a sobering dose of Alabama reality. Since our last newsletter, the state has executed two more of our brothers. They killed Jimmy Dill on April 16 and Willie "Chub" McNair May 14th. Robert Coral died of "natural causes" in April. I realize that to many these are just names on a list but I'm telling you, the world is a lesser place without them. They will be missed and mourned.

The state plans to kill Jack Trawick on June 11th. I can't think of a time when Hope was needed more. My wish is that soon there will be no need for PHADP. Until then, please help us to keep Hope alive.

Waiting to Exhale

Anthony Tyson • January–March 2009

We have all experienced it: that moment when we're just relieved when something was finally behind us and we were able to exhale. Currently eyes are being opened to the truth and reality of the death penalty. Not only does it not deter murder, but it is a prime example of senseless spending. Why would anyone close a school to be able to continue executions? Our own attorney general ran on the premise that he wanted to protect our kids. Well, since my kids are included in that promise, how about doing so by preventing their demise by not preparing for their failure. Because that is exactly what is happening. When you consider that we have over two hundred inmates on Alabama's death row, the largest in the country considering our population, you are planning to spend over 200 million dollars to see no change. Wouldn't it make more sense to spend that money on education and after-school programs that will keep kids away from gangs, drugs and other criminal activities? If a seed of confidence and encouragement is not planted into a child at a young age, you are setting that child up for failure and the chances of them visiting some kind of institution before his/her adult years arrive. But this argument has been made over and over again. One minute, we here at Hope feel so close to our goal; then, the news comes on and shows some horrific crime. And each time this happens, it feels as though so many on Union Street in Montgomery are happy.

We hear about other states discussing the possibility of abolishing the death penalty. Alabama however, seems to hold its breath and hopes no one will see its flaws. How can the state not offer DNA testing without a court order? Or legal assistance post conviction? Men here have to climb the channel of appeals and be rescued by federal judges. In the last year alone, seven men here have been given relief in the federal courts.

Others have woken up. We applaud the governors of New Jersey and New Mexico, and also the district attorney in Dallas, Texas, who has taken it upon himself to look into the innocence pleas of several men in prison. What a great example of integrity! Faced with adversity and peer pressure, but despite the odds, does the right thing anyway. And to all the other states that have even considered the possibility of shutting down, repealing or abolishing the wasteful spending and senseless killing by the government that capital punishment entails, we say, keep trying! Closing down schools now will definitely cost you later. And you can take that to the bank! All these concerns and more are circulating the country at an alarming rate right now, for good reason, especially during these tough times. Still, I believe Alabama's day is coming. Meanwhile, I and others like me are waiting to exhale.

A Christian Perspective

Ronald B. Smith • January–March 2009

This has been one of the toughest years I have spent here at Holman. We have lost six of our brothers on the row, two who expired from natural causes and four who were executed. And the state is not finished yet. They have set an execution date for Jack Trawick on June 11th. All this is happening as Project Hope to Abolish the Death Penalty commemorates its twentieth year in existence. Begun in the humble environs of the Holman Unit, Alabama's death row, it remains guided and directed from those same humble environs, aided, assisted and befriended by caring and concerned supporters to abolish the death penalty by educating the public.

The founders of Project Hope to Abolish the Death Penalty faced numerous challenges, as do we, the current members of the board of directors. None of us has received any special training for the various and assorted roles and duties we find ourselves doing. Applying for grants, putting out a newsletter, not to mention networking with like-minded groups and individuals. This does not take into account the running of the various PHADP sub-groups in which information the board receives from various sources is disseminated to our peers on the row.

We keep ourselves and each other motivated and I can speak from experience when I say that we have all needed a morale boost that only other board members could provide. Bad news from the home front or an unfavorable ruling from the court can make a person feel helpless and dispirited. But we are not alone. We stand, at times literally, shoulder to shoulder in this fight against the death penalty. We play together, pray together and grieve together. I can't say enough about the men I have served on the board with and those currently serving on the board. And lest I forget our Outmate [Esther Brown] who knows who she is and what she means to me and us. With her on our side we persevere and accomplish much more than we ourselves often expected.

And I want to personally thank all our supporters past and present. May God repay the kindness you have shown us. Please continue to keep us in your thoughts and prayers. The fight continues and so does Project Hope to Abolish the Death Penalty.

DOING OUR BEST TO KEEP HOPE ALIVE!

A Blessed Long Journey

Arthur Giles • January–March 2009

Soren Kierkegaard said, "Adversity not only draws people together but brings forth that beautiful inward friendship!" My name is Arthur Giles and I am incarcerated on Alabama's death row and a member of Project Hope to Abolish the Death Penalty. This year we celebrate our twentieth anniversary of the founding of PHADP and our involvement in the struggle to abolish the death penalty. We are an organization that was founded by our dear brother Jesse Morrison while he was on death row himself!

When I arrived in 1979 I was placed in a cell next to Jesse and upon introducing ourselves, he seemed like a very caring and giving person. Being nineteen years old at the time, ignorant and stubborn as a goat, one could say that I could not have been placed in a better spot than in a cell next to Jesse. Like I said, Jesse was a caring and giving person and when I say giving I don't just mean in the material sense, but in giving of his time to an individual! Something that I needed. He freely gave and took every opportunity he could to instill in me the importance and value of education, while inspiring brotherhood, hope and unity among those around him.

When he asked me to join Project Hope to Abolish the Death Penalty, how could I not but feel deeply honored, as the words flashed across my mind, "to whom much is given, much is expected!" Upon becoming a part of the family, not only did I quickly learn what my brother Jesse had created, but that it gave men like myself an opportunity to be a part of something good, meaningful and special for the first time in our life. Also, as time went on, this family and our supporters taught me that what good one gives of himself always has a way of coming back around to him. You also taught me what humanity really means and that standing up for life and justice in this world of ours is always right.

Though our struggle has been hard and long, I think what we believe in and stand for is the reason for and a testament to our longevity. Our battle is not over yet. The first half of this year has been topsy-turvy for us with the painful losses of our four brothers. "We suffer defeats along the way: Yet to victory we are born!" (Ralph Waldo Emerson). I strongly feel and believe our victory is just around the corner. As I expressed, it has been a long and hard-fought battle for us, but I can't be any more pleased and proud of who we are and our perseverance as an organization and family. Which is why I send a special thank you to all our loyal supporters! Remember, victory often comes at times when one least expects it.

GREETINGS FROM

the Editor's Desk

Jeffery Rieber • July-September 2009

As you may know, the state executed Jack Trawick on June 11, 2009. Also, Gerald Lewis died from medical complications on July 25, 2009. Both will be missed.

In the "don't make me laugh" category, Alabama passed a new access to DNA testing law in an attempt to not be the very last state with no DNA law on the books. However, a renowned attorney who specializes in capital law said that rather than making access to testing easier, this law actually raised the bar for those attempting to qualify for DNA testing. As they say on *Saturday Night Live*, "REALLY, ALA-BAMA?? REALLY?!?!

New Jersey, on the other hand, seems to have the right idea. Since they imposed a moratorium in 2006 and abolished their death pen-alty in 2007, murders there have declined each year. The number of murders has already declined by 24 percent in the first six months of 2009 compared to the same period in 2008, which was lower than 2007. 2007 saw an 11 percent drop when compared to 2006.

Shouldn't it be obvious to everyone that maybe we have the wrong method of fighting murder if, when we STOP using that method, mur-der rates drop steadily? Sometimes, fighting fire with fire is just the wrong way to go.

I don't usually mention specific articles in my editorial but when I read Omar D's "The Kentucky Derby," I told him I was jealous and mad at myself for not thinking to write it myself. It makes a very important and often overlooked point, and the best part, to me, is that he used Clay Crenshaw's own words to do it. I encourage the reader to take note of the enclosed article. Good job, Omar D.—keep up the good work!

After our last issue came out (twentieth anniversary), we received an outpouring of congratulatory responses from our supporters. It made us all feel so good, to be reminded that our efforts are appreciated, that we decided to print a couple of them in this issue. Our deepest thanks go out to all of you, our supporters, who make this work possible.

Until next time, help keep Hope alive.

The Kentucky Derby

Omar D. • July-September 2009

I read a column recently in the *Montgomery Advertiser* that made me think of a greyhound racing in the Kentucky Derby. Clay Crenshaw, a prosecutor in the Alabama attorney general's office, wrote it. He was commenting on a previous column written by Thomas Wells, which criticized Alabama's death penalty system.

Mr. Wells, whom Mr. Crenshaw gladly pointed out, is a Birmingham lawyer that serves as the president of the American Bar Association and whose legal practice focuses on environmental law and product liability cases.

In order for Crenshaw to set the stage, he boasted, "Because I have a front row seat in death penalty battles as a prosecutor in the Alabama attorney general's office, over the past twenty-two years, I have acquired detailed knowledge of capital litigation law. As someone with long personal experience in this area, I feel it is necessary to offer the following counterpoint to Mr. Wells' column."

By pointing out their respective credentials, Crenshaw had two things in mind. He wanted the readers to come to the conclusion that Wells was unqualified to speak out against Alabama's death penalty system and therefore should disregard what Wells had said. But, by all means, to believe everything he was saying. I, along with my eleven and a half years of being on Alabama's death row and firsthand knowledge of how the system works, came to a different conclusion. I took it as Crenshaw saying it's wrong for non-criminal law attorneys to speak out against Alabama's death penalty system, but okay for them to represent someone facing a sentence of death.

Mr. Crenshaw is well aware of how inadequate legal representation is for indigent defendants in Alabama. He knows that lawyers whose legal practice focuses on bankruptcy, property liens, and family law oftentimes represent us at trial and on appeals. When it comes to criminal law, they have little or no experience. I found it very ironic for him to use the term "death penalty battles" when describing what he does against lawyers who, again, have very little or no experience in criminal law versus his twenty-two years of capital litigation (criminal law).

I am not saying that non-criminal law attorneys are unqualified to speak out against Alabama's death penalty system. If anyone cares to look with neutral eyes, they would see how unfair, unjust and racially biased this system is, as well as how elected judges abuse the state's judicial override provision. They are afraid to seem soft on crime. However, I am saying that a greyhound will never win in the Kentucky Derby.

One Plus One?

Booman • July-September 2009

Over the years, I have read hundreds of articles and studies on deterrence and the death penalty. I've read how it does deter, and how it doesn't. I have yet to read about what those who are closest to the issue have to say on the matter. For that reason, I will tell you my thoughts on the subject.

I can't speak for anyone else here but I can say that most of the guys on Alabama's death row that I've discussed this topic with either knew nothing of the death penalty at the time of their crime or were not clearheaded enough at the time for it to be a factor. As for myself, I can honestly say I fell into both categories. I wasn't aware Alabama had a death penalty, nor was I sober enough to give it any thought. In either case, it seems to me that through ignorance or indifference, or both, the death penalty failed miserably in its aim to deter.

It also seems to have failed to deter those here who knew of the death penalty, and that their actions would warrant it, from committing their crimes. There are far more than you would think. Given that there are two hundred plus on Alabama's death row and hundreds more who narrowly escaped coming here, anyone with the power to reasonably add one and one, must, in my opinion, conclude that the death penalty has no deterrent effect what so ever.

Of course, that's just my opinion on the matter.

It's the Southern Way

Nicholas Acklin • July-September 2009

Don't be fooled by the shouts from the mountain tops that "change has come." The South remains the South of old. The "hang 'em high" mentality continues to flourish. We in the South are known for our hospitality and moral attitudes. Outside of the South, we are said to be "slow" or "green." There is a saying well known in the northern states, "Don't get 'caught up' in the South, cause once they get you, they got you." It's a knock on how backward our justice system really is.

One can argue that I am only venting because of my current situation. True, but only now do I know and have experienced southern justice! The reality is, once you find yourself among the "others," your eyes are opened to how unfair our system is. The death penalty seems to be the pride of the South. I've come to realize that there are few that actually care about the fairness of the death penalty. The mentality is, as long as it doesn't affect me or my family, it's not important. Because of this way of thinking, many have found themselves with "the shoe on the other foot," now realizing how unfair this system truly is.

If we'd treat others the way we want to be treated, we'd have a better justice system. Instead, revenge fuels us and leads to more ignorance. Our laws are getting worse. The lock 'em up and throw away the key mentality runs rampant. As a result, the good ole southern way has our prisons overcrowded, education at a low and there is still a seemingly segregationist mentality of "us" and "them." And you wonder why Republicans fight against restoring voting rights to ex-felons. It's because eyes have been opened to the traps, corruption, and failure of equal justice.

I hope for the change we all deserve, and not one that's just beneficial to the few. I believe that change will come, but only when we can seek equality for all, a New South. Until then, we will continue to die a slow death, all of us.

the Editor's Desk

2009 was PHADP's twentieth year of existence and it has been a trying year with eleven men on death row losing their lives. Six were executed and five died of "natural" causes. This year, Alabama executed more people than in any other year since they reinstated the death penalty in the 1970s. We have also lost friends, family and supporters on the street. One beautiful human being we lost, Shirley Cochran, was friend, family and supporter all rolled into one. Shirley was our big brother and ex-death row inmate Bo Cochran's wife. She was also a surviving family member of a murder victim and an ardent supporter of PHADP who always made the time to speak at events in an effort to end capital punishment. Shirley was always there for us. We mourn her passing and send our love, support and compassion to our brother Bo. Shirley made a difference and she will be missed.

This issue is not, strictly speaking, about the death penalty. It is more about the men who write for the newsletter. The articles are not all happy-go-lucky, but they are real. I started out wanting an issue full of cheer and heartwarming stories, but when I read the submissions, I realized that what I had hoped for would have been a lie. The articles are as different from one another as the men who wrote them. Each contains personal truths about that individual, and maybe that is more important than putting on the happy face for the holiday season. I know we all have different ways of dealing with our situations, different ways of trying to make sure that our daily lives have meaning. And, really, isn't that true of everyone, no matter our circumstances?

Here's to hoping that the new year will be a better, more productive, less tragic time for us all. There have been a lot of behind-the-scenes negotiations with the administration here in an effort to keep our group meetings intact, and as of now, things are ok, but the struggle continues and we are doing all we can to keep PHADP alive.

We thank each of our supporters for helping us through a difficult landmark year. May you all have a loving and happy holiday season. And, as always, please help keep Hope alive.

Thanksgiving

Derrick Mason • October–December 2009

Every year, as this time approaches, my mind goes back to those good times that I experienced as a kid. But Thanksgiving then and Thanksgiving now, I see in two very different ways. As a youngster Thanksgiving was more about eating (of course) and being surrounded by the warmth of family, visiting family in the country . . . and yes, again, eating! But now it has begun to take on greater meaning. It still means good eating (smile) but now I begin to really factor in and give serious thought to those things that I am really thankful for. Being in a place such as this (prison), I am thankful to have made it to another year. So many guys get sick in here and die before they have an execution date set. Although I have recently gotten over the flu shot that was given out about four weeks ago, I am so very thankful for my health being intact. I thank God for that.

I'm thankful for the love of family and friends that so many in my situation don't enjoy. I'm thankful for the love that I have from supporters and workers such as Esther Brown, a beautiful human being. I'm thankful for the friendships that I share with my brothers in PHADP. Being thankful is a beautiful thing, for it wards off selfishness. Even God appreciates thankfulness! As Christians, we are admonished to bring thanksgiving on our lips when we come together in prayer.

As I was preparing to write this article, I shared with my neighbor the subject matter that I wanted to discuss and he dropped a lil' nugget on me that I just couldn't leave out. At this time, we also want to allow our thoughts to consider those victims' families who will be missing a loved one at the Thanksgiving table this year. My thoughts are that God would bring blessings on their homes.

And lastly, I am thankful for all of you—our beautiful readers and supporters out there in the free world! Be blessed.

Oh yeah, and all that good eating (smile)!

My Everyday

Tony Barksdale

October–December 2009

A brave face,
trembling knees,
sweating palms,
the sound of keys,
handcuffs jingling,
the tier lights shine,
conversations cease,
even within the mind,
listening, waiting,
the heavy boot steps heard,
are our wind chime,
is it a time to hope,
or a time to fear,
if it's the mail, please stop,
if it's not, steer clear,
to all my readers, even my enemies,
I'm glad you aren't here . . .

My everyday

From the Editor's Desk

Jeffery Rieber • January–March 2010

The good news is, we are two months into the new year and Alabama has not executed anyone. The bad (but not surprising) news is that the state is still trying as hard as it can to remedy that.

We are thankful that Robert (Lil' Rob) Melson received a stay of execution. He was scheduled to be put to death on February 18th but it was stayed, pending the outcome of a Florida case with similar issues (*Holland v. FL*).*

The American Law Institute (made up of four thousand judges, lawyers and law professors), which created the intellectual framework for the modern capital justice system, has declared the entire death penalty system to be a failure and no longer supports it. Law students from now on will be taught that the very institution responsible for creating it now says that the whole experiment of capital punishment is a moral and practical failure that should be abolished. We agree completely.

The list of Alabama judges (inside) who override jury recommendations for life [without parole] and instead impose death sentences was researched and compiled by some of the PHADP brothers here on the row. Thanks go to each man for his time-consuming hard work and effort.

Before I go, I want to mention some logistical problems we are experiencing at the moment. The typewriters for death row were recently broken and that leaves with no way to complete our usual work on the newsletter. The men here take great care with, and pride in, creating each issue. We hope to be back on track with the next issue. As for this issue, our love and thanks go to Esther for pulling our bacon out of the fire by doing the work that we are unable to do. Without her, this issue would not be in your hands right now.

---

* The court ultimately ruled in *Holland v. Florida* (2010) that "equitable tolling," or a pause in a statute of limitations, can be upheld if the petitioner has been pursuing their rights diligently and that an extraordinary circumstance prevented timely filing (560 US 631).

The Prodigal Son

Anthony Boyd • April–June 2010

Hello, PHADP friends and family. This has been a long time coming and it's good to be back. For those who don't know me . . . my name is Anthony Boyd. I used to sit on the board of PHADP as the sergeant-at-arms, but I stepped down due to personal issues. I stepped down and back, but never out. These guys are, and always will be, my family and I wouldn't leave them high and dry. So I've always been supportive and here to do anything they needed. However, for Jeffery, that wasn't enough . . . so I'm back! (smile)

I had been attending meetings from time to time, as an observer and the occasional sounding board. Now, with time having passed, and my personal issues better under control, I've become more active. Recently, I was voted onto the sub-board (because Jeff said I must start from square one) and I serve as the sgt-at-arms in the newly formed Group 3. I am very happy to be back full time and more active. More articles will follow, but I just wanted to take this time to introduce myself to those who don't know me, and to say to those that do . . . I'm back. (smile)

I've missed you all and want you all to know that I am impressed with the great strides made by PHADP, and I'm proud and honored to be in such great company. Thanks to all our supporters, friends and advisors for staying strong and staying the course, even when some of us tend to lose our way.

With love and support like yours, we can't lose. God bless, and love to all.

Out to Pasture

James Largin • April–June 2010

My keeper came this morning and put my feed in the stall for me. I ate it. It's hard to get excited about my fodder. He came back a little later and let me graze in the pasture for an hour. That's not very long when you consider that I won't get to go out again today.

I welcome this time to graze. Since I eat and relieve myself in my stall, as well as sleep there, it's nice to get out.

The other bulls and I enjoy the air and the grass. We frolic in the field, but our eyes never stray far from the red door at the edge of the pasture. That is the door to the slaughter house. They can dress it up anyway they want to, but they murder us in there. It's very cold and calculated. They are all business when it comes to the slaughter.

Unfortunately, I am not a cow. I am a man. My stall is an 8×5 cell. This is "life" on death row at Holman Correctional Facility. The slaughter house is real.

The Reason I Joined

Randy Lewis • April–June 2010

Since my youth, I have been interested in pursuing an education in criminal justice. My motivation comes from fights for justice that were fought long ago, such as the Civil Rights Movement, the Black Panther movement and the Islamic movement. People who have inspired me are Dr. Martin Luther King Jr., Malcolm X and Huey P. Newton.

As a youth, I saw how prejudiced the law was/is toward minority groups and how the law was being applied in a biased manner. I became more enthusiastic about becoming involved with the law when I was falsely accused of capital murder on April 27, 2006, wrongfully convicted on May 17, 2006, and wrongfully sentenced to death on June 24, 2006.

When I arrived here on death row, June 26, 2007, a man was executed. Once I was assigned a cell, I immediately began to request legal information. A brother here on death row informed me of PHADP, and how to become a member. He said that PHADP is an organization dedicated to ending the death penalty, but they also have classes in which they pass on their legal knowledge, gained through time, experience and research, to anyone who wants to attend. Three months in, I became a PHADP member. I joined because 1) I'm all for a grassroots movement for positive change, 2) I'm all for self education and learning, 3) PHADP is the only way I can do something positive while, at the same time, help myself and assist my attorney by keeping them updated on new state and federal laws and rulings and how either may apply to me.

The brothers of PHADP are very kind and very helpful. When I'm confused and need answers, I can always go to the Hope brothers for their assistance. PHADP is not just an organization or place of being for me; it is the closest thing to family in my eyes, and I appreciate the brothers welcoming me with open arms and for their (our) efforts to make a change.

An Apology

Omar D. • April–June 2010

There seems to be a double standard when it comes to making an apology. There also seems to be a rule on when it is not okay to say one is sorry. It's clearly seen when it comes to politicians and prisoners, the poor and the rich.

Lately, we've been hearing a lot of politicians apologizing for their infidelities of one sort or another. They are quick to hold a press conference and pour out their hearts to their families and the public. All of it is done to save his or her political career. The thing about that is, it's about the only time you will hear one apologize. Never will it happen when a person has been exonerated due to DNA evidence. Never will it happen due to the withholding of evidence or prosecutor misconduct. It's like they don't care about ruining a person's life and causing them to miss out on the rearing of their children, graduation and marriage. We are so often taken advantage of. Why is it like this? Do we not deserve to hear the phrase, "I'm sorry"? Does our family not deserve to hear it? Is it so hard to admit their mistakes?

I truly hate that there seems to be a different code of conduct or code of ethics when it comes to atonement. Of course, an apology will not change what happened, but it definitely will go a long way into making things right.

PHADP vs. VOCAL

Anthony Tyson • April–June 2010

Some would think that Project Hope to Abolish the Death Penalty and Victims of Crime and Leniency (VOCAL) are at odds with each other. But both groups are striving to promote justice. Both sides believe in the rights of the victims. And both sides feel that killing is wrong. VOCAL, for all of you that don't know, is an organization that supports and aids victims of violence. And they seek justice for victims of violence.

Recently I read an article in the *Montgomery Advertiser*. I saw where VOCAL hosted a vigil along with the attorney general to uplift victims of violent crimes. It was titled "Violence against the Young." Little kids had been abused and murdered, some by their own families. It was a hard article for me to read, being a father and all. I tried imagining myself in those families' seats and asked the questions, "What if my son had been murdered and tortured at an early age? Would I want the criminal to receive the death penalty?" As I sit here on death row the answer is easy. NO! But would I have advocated for it before coming to death row? Probably so.

So, as we fight to end the death penalty and VOCAL continues to fight for justice on behalf of the victims, the way I see it, we are really a part of the same fight. The only big difference is that we see and define justice differently.

But we do sympathize with all the families who have been victims of crimes all over the US, especially those affected by the crimes that happen here in Alabama.

Although I know we will never be welcomed with an open handshake to join VOCAL in the fight for justice on behalf of victims of violence, our hands will never be closed in prayer.

Change

Craig Newton • April–June 2010

I think about change in my life as an analogy of a caterpillar. Before a caterpillar receives its wing it crawls upon the face of the earth, which makes it subject to all kinds of dangers. It could get stepped on, fall prey to birds or other animals, or weather conditions. It is not guaranteed that the caterpillar will make it to the tree branch to build a cocoon around itself. But if the caterpillar does make it and builds the cocoon around itself, then a tremendous event takes place: metamorphosis.

Life to me is the same way. When I was out in the streets I was crawling on the face of things which left me subject to so many mishaps. But being in the cocoon of this cell has brought about a metamorphosis in my life. My wings are knowledge, wisdom, and understanding of life, myself, God and events, etc. Now I'm no longer subject to crawling. I can fly above the things that I used to do. Everything in life goes through stages of development, which in essence is called change. Seeds must grow into trees. They are planted, and over the course of time, change is taking place even though you can't observe the change because the seed is covered in dirt. Just because politicians, district attorneys, police, family, etc. can't observe the change that is taking place with death row members because we are hidden in cells, blocked from the view of society, doesn't mean that change is not taking place. One day, you go outside and see that from the darkness in which the seed was planted has emerged a beautiful sprout.

the Editor's Desk

Jeffery Rieber • July–September 2010

My worldly fortune for an air conditioner! Yes, the Deep South Dog Days of Summer give new meaning to the words hot and sticky. Many people on the street think we have air conditioning here. Well, we don't. And only getting to shower every other day, in 118 degree heat index, is my personal definition of hell. :) Since I'm indulging in a little navel gazing at the moment, I'd like to address what Esther and I call the "poor me" syndrome and how it relates to death row. I think everyone in the world, on occasion, feels sorry for themselves in a given situation, even if it is due to their own actions. Everyone does it in one form or another, and death row convicts are certainly no exception. While it may be natural to feel it, that doesn't mean people want to hear about it. I realize that it can be offensive to hear a person convicted of taking a life lamenting their situation. So, as the editor, I try to keep it to a minimum in the newsletters, but please understand that to pretend we don't have these moods, to pretend we don't hate it here, would be a lie. We try to show our best face but it is possible that the recent executions and the intense heat have contributed to more navel gazing than would be usual otherwise.

It is my sad duty to report that three more of our brothers have been executed since our last newsletter, and two more have pending execution dates. Thomas Whisenhant was executed May 27th, John Parker was executed June 10th, and Michael Land was executed August 12th. I can't express how much these men will be missed. Holly Wood has an execution date set for September 9th. Phillip Halford has an execution date set for November 4th. Please keep an eye open for the execution alert notices and contact the governor when the time is right. Thank you.

In closing, I would like to thank all those who participate in the execution vigils. Your sacrifice, caring and dedication do not go unnoticed.

Please, help keep Hope alive.

I Have Fallen

James Largin • July–September 2010

I recently arrived here on death row. It's a long way from home. Before my conviction I was an engineer. I designed electrical systems, lighting systems and machines. I had three dogs. I lived in a nice house in a good neighborhood. I loved the outdoors. I hunted. I had dirt bikes. I had my hot rod projects. I went to church.

This is my first time to go to prison. Last year, I was sentenced to death. Now I have an 8'×5' cell. I have no job or trade here so, if I want coffee or cigarettes, stamps, paper or snacks, I sell the food off of my tray. Now, I wash my clothes in the toilet. If I send them out to the laundry, more than likely, they'll be stolen. I can't afford a TV so I sit in my cell sweating as I read from our limited library. Most days, I don't leave this cell.

Occasionally, I can go outside for an hour. I read the Bible. I pray a lot. All of my life is gone now. I can't pursue my interests. I've lost friends and family. There's really only one thing left for them to take. They'll strap me down to a table, they'll give me a drug to paralyze me so I won't jerk or scream if the ultra-short-acting anesthetic wears off too soon. They'll stop my heart at some point.

Once my body uses up what it can in my blood, I'll die. They'll put me in the cheapest box they can find. I'll be wearing prison whites in my box. I'll be buried as a pauper.

Untitled

Randy Lewis • July-September 2010

Have you ever felt like stopping believing, giving up on dreaming, crashing out before the start of your season—give me one good reason why my heart should keep on beating? Why should I continue to sacrifice my soul, when all it does is keep on bleeding? Nobody feels my pain, they're trying to shackle my brain, to keep me locked in chains; as they vindictively pursue strapping me down and then poisoning my veins. I struggle for change as I fight for change, but the thought of sunshine brings pain, so I ask for cloudy days and rain. Put yourself in my shoes, what would you do, when the demons are looking for you? I am lost and confused. Suicide seems easy for some, but it's something that I will never do. So, what should I do? Who should I pursue? God seems plausible, but all I see is you.

Generations

Carey Grayson • July–September 2010

It seems to me that Alabama has fine-tuned its machine a bit. The execution dates are rolling in and an entire generation of men are falling beneath the wheel. With every year, the time grows shorter and it seems that the executions are more frequent. I can see my time approach in the faces of those who go before me. I hear the clock tick and the gurney calls my name. It grows harder and harder to find hope for a future as fellow after fellow walks around the corner. (Going "around the corner" refers to going around the corner to the death cell and execution.) I do not know this next generation that has arrived unannounced to me. This must be how my grandfather felt as his era passed and the next began. In truth, I find myself understanding him better as my time grows near. Like him, I have no interest in knowing these newcomers, for to know them is to lose them, to lose them is to mourn them. I have too many to mourn as it is. I will accept no greater burden. I will mourn no more friends than I have to. The machine is well-tuned, and as this generation passes, so shall I pass with it. I am not afraid.

The Six Million Dollar Man

Arthur Giles • July–September 2010

I have been on death row, snared in the state's death program, for thirty-one years. Earlier this year, I read a news article where in the state of Florida, an inmate's average stay on death row is thirteen years and it costs the state 3.5 million dollars to execute the inmate. Here in Alabama, no entity of the government or the state's attorney general's office will tell the citizens of Alabama what it costs them to execute an inmate. Why is that?*

Is it because the state is ashamed or what? A bad policy equals a lack of humanity! Understanding that the economy is higher in Florida than in Alabama and the state's refusal to give a figure, I only have the figure of the state of Florida to surmise what it has probably cost the state of Alabama to have kept me in its death program for thirty-one years. I recognize that I don't fall into the average category here. So, instead of using the whole 3.5 million as if I were an inmate on Florida's death row, I'll say, give or take, it cost the state of Alabama 2.5 million for every thirteen years that I have been in the death program. Since I have been here for thirty-one years, one can probably call me "The Six Million Dollar Man" and counting! There are a little over two hundred men and women in the state's death program. Millions of dollars are being thrown away just to extinguish a life. This means the death of a citizen is worth more to the state than a whole economy. I find this totally appalling and you should too! The state is supposed to be a servant of the citizens, not a killer of its citizens!

All this money could be better spent on educating the children and finding programs for families throughout the state. Instead, the state has chosen to terminate teachers and slash public programs, but not its death program, the bread and butter for many politicians' election

---

* See PHADP's letter to the Alabama Media Group, July–September 2019, p. 303 of this volume.

and reelection campaigns. Now I understand why the Annie E. Casey Foundation, a charitable organization that focuses on public policy, ranked Alabama forty-seventh in the country when it comes to policy and reforms for children and families. There is no telling how well off the state of Alabama would be if the politicians could write those programs a check as they continue to do for the death program.

Strength—Maturity—Hope

Nicholas Acklin • July–September 2010

I recently received a letter from a friend who was sharing with me the story of Nelson Mandela and his twenty-seven years in prison. She shared with me how he credited the "Invictus" poem for helping him get through those twenty-seven years. My immediate thought was that after twenty-seven years in prison, one's heart should be hardened. Of course, upon thinking of my fourteen years of incarceration, I withdrew that thought.

It does take a strong-minded individual to serve twenty-seven years in prison and maintain his/her sanity. Speaking for myself, I can't say it is a matter of a strong mind, necessarily. For me, it is the constant desire to once again be with my family: for once in my life, to be surrounded by family, now as a mature man, having experienced many harsh realities in my life.

Though many things happen that could harden my heart, thankfully something within me and a higher power has gotten me through. There is always the opportunity for change, maturity and rehabilitation. Though Nelson Mandela was a political prisoner and I a prisoner for a crime of violence, still within the two life stories, there lies strength, maturity, and most of all, hope. I continue to hope for a similar outcome: to be free and offer to my family and society the mature individual I have become.

the Editor's Desk

Carey Grayson • October–December 2010

I'm not the usual writer for this column, but we decided that as assistant editor, it is time for me to contribute in a manner other than advisory. I do hope you're not disappointed with my attempted coup.

As you all know, this is your end year / Christmas issue. I will be reviewing the year's prominent events for those of you who don't remember and as a reminder for those who do. We have had an exciting year and I'm sure we will have plenty to review.

First off, I would like to mention the brothers we lost this year to the state killing machine. They have had a busy year, to our great regret. On May 27th Thomas Whisenhant was executed, then John Parker on June 10th, Michael Land on August 12th, Holly Wood on September 9th, and most recently Phillip Halford on November 4th. Five men fell to the vengeful blood lust of the state this year despite the shortage of a key chemical needed to carry out these executions. All will be missed and none forgotten.

On a lighter note, I would like to speak on our own personal Santa, or in this case, Mrs. Santa. A year-round job that she does like no other could. She is our light, the backbone of PHADP. Everyone loves and respects her for who she is and to our great joy she knows each of us and loves us for who we are. It is an honor and a privilege to know and be known by this woman. Merry Christmas, Esther Brown. May all your wishes come true.

I would also like to give a shout out to our supporters. Without you, we would be hard pressed to keep this train rolling. You are greatly appreciated and we hope that you will continue to support our efforts. We have recently acquired a new avenue for you to keep up with what's going on with PHADP as well as offer your comments and ideas. We are now on Facebook and welcome you to visit us there. On the same note, we now have a German PHADP website. You can find info on both in the Alabama News Section of the newsletter.

Merry Christmas, everyone, and a Happy New Year.

PHADP—On the Inside

Jeffery Rieber • October-December 2010

It has been pointed out to me that most of our supporters are aware of PHADP's efforts and actions in the free world but very few know what PHADP does and means inside the prison walls. While our main function is working to end the death penalty, operating on death row presents us with the need to be much more than an abolitionist organization.

Understand that a death sentence doesn't only mean that we have been found guilty of murder. It means that society has judged us to be totally unworthy of life, leaving us with little impetus for positive change. Most of us are undereducated and suffer from the effects of years of chronic substance abuse. Add to that the atmosphere of prison life, which discourages personal growth with its distorted "Convict Code of Survival" fomenting discord between groups and individuals, and you begin to see the setting and conditions in which PHADP on the inside works.

Not everyone here chooses to be a part of PHADP. The temptation to stagnate and do nothing is great. Each member must daily make the decision to take the more difficult road of trying to grow as a man. Being a member of PHADP is rewarding work, but it is work nonetheless. It comes with certain responsibilities and expectations. All members, for instance, are required to write a number of articles per year for our newsletters. This means that the "Old Heads" (men who have been here the longest) get together with the newer guys in order to help them whenever it's needed: to encourage them, build their confidence, and assure them that the writing gets easier with each completed effort.

The same is true of learning about the law and rules of the capital appeals process, which we are all going through. The men who have gone through the early and mid stages of their appeals teach the newer men how to best assist in their own appeals.

Keep in mind that prison is not a place where one wants to reveal any kind of perceived weakness or shortcoming. It takes a great deal of courage and a certain amount of faith in who you are dealing with to admit that you may need help. But once this leap of faith has been taken, the giving and receiving of time, attention, assistance and effort tends to create a feeling of brotherhood. We become FAMILY.

We attend board and group meetings together where we share updates on the current events of the abolitionist movement and where we share our thoughts and ideas about the direction PHADP should move in next. We hold and attend execution vigils together where we recognize each individual who gets an execution date, and we stand together in peaceful protest of state-sanctioned murder.

The board of directors asks each new man to attend a meeting, where we welcome them (imagine that conversation: "Welcome to death row"). We tell them about PHADP and invite them to join in our efforts. We offer them what insights we can give about living here on the row and we encourage them not to give up, not just to mark time waiting for the executioner.

There are not a lot of opportunities on death row to continue or even to begin to lead a productive life. Project Hope to Abolish the Death Penalty is one such outlet.

After twenty years here, one of my greatest pleasures is seeing one of the Old Heads who received help years ago passing that on by giving help and encouragement to the new guys.

The men here are very much aware that working for PHADP will not end the death penalty in Alabama soon enough to save our own lives. All of our efforts and shared experiences in PHADP bring about a feeling of belonging—for some, maybe for the first time. PHADP affords us the opportunity to do something positive here on the row while giving us the added gift of family. Put that together with the feeling of satisfaction that comes with personal growth, and I say that is very worthy indeed.

Untitled

Ronald B. Smith • October-December 2010

DEAR FAMILY AND FRIENDS,

Greetings and salutations! Merry Christmas and Happy New Year! Oh what a year it has been! A few of our friends and brothers now departed. One would think that, considering our circumstances, there would not be a whole lot of celebrating or joyfulness taking place on the row. Those people of course would be wrong. Not only do we celebrate the short visits from family and friends that we receive during this time of year, but we also take pleasure in phone calls, Christmas cards, and letters we receive. Then there are our Christmas packages. With added calories to burn and an attitude of finding joy wherever it may be had, we embark on a season in which grown men such as myself, some of whom have children, find themselves gazing with childlike wonderment at our TV's at animated shows such as *How the Grinch Stole Christmas* and *Merry Madagascar*. Also, old standards such as *It's a Wonderful Life* and *A Charlie Brown Christmas* watched for the umpteenth time. Chuckles and snickers, a few giggles and the occasional sniffle signifying memories of past viewings in very different environs. If you can remember the first time you saw *Miracle on 42nd Street*? Where were you at the time? Were you surrounded by family? Brothers and sisters perhaps? Maybe sitting on your grandfather's lap? What did the house smell like? How did you feel thinking back to that time?

Holiday gatherings bring family, friends, and co-workers together during the Yule time. Such is true even on death row. Each tier has a library day and the weeks before and after Christmas and New Year's are full of potluck get-togethers in the library. The PHADP board is holding three such get-togethers this year: one for Thanksgiving, thanks to Mr. Christophe Silex's generous donation for that exact purpose; a Christmas party; and a New Year's party. I can assure you that a group of guys such as the board and sub-board are fueled by the good wishes of our supporters, gleaned from cards and letters, the before-mentioned added calories from the shared goodies, prison casseroles, sandwiches and snacks from the prison canteen and Christmas packages, not to mention Santa's helper, Mrs. Esther Brown. I have often wondered if she actually knows the secret to Santa's real workshop? (As opposed to the fake one graphically overexploited in children's books, cartoons, and movies.) Just a thought I have sometimes this time of year. And I am sure if Santa trusts anyone, it is Esther.

Then there is the neighborly gift-giving. During this season, even guys who do not get along with even the friendliest, most well-mannered and generous neighbors for the most of the year will somehow find it in their hearts to give a little something to our less well-supported brothers on the row. Who would have thought, right? Well, it happens. Grinches, Scrooges, and the coldest Jack Frosts giving of their own meager goodies so that the less fortunate on the row have something to feel fortunate, one might even say merry, about this time of year. And I am not talking fruit cake. I'm talking good stuff like real Nutter Butters and Keebler Fudge Stripe cookies. (And you got to admit those elves really know how to make a fine cookie.)

During this time of year filled with holiday gatherings, gift giving, and jolly memory making, take time to remember the true reason for the season. And say a prayer for me and my brothers. Who knows, maybe your prayer will be the one that turns the tide to keep Hope alive! Meanwhile, we'll do what we can do from in here. And here's hoping we get peace on earth and good will toward men. Even those on death row.

How I See Tomorrow

Ulysses Sneed • October–December 2010

How will I see tomorrow, without me getting abstracted from the past? I wish this was a joke, but I'm in no mood to laugh. When I done seen the death, seen the pain, seen the sorrow and the mothers tremble from the grief that grabs them tight like a cold winter night. You can't cover that stuff with no coat. It seeps within, runs thick through their veins as they watch their child lie deceased from the needle or some other wicked way, and I keep thinking about my last days. Keep thinking about watching as the state buries another brother. I wonder if I can lend him a blanket to keep him warm on his journey? I wish I could embrace his family, but what can I say when my tears block my view as well. I keep wondering if I bleed just to keep from the psychological lashings. I think about the love and I consider the hate.

I write this because I hate when the agony overcomes me, trying to separate me from a thing called sanity. There have been plenty of nights when I buckled down on my knees, eyes watery with both fear and care because I admit, I am scared, and try to imagine being free from the adversity that swells through me. I gotta reach for the heavens and grab back that sanity. I remember I used to call out for Christ all day, every day to make things better for me.

So much to say about that word "tomorrow." Where will I be tomorrow? I look forward to tomorrow, because thinking of yesterday keeps me humble, and looking forward to a bright, better, and more productive future keeps me going. Remember, whatever your thoughts, good or bad, they will manifest in your life.

PART IV

It's the Southern Way

2011–2015

the Editor's Desk

Carey Grayson • January–March 2011

Hi there, this is Carey Grayson coming to you from the editor's desk. My plot to take over has succeeded and I am now in charge!

We have some good news and some bad news to go over. I say we start with the bad and end with the good.

On the 13th of January, our friend and brother Leroy White, a board member of PHADP for many years, was murdered by the state. Our ex and current attorneys general have already asked for three other dates for Glenn Boyd, Jason Williams and Eddie Powell. Please keep Leroy's memory and good thoughts for these three men with you throughout the day.

Alabama is again the leader in death sentencing and executions per capita in the nation. In 2010, Alabama sentenced more people to death than Georgia, Maryland, Virginia, Arizona, South Carolina, Oklahoma, Kentucky and Louisiana combined! More than Texas, which has 20.1 million more people than Alabama. Do the math and try not to cringe.

On a lighter note, the FDA has its hands full with a lawsuit filed by a DC law firm on behalf of death row inmates in California, Arizona and Tennessee. The suit claims that the FDA knowingly and willfully assisted states in getting illegal drugs for executions into the country.* The FDA's own rules deem this drug to be illegal for entry into the country, but they have waived their own rules and allowed the drugs to be imported. It will be interesting to see how this case turns out.†

---

* James Ridgeway and Jean Casella, "Death Row Inmates Sue the FDA over Execution Drugs," *Mother Jones*, February 10, 2011, https://www.motherjones.com/crime-justice/2011/02/death-row-inmates-sue-fda-over-execution-drugs.

† In 2012, a federal district court ruled in favor of the plaintiffs, blocking the FDA's ability to receive foreign shipments of execution drugs. See Zoe Tillman, "Judge Blocks Shipment of 'Unapproved' Drug Use in Lethal Injections," *The BTL: Blog of LegalTimes*, March 27, 2012, https://legaltimes.typepad.com/blt/2012/03/judge-blocks-shipment-of-unapproved-drug-used-in-lethal-injections.html.

Also, as I write this, Esther is at the Justice and Mercy (JAM) conference, making us look good at our jobs. Gotta love that woman!! The turnout is expected to be good, with one hundred and twenty people pre-registered, the Rev. Forte and three others from Eufaula among them. Wish them good hunting.

Project Hope to Abolish the Death Penalty

Inmates, Families and Friends Working to End All Killing

11076 Country Road 267, Lanett AL 36863
Phone 334-499-2380, e-mail *vineyfig@mindspring.com*

ARTICLES OF ORGANIZATION

I. The name of this organization is and will be referred to as Project Hope To Abolish The Death Penalty.

II. This organization is a non-profit, non-denominational religious organization and is not organized for the private gain of any one person.

III. The purpose of this organization is to influence the public opinion regarding Capital Punishment through education.

IV. The property of this organization is irrevocably dedicated to charitable purposes, and no part of the net income or assets of this organization shall ever be inure for the benefit of any director, officer, or member of the forementioned organization. Nor shall any private person make gain from the proceeds of this organization.

V. The main office for Project Hope To Abolish The Death Penalty is located at: 11076 County Road 267, Lanett, AL 36863

VI. Project Hope To Abolish The Death Penalty will be comprised of two entities: (1) Board of Directors (2) Executive Committee.

VII. Any chapters of Project Hope will be chartered through the main office located at 11076 C.R. 267, Lanett, AL 36863, by a unanimous vote of the members of the Board of Directors of Project Hope.

XIV. The Executive Committee will consist of the following positions: President/C.E.O.,Vice-President,National Director,Treasurer, Secretary,Administrative Assistants,Board of Advisors.

XV. The official publication for Project Hope to Abolish the Death Penalty: "On The Wings of Hope", Newsletter: Brian Baldwin, Editor "A Christian Perspective", Newsletter: Gary Brown, Editor

All of the above is a true and accurate statement, as to the organization referred to as Project Hope to Abolish the Death Penalty.

PHADP
11076 C. R. 267
Lanett, AL 36863

PHADP
41 White Ave.
Worcester, MA 01605

FIGURE 28. PHADP's original Articles of Incorporation

PHADP on the Inside, Part 2

Carey Grayson • January–March 2011

In the last issue, I wrote about the spirit of family that has been forged over the years in PHADP. My focus was on telling you about some of the little known activities taking place within Hope here on the row. Things that are unique to PHADP and don't occur in other abolitionist organizations. Things that are, through necessity, out of the box and innovative ways to address the inherent challenges of staffing and running an organization from death row.

In this issue, I will outline the actual structural mechanics of our organization, which resemble many others, but also necessarily deviate from the norm. I hope that this article, along with the one in the last issue, will leave you with a better understanding of how our beloved little organization works.

PHADP on the inside is made up of the following: the board of directors (big board), the sub-board (little board), and five Hope groups.

The big board consists of seven men who, over the years, were each voted into their present position by the existing board members whenever an opening occurred. The big board meets every Wednesday. PHADP's Articles of Incorporation (fig. 28) dictate that there be a chairman, vice-chair, coordinator, assistant coordinator, secretary/treasurer, sergeant at arms, and a director of information. This is the voting body, or steering committee, of PHADP. While the chairman and the executive director (of whom I'll speak shortly) have basic decision-making freedom in certain day-to-day business operations, the board of directors is tasked with weighing the pros and cons and voting on all major decisions. The chairman speaks on the phone almost daily to the executive director (our conduit to the outside) to handle ongoing business and to gather information for the Wednesday board meetings.

At board meetings, we go over the week's events and discuss past and present business with an eye toward our direction for the future;

we have a heavy influx of material to digest and act on comprised of PHADP email, snail mail, phone contacts, Facebook posts, and website activity along with the reams of death penalty news from all over the world, which is printed and sent in to us by a dedicated Hope member. We handle any bookkeeping chores and send THANK YOU cards and tax receipts to our donors. We speak via telephone to our "Outmate" executive director Esther Brown. The Wednesday phone calls are a tonic for all involved because Esther is like our board member-at-large and these calls are the closest we can come to all being in the same room at the same time. Everyone comes away with their batteries recharged and ready for another week.

For ten years now, we have enjoyed the help, support, and advice of our executive director Esther Brown, who has given us the benefit of her knowledge, experience and wisdom along with her incomparable people skills in networking and growing the organization. Honestly, most people with her resume and skills would demand and get the top job at an organization like ours. One of the things that makes Esther so special is her understanding of the idea that moving control of PHADP from the board of directors, all of whom live on death row, to any person or group on the street would diminish the organization. One of the things that make her such an asset is her willingness to bring all of her efforts and influence to bear while working within our organizational framework. We are lucky to have her.

The sub-board was instituted ten years ago as a training program for future big board members. There are up to four people on this board who have each been chosen, discussed, and voted in by the board of directors for having distinguished themselves as members of one of the PHADP groups. The sub-board attends the board of directors meetings every other week to familiarize themselves with the duties and responsibilities that will be expected of them if/when they fill a spot on the big board. It also allows the big board members to observe prospective board members under working conditions in order to establish if they have chosen their replacements well.

Unlike other abolitionist organizations, death row inmates hold the main decision-making responsibilities in PHADP, necessitating that we make wise choices when voting in new sub-board members.

The sub-board members are chosen from the five Hope groups. As we can only meet in groups of fifteen or less, the members of PHADP inside are divided into groups that meet on consecutive Wednesday nights. The groups are the main body of Hope on the inside and it is one of these groups that each new death row member is invited to join. Each group has a group leader who is also a board or sub-board member. The group leader is responsible for disseminating all information and data gathered at the board of directors meetings. Issues are discussed and debated and ideas are formed. For many, this is their first foray into the world of social change through group activities. Some find that they enjoy it and thrive on the experience. Others find their time better spent elsewhere and drop out of the group. Either way, something is learned.

Space issues preclude my going into further detail. There is much more I would like to talk about. For this article, though, a basic structural outline will have to do. I'm thinking that there may be more to come, in this "PHADP on the inside" business.

Stop the Madness

de'Bruce • January–March 2011

Alabama has elected a new governor. One of the first cutbacks was in education.* Alabama ranks near the bottom of all the states when it comes to education. Schools are being closed due to lack of funding, while Alabama continues to spend more money on prisons than on education.

Where does this leave the children in Alabama? Studies have shown that the better the child is educated, the less likely it is to end up in prison. The average person on death row did not finish high school. Many never attended high school or even learned to read.

Education is the key to success, and without a good education the child is doomed to fail. This is the type of idiosyncratic nonsense that keeps Alabama behind. If Alabama keeps closing schools and having more cutbacks on education, we are giving up on the children and throwing our babies out with the bath water.

A good education is also crime prevention. Most crimes are committed for money. When a person has the education to get a good job, they are less likely to be hanging out on street corners and committing crimes to get money. We can clean up our streets and make them safer when young people have a bright future to look forward to, and they have something other than the streets and gangs to turn to.

We need to fill up the classrooms and not the Alabama prison system. Our children are the leaders of tomorrow. Do we want them to become the leaders of street gangs and groups within the Alabama prison system? Or do we want them to be the type of leaders that can make this world a better place?

---

* Newly elected governor Robert Bentley announced 3 percent proration, or across-the-board cuts, in the Education Trust Fund for fiscal year 2011. See "Alabama Gov. Robert Bentley Declares Proration for Schools, Says General Fund Next," AL.com, February 28, 2011, https://www.al.com/spotnews/2011/02/alabama_gov_robert_bentley_dec.html.

Education is a necessity, not a privilege. I am speaking from experience on what can happen when a child gets stuck in a system that does not put education first in a child's life. I know what it's like to have teachers trying to teach with outdated textbooks; to have teachers who would go to sleep and say whoever wakes him up will get a failing grade for that day. I am a living example of what can happen. Let's stop the madness and lift up the young leaders of tomorrow so that we can become a first class nation with justice and equality across the board.

"Don't Think About a Zebra!"

Jeffery Rieber • April–June 2011

I have a good friend who used to work as a psychiatric social worker. She is always head-shrinking and analyzing me. :) We talk about everything from dreams, fears and addiction, to relationships, emotions and the "path not taken." It's not always a fun thing to do, but it is always revealing.

One day she asked me, out of the blue, "What do you look forward to when you wake up in the morning?" I went into an instant tail-spin because I knew that I had no answer other than trivialities. My brain was screaming, "this is not a safe topic; this way lies despair!" Most death row inmate's futures are not to be looked forward to, and I was wondering why my friend (who is well aware of this death row reality) would be picking at this particular scab. I gave her the only honest answer that I could think of: that NOT thinking along those lines is what keeps me from losing it in here.

Turns out, that's not what she was driving at, but by coming at me in that way she made me better appreciate the "good times" AS they happen, to recognize them while they are occurring and "squeeze" them for all they are worth. Don't wait for them to become fond memories: see them for what they are in the present and cherish them.

You know that old mind-trick where you say "You can think of anything at all, but DON'T think about a zebra," and of course they can't help but think about a zebra? Well, since our conversation, I find myself doing a crossword puzzle with my friend Boo (which is a lot funnier than it sounds) or something else that has me laughing, and the zebra will pop into my head. I get a third-person, observer's view of the moment and I'll say to myself, "Yep, this right here, right now, is a good moment." It really does work for me, I definitely get more out of these moments when I'm able to recognize them in real time.

She wanted to, and has, given me something to look forward to when I wake up each day. Now, I look forward to my zebra moments and that little extra something that comes from being aware of them as they happen. Thank you, friend!

Mansion of Good and Evil

Arthur Giles • April–June 2011

In the modern era of the death penalty, an Alabama governor has granted clemency only once. On his last day in office, Governor Forest "Fob" James commuted Judith Ann Neely's death sentence to life in prison in 1999.

I often wondered which Alabama governor had signed the most death warrants sending their deaths during their tenure in office. I finally learned the answer in a newspaper article featuring former governor Bob Riley on the subject. The article stated that during Governor Bibb Grave's reign in the 1920s and the 1930s, he sent forty-nine inmates to their deaths before the state took over executions, moving the barbaric practice behind the state prison walls in 1939, at which time Governor Frank Dixon's term began. It lasted until 1943 and he was responsible for sending thirty-three inmates to their deaths. Next comes Governor Bob Riley, who between 2003 and 2010 signed twenty-five death warrants. The last warrant he signed just before leaving office on January 17th was our brother Leroy White, but his execution will be listed under Governor Robert Bentley's term. However, in the twenty-first century, former Governor Riley leads with the most signed death warrants. What I find extremely hard to believe, is that out of twenty-five human beings who came to him for clemency, he could not find one worthy of mercy. Twenty-five human beings! A political slaughter house is what it was.

While reading the article, two things lingered with me. Governor Riley stated that before he signed a death warrant he always listened to the pleas of both sides, especially the pleas of the victim's family. When I read that, I could not help but ask myself, what happened in our brother Leroy White's case? Because if my memory serves me correctly, not only had the jury voted for life and was overridden by the judge, but Mr. White's daughter forgave and even visited her father.* (The victim was Mr. White's estranged wife.) So the daughter, along with other family members, pleaded with the governor to spare the life of the only living parent she had left. The governor turned a deaf ear, signed the warrant, and the daughter became a victim for the second time—this time, as a result of Governor Riley, who could have brought her and her family justice, which would have meant mercy and closure, by sparing the life of her father, which is all they were asking for. I'm still trying to figure out the sick logic of Governor Riley's decision. I guess that falls under the second thing, which is that he stated at the end of his term that when he turned down requests for clemency it was because he believed the inmates' cases had been thoroughly reviewed by the state and federal appeals process, which justified his decision. And here I thought he listened to the victims . . . !

Now we have Mr. Robert Bentley, the Baptist deacon and physician who wears our Lord and Savior on his sleeve like a badge of honor. Yet, even though our brother Glenn Boyd had a judicial override in his case, which gave Governor Bentley a real opportunity for clemency, he chose not to show the people what Christ truly stands for: compassion and mercy. Instead, Governor Bentley signed our brother's death warrant and afterward stated the same thing former Governor Riley always said. Hmm! Have you noticed the sentence that they conducted a "full review" seems to be a statement passed down from governor to governor to use and hide behind.

I think we would stand a better chance in returning to trial court and seeking clemency from a jury of our peers than from a Christ-proclaiming, yet double-minded, double-talking political and merciless governor! Nevertheless, as we continue to pray for Governor Bentley to stop this evil, also let us continue to pray for Governor Bentley and for the men and women who uphold this killing system, that they will one day leave final justice in the hands of a just God.

---

* For more on judicial/jury override, see "Interview," pp. 32–33 and 40n6; "Untitled," January–March 2012, p. 220; "Alabama (Un)Just Being Alabama," p. 254; and "Political Put-Away," p. 258 of this volume.

the Editor's Desk

Jeffery Rieber • July-September 2011

In the modern death penalty era, elected Alabama judges have discarded one hundred and seven jury verdicts of life without parole and imposed death sentences, instead. Alabama has 4.5 million people, yet last year, we imposed more new death sentences than Texas, which has 24 million people. Texas doesn't have judicial override.

Consider these facts: 1) Many are not aware that all capital jurors in Alabama are DEATH QUALIFIED. This means that every juror is asked if they are willing to impose the death penalty. If they're against the death penalty, they are summarily removed from serving on the jury. 2) In Alabama, unlike most states, the law does not require that a jury be unanimous in order to give a verdict of death. 3) Alabama judges are elected, again unlike most states, and are therefore subject to political pressures involved in getting elected and staying elected.

These are just three of many examples of reasons why Alabama's capital punishment system is already very heavily skewed in favor of the death penalty as opposed to life without parole. Allowing judges to override jury verdicts of life is just adding insult to injury. It is, literally, overkill. Override is overkill.

In this publication, our general policy is to abstain from pleading our individual cases. This forum is not intended for that. As a result, we usually speak on issues in a broad overview method. This has the benefit of being inclusive but it also has the drawback of omitting the personal examples of issues that might serve to better make a particular point. In illustration, I found out after my trial that I was the judge's first capital case. She had just been elevated from traffic court.

Judges like to say, in explanation of override, that they have capital trial experience that jurors don't have, so they are the better arbiters of appropriate sentences. My case challenges that because my judge and my jury experienced their first capital trial together, yet, the one person who had a personal stake in the outcome was allowed to throw away the considered judgment of the twelve jurors and, instead, impose her own will. If she wanted to keep her new job, she had to prove that she was tough enough to roll with the "big dogs" and work within the good ol' boy network that still pervades the Alabama system.

It saddens me to report that, since the last newsletter, two men were executed, one committed suicide, and Alabama has set yet another execution date. Jason Williams was executed May 19. Eddie Powell was executed June 16. William "Corky" Snyder took his own life July 12, and board member Derrick Mason has an execution date set for September 22. Derrick's fight is our fight, and it isn't over, by a long shot. PLEASE lend your help by contacting the governor and expressing your abhorrence of state killing. Help keep HOPE alive.

AL vs USA Executions

July–September 2011

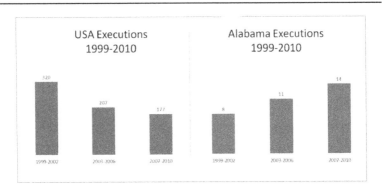

USA Executions
1999-2010

Alabama Executions
1999-2010

Alabamians polled clearly believe it is possible for an innocent person
to be convicted and executed with the current system.

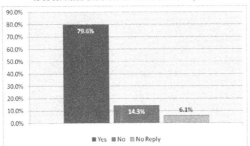

Question: "Do you believe an innocent person may be convicted and executed?"

Survey by Capital Survey Research Center for Project Hope to Abolish the Death Penalty
To see full survey results visit: www.phadp.org/2005_poll

The majority of Alabamians polled support suspension of the death
penalty for its fairness and accuracy to be studied and confirmed.

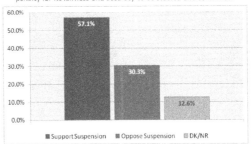

Question: "There have been cases in which someone sentenced to be executed was found not guilty based on new
evidence, usually DNA testing. How do you feel about suspending the death penalty in Alabama until questions about
the fairness and accuracy of the death penalty have been studied and confirmed? Do you:"

Survey by Capital Survey Research Center for Project Hope to Abolish the Death Penalty
To see full survey results visit: www.phadp.org/2005_poll

Execute Justice Not People!

de'Bruce • July-September 2011

When I was sentenced to death, the district attorney told me that this day is the first day of the rest of my life. As he walked out of the room, someone asked me, how does it feel to get the death penalty? There was a lot that I wanted to say, but I stood there in a catatonic state.

As I arrived at Holman and walked down the hallway, I said to myself, So this is what they mean by walking through valleys of the shadow of death. All I could think about was how the people before me who had to walk down this long hallway must have felt.

When I got to the cell block, I was put in a cell that is five feet wide and eight feet long. I was looking for a place where the walls dripped with melancholy. I was asked to go to church and I said I didn't know God came to death row. What I found was nothing like what I thought. All the horror stories I heard weren't true. No one was running around like an animal trying to kill anyone. What I learned was just because the prison doors are slammed shut the person doesn't lose the qualities that make them human. It is then when they need them most.

I will never forget the date March 20, 1992—the first execution I witnessed as I stood in my cell and looked through the bars out the window. I watched the prison guards take Larry Heath to the execution chamber. I remember the loud noise made by the generator used to power the electric chair and the smell of burnt flesh and hair that morning. The bleach that was used to try and cover the smell only made it worse. Tears rolled down my face for a person I had never known. That was a human who was murdered by the state of Alabama. And the people in charge said that killing is wrong and to show that killing is wrong they are going to kill anyone charged with killing someone.

Murder is wrong, no matter who is doing it.

From the Editor's Desk

Carey Grayson • October–December 2011

Greetings from the Season, folks!! Or, maybe that's Season's Greetings. Either way, Merry Christmas and a happy New Year to you all. This is Carey Grayson coming to you from the editor's desk again and I have a lot to tell you.

Where to start? Well, how about the great news? PHADP has become the proud recipient of RESIST's three-year $4,000 grant! This will truly help us in these tough economic times.

PHADP has also been getting some overseas attention in the form of the *Guardian* (UK), the *Times of London*, and *Reuters*.[*] The *Japan Times* has also done an article on Alabama's habit of killing the mentally handicapped. Esther has been working hard in the state media with interviews with the New American Dream radio hour and three interviews with the Huntsville radio station WEUP with Mr. David Person. The *Huntsville Times* also quoted Esther during Derrick Mason's time of execution, a time of great loss for PHADP and the world.[†] I can think of no one better to convey our thoughts.

On a less pleasing note, Alabama has executed six men this year, one of whom was a PHADP board member and a dear friend. We will miss you all, and continue to fight in your names. We would like to thank Patrick Jackson, of the Tuskegee student chapter of the NAACP,

---

[*] Ed Pilkington, "Alabama Executes Christopher Johnson Despite Mental Health Doubts," *Guardian*, October 20, 2011, https://www.theguardian.com/world/2011/oct/21/alabama-executes-christopher-johnson-doubts; Kaya Burgess, "If You Make a Mistake There's No Turning Back," *Times of London*, November 7, 2011, https://www.thetimes.co.uk/article/if-you-make-a-mistake-theres-no-turning-back-5zwrdmb8l92; Kelli Dugan, "Alabama Set to Execute Man for 2005 Death of his Infant Son," *Reuters*, October 20, 2011, https://www.reuters.com/article/us-alabama-execution/alabama-set-to-execute-man-for-2005-death-of-his-infant-son-idUSTRE79J3MQ20111020.

[†] Keith Clines, "Derrick Mason Apologized to Victim's Family Years Ago, an Anti-Death Penalty Official Said," AL.com, September 22, 2011, https://www.al.com/breaking/2011/09/derrick_mason_apologized_to_vi.html.

and the Auburn student chapter of Alabama Arise for co-hosting the Journey of Hope events at Tuskegee and Auburn, respectively.

We also would like to congratulate Esther on her newest award from the Alabama NAACP for her work as chair of their Moratorium Committee. In case you haven't noticed . . . this woman ROCKS!! :) We would also like to congratulate our newest sub-board members (David Wiggins and David Riley) as well as our Director of Information (Brent Martin): your dedication has been noted and we are proud to work with you.

Our thanks go to all of our great supporters within the states and outside of them. Without you, we couldn't do what we do, so thank you all.

And to all of you out there, we at PHADP wish you a very happy holiday season and a Happy New Year! I want a Corvette in case anyone was thinking of playing Santa. Just saying.

The Heart and Soul
of Death Row

LaSamuel Gamble • October–December 2011

In 2012, LaSamuel Gamble would be resentenced to life without parole in exchange for waiving his right to appeal his sentencing.

To the average person, this would be the last thing that comes to mind about death row: despite what you may have heard from the TV or read in the newspaper, there is an unspoken brotherhood on the row. I am not going to sit here and tell you that everyone loves each other, but I can say that each one of us has respect for one another because we know that we are fighting for the same cause: to stop the death penalty or get off the row.

I cannot tell you how deep our bond is when someone gets an execution date; you would have to see it for yourself to believe it. The brotherhood is unreal, like none I have ever seen, not even with my own family. And I am sure some of the brothers here feel the same way.

We developed friendships that will last a lifetime, just like you would do with your brother or cousin. A bond that will stand the test of time. So, when you or one of your brothers receives an execution date, it takes a little out of you because of the love and bond that you have built over the years. And it makes you wonder, am I next?

It's hard not to put myself in my brothers' shoes because I could very well be in the same situation where I would have to say to myself, I am going to die at 6:00 and I will never see my loved ones again. It's hard to imagine, but that is life as we know it.

Even though society may say we are cold-blooded animals, they do not see the love that is shown to each brother who comes to death row, those who don't have loved ones, no one to care for them. That is when the heart and soul of death row comes shining through. That will make the darkest heart shine bright.

Season's Greetings!

David Riley • October–December 2011

Our last newsletter comes out around the holidays. The holidays can be depressing for all on death row. We must deal with the prison conditions, not being with family and loved ones, and knowing that they also feel the pain of our absence.

One of the hardest holidays to face is Thanksgiving. Thanksgiving is supposed to be a time to be thankful and celebrate what you have. At times this is difficult. I'm on death row. I live in a 5×8-foot cement box. I'm painted as a monster to society by people who don't even know me. And with politics playing a major role in the death penalty, an issue that should save my life or someone else's is easily covered up or overlooked. Therefore, my life ending with a drug that comes in a box with a label that reads "for animals" . . . I have to keep looking for what I have to be thankful for.

I am thankful for the people who don't know me, people I've never met and have never heard of me, but take a stand against the death penalty. I'm thankful for all our PHADP supporters because we wouldn't be able to do what we do without you. I'm thankful for the people who feel my life and the lives of my brothers on death row are worth fighting to save. I do have many other things I am thankful for. I wanted to take this time to let you and all our supporters know your love and support helps ease the pain of our hard times and pain. I want to end this by wishing you and your loved ones a very Happy Thanksgiving and Happy Holidays. Have a blessed and safe holiday season.

Untitled

Ronald B. Smith Jr. • October-December 2011

The holiday season spent on death row can't be described in general terms as it is such an individualistic experience. It is different for each and every one of us. Some seek communion with their neighbors. Some call home in the hopes of communicating with their loved ones. Some of us have kids. Some seek a cocoon of self-pitying solitude and depression. Some pray. Some curse or something in that vein. Some are truly thankful for what they have even if it is not considered much in a commercial world. Some, like many of their free-world counterparts, are never satisfied and sadly will never be satisfied. Some of us stay busy while others relax. Some will laugh and some will cry; some will stress out over their cases or not getting everything they wanted in their Christmas packages. Or not getting their Christmas packages when they expected. Some will worry about their family members. Some will receive good news from home and some will hear bad news. Some will watch basketball. Some football. And some will watch anything but sports. Some will eat alone and some of us will break bread, plan and prepare meals in conjunction with our neighbors. Our brothers. If any of this sounds familiar then maybe just maybe we aren't as different from the rest of society as the politicians would lead you to believe. As for me, I will awake on Christmas morning, thank God for allowing me another day. Then I will open, read and enjoy all the Christmas cards I received. I save and open them on Christmas morn like presents. Something to look forward to. Then I will pester my neighbor Mark and exchange greetings with several of my other tier mates. Then most likely some Christmas cartoons—yes some death row inmates enjoy cartoons. And then some football followed by a call home to talk to my son, my folks and my sister Cassie. My brother Bryan passed this year and I will deeply miss talking to him. I will then await the state tray upon which I will choose what to eat right then and what to put up later to go with the burritos or sandwiches Mark, Jeff, Boo and I have planned. More sports on television complete with arguing close calls with various neighbors especially if they are rooting for the opposite team. Then the "feast" with my neighbors will be assembled and eaten while we reminisce about past "feasts" such as the current PHADP chairman's infamous fish tacos which made me sick for several days after ingestion. We will also reminisce about the brothers who are no longer with us to share our "feast." Things usually taper off and get pretty quiet at this point as we drift into our own reveries of Christmas pasts. And that is how I will more than likely spend my Christmas unless Santa sends the stealth helicopter piloted by Angelina Jolie that I have been asking for. Yes, some death row inmates still believe in Christmas miracles.

A Friend Is Gone but Never Will Be Forgotten

Randy Lewis • October–December 2011

I arrived on death row on July 26, 2007. I met Derrick Mason on July 27, 2007. He came out that morning and fed me breakfast. He introduced himself to me and we began to talk from there. He gave me an extra tray and then sat down in front of I-1A and we talked until he locked down. All I wanted to talk about was my innocence and the law. He told me about PHADP as well as how [Anthony] Tyson was well equipped in the law. From that point forward we became the best of friends until the day of his departure. Even though he is not physically here with me, I still consider him a good friend. We never had an argument—never. He knew that I was doing bad on finances so he used to look out for me when he was able, when God blessed his finances to do so. This continued up until his departure. Derrick also used to buy my chicken, fish and corn dog trays from me so that I could keep what I needed on hand. He and I didn't consider the tray deal as him buying them from me, but just as a way of me saying thanks for looking out for me during these rough times. He said to me, "I understand you are doing bad right now, but don't worry about that because I consider you family." I told him likewise.

Derrick and I used to talk everyday. He was in I-4 and I was right above him in a new assigned cell, I-18A. The last time I spoke to him was on September 21 when he was coming off the visitation yard from a visit with his family. He, Tyson, and I talked briefly before the officers took him back to the death cell. We all were full of joy and high hopes for a miracle. The last time I heard his voice was on September 22 when he came from another visitation with his family. He called out, "Alright I-side!" I tried to break down the door hollering at him. I was hollering, "Alright, I love you bra, Alright!" I know that he knew that already but it is always good to hear it, especially from someone who really sincerely means it. Thanksgiving and Christmas will not ever be the same without you, bra. And I still love you.

My birthday was the week of his murder, September 19. It wasn't a good one because I knew what that week might bring.

the Editor's Desk

Carey Grayson • January–March 2012

Hi folks, this is Carey Grayson coming to you from the editor's desk. Don't tell him my feet are on it OK? Well, I am out of the doghouse and back into the swing of things and I must say it's good to be back in my cell. Never thought I'd say that did ya. LOL. Me either! But it's true.

On a darker note, especially for myself and my PHADP brothers and adopted mom, the lovely miss Esther Brown: we have two executions set for the next two months. Tommy Arthur has a date set for March 29th, and Carey Grayson (me) is scheduled for April 12th.* Keep us in your prayers and send all the happy thoughts you can. OH! and if anyone wins the lottery, let me get a loan. Hee hee.

Aside from these aforementioned events, life at Holman remains the same and I'm still shootin' for chairman! Although, if it's as much work as it looks, I may change my mind. You folks have a great day and stay out of trouble. Peace! I'm out!

---

* Carey Grayson and Tommy Arthur both received stays of execution after a federal appeals court agreed to review Alabama's lethal injection process. Arthur was executed May 26, 2017. Grayson remains on death row. For more, see "Alabama Supreme Court Stays Execution," Equal Justice Initiative, April 9, 2012, https://eji. org/news/alabama-supreme-court-stays-carey-grayson-execution.

Doing What You Can

Nicholas Acklin • January–March 2012

I've been an active member of Project Hope to Abolish the Death Penalty for fourteen years now. In those years, I have experienced many things. There have been ups and downs, as well as gains and losses. I have taken all in stride, but with the intention to grow from each experience.

Some may say that it is the big things that they have experienced in life that have made the biggest impressions. I can say it has been the big things as well as the small things. For me it has been the small things that have made lasting impressions on me. In an environment where there is struggle every day, both mentally and physically, it can be easy to be sucked in by those struggles.

Thankfully for me, when the struggle can seem to be too much, the small things offer me strength.

I think about the pen friends I've come to know over the years and their emotional support, it strengthens me to keep going. These are people that have never known me before my incarceration, don't judge me, and have faith in me and for me. Recently, at one of our PHADP co-sponsored events, a young lady dug into her purse and donated all the money she had ($14) to the cause. What an impression that act had on me! An act of doing what you can, when you don't have to.

To my pen friends, and this particular young lady, I say thank you. Thank you for doing what you can, which encourages me in the midst of the struggle.

KEEP HOPE ALIVE!

Untitled

Anonymous • January-March 2012

The practice of judicial override—the authority of a judge to overrule a jury's sentencing recommendation—would be abolished by Alabama in 2017 but not made retroactive. According to the Equal Justice Initiative, 91 percent of overrides imposed the death penalty where juries had recommended life imprisonment.*

Override is legal in only three states: Alabama, Delaware, and Florida. Florida and Delaware have strict standards for override. No one in Delaware is on death row as a result of an override and no death sentences have been imposed by override in Florida since 1999. In Delaware and Florida, override often is used to overrule jury death verdicts and impose life—which rarely happens in Alabama.

Alabama's trial and appellate court judges are elected. Because judicial candidates frequently campaign on their support and enthusiasm for capital punishment, political pressure injects unfairness and arbitrariness into override decisions.

Override rates fluctuate wildly from year to year. The proportion of death sentences imposed by override often is elevated in election years. In 2008, 30 percent of new death sentences were imposed by judicial override, compared to 7 percent in 1997, a non-election year. In some years, half of all death sentences imposed in Alabama have been the result of override.

There is evidence that elected judges override jury life verdicts in cases involving white victims much more frequently than in cases involving victims who are Black. Seventy-five percent of all death sentences imposed by override involve white victims, even though less than 35 percent of all homicide victims in Alabama are white.

---

* See the full report, "The Death Penalty in Alabama: Judge Override," Equal Justice Initiative, July 2011, https://eji.org/wp-content/uploads/2019/10/death-penalty-in-alabama-judge-override.pdf.

There are considerably fewer obstacles to obtaining a jury verdict of death in Alabama because, unlike in most states with the death penalty, prosecutors in Alabama are not required to obtain a unanimous jury verdict; they can obtain a death verdict with only ten juror votes for death. Capital juries in Alabama already are very heavily skewed in favor of the death penalty because potential jurors who oppose capital punishment are excluded from jury service.

A Christian Perspective

Ronald B. Smith • January–March 2012

A lot is happening and has happened recently in Alabama surrounding the issue of capital punishment. Some of it hits so very close to home as two more of my brothers on the row have execution dates set. One of these brothers, Tommy Arthur, is a Marine Corps veteran and a long-time friend of mine. One of these brothers is a PHADP board member, a man I have sat next to on Wednesdays for the last several years. We have talked, eaten, laughed, and commiserated together. We also share the same law firm. We are on the same tier here at Holman and have gotten close over those years. As you can imagine, this is exactly the situation that PHADP is trying to put an end to once and for all. Personally, I am tired of saying goodbye to men I have come to know and love. I am weary of the emotional and mental toll it takes on my brothers and me.

I am not known for my sentimentality. I don't always get why people feel what they feel about certain things, or why they feel so strongly about things I care so very little for. But as a neighbor of mine said recently, "sometimes even a blind squirrel will find a nut." Well, that is all well and good when the squirrel in question is not in any danger of starving to death. But sometimes the blind squirrel needs a helping of kindness and compassion to get through the day. As an emotionally "blind squirrel," I rely on my PHADP brothers to clue me in on emotional issues. My brother Boo [Carey Grayson] has done this for me several times when I was uncomprehending of the passion of other peoples' emotional states. Now I find myself contending with my own feelings concerning his upcoming date and the loss it will bring but also figuring out how to go about not making things worse for Boo. I also struggle to continue to lead my younger and newer to death row brothers by setting a good example when what I truly want to do is, in the vernacular of the row, "act a complete fool," which of course will do nothing in the way of making things any better. So I pray. For

Boo. For me. For you. And I hope. And I rely on faith. After all it only takes a mustard seed, right? I wonder how long a blind squirrel can live on a mustard seed?

I'll keep you all posted. Pray for Boo. For me. For you.

Keeping Hope Alive and Growing!

the Editor's Desk

Jeffery Rieber • April–June 2012

I have finally managed to wrestle my office back from that pesky assistant editor, Carey Grayson. (I think he's been putting his feet up on my desk.) Speaking of Carey brings me to our most happy news: I am relieved to report that our brother Carey Grayson and Tommy Arthur have both received stays of execution due to a challenge to the execution protocol. This is wonderful news and we are so glad to still have them both with us. May the state come to its senses and end capital punishment without further killing.

We have been encouraging our members and new guys here to write for the newsletter. This issue features some of them as well as a list of contributors who were not printed due to a lack of space. The effort these men put into writing is recognized and appreciated. I look forward to printing more of their work in the future. Opinions, as always, are the authors' own.

The big news, nation- and world-wide, is that the state of Texas has indeed executed an innocent man. We owe this ground-shaking revelation to the investigative work of a dedicated team at Columbia University. Find the story, as well as all proof, at www.thewrongcarlos.net.

The news about Texas OUGHT to be enough, by itself, to lead any and all fair-minded people to oppose the death penalty. However, if the United States Supreme Court requires evidence of the nation trending away from capital punishment, then we offer the five states in five years that have done away with their death penalty, including Connecticut (the fifth), which abolished their death penalty on the 25th of April. Also, California (with the nation's largest death row) will likely be the next to abolish, as they have placed it on the ballot for a vote in November and all signs point to their voting it out of existence.[*]

There are many encouraging, possibly game changing, events occurring at the moment that I don't have space to mention individually. Let us hope that the end of capital punishment is not far away. As always, please help to keep Hope alive. Until next time.

---

[*] Capital punishment remains legal in California. However, Governor Gavin Newsom ordered a moratorium in March 2019 that is still in place.

the Editor's Desk

Jeffery Rieber • July-September 2012

---

*In 2012, people on Alabama's death row—including members of PHADP—filed
suit against the state of Alabama, challenging the constitutionality of its three-
drug execution protocol, which included the sedative midazolam.*[*]

As we prepare to publish this third issue of 2012's newsletter, I am
pleased to report that there have been no executions in the state of
Alabama to date this year, and none scheduled. This is due to the still
unresolved legal issues concerning the execution protocol. Realistically,
we know that this can not go on forever, but we are definitely enjoying
the respite from being a leading execution state.

As a result of our program to get more of Alabama's death row population engaged in writing articles and poems, etc., for the newsletter,
we will be posting on Facebook some of the submissions that do not
make it into the newsletter due to a lack of space. This will allow many
more voices to be heard and will also reassure the writers that their
efforts will not go unpublished when possible.

In other news, one of the most important tasks we board members
have is to prepare other inmates to take over from us when we leave.
Among many other things, this includes editing, typing and formatting the newsletters. This issue was edited and typed by two men who
have never done it before, Anthony Boyd and Anthony Tyson. There
may be more typos than usual but please be kind and remember that
this is their first effort in this area. And while it may look like a step
backward, it is in reality a step forward.

I hope that our readers find this issue interesting, and we thank all

---

[*] See also "Lethal Injection," p. 267; and "Greetings from the Editor's Desk," p. 287 of
this volume.

of our family of supporters for their dedication to ending the death penalty in Alabama. Please, help us to keep Hope alive.

Untitled

Steve Hall • July–September 2012

An optimist sees the glass as half-full.

A pessimist sees the glass as half-empty.

A realist knows that sooner or later someone has to wash that damned glass.

I'm a realist.

I've been here on death row now for over eighteen years. Not as long as some—longer than many. I've seen guys come to death row, and I've seen some guys get lesser sentences. Some even went home. I've seen many murdered by the state, some of whom came to death row long after I did.

There have been forty people executed since I arrived on death row. I personally knew over half of them. Some I knew well; others I just talked to. Some were even close enough to call "friends."

I've seen guys die for one reason or another, before the state got to them. And I've even known some guys who took their own lives.

I've seen death row stand strong as a whole against a wrong done to us by the administration, and I've seen death row divided no matter the wrong.

When I came to death row in 1993, there were only about one hundred of us on the row. That number has more than doubled now.

I've spent almost half my life on death-row. I've never held, let alone used, a cell phone, and the internet is as much a mystery to me as astrophysics. I fully expect to die here . . . despite the hard work and optimism of my attorneys over the years. I'm a realist! I know that the state holds all the cards. Yes, my attorneys could find a really good issue or two for my appeals. Yes, the law could change—it's done so a few times, just not enough to really benefit me. Those are realities as well, and I acknowledge them, but I also know the odds are slim that anything like that will happen before my time is up.

So, what's my point in all this rambling?

GHOSTS OVER THE BOILER   226

Just this: of all the articles I've read in the Hope newsletter, and other such newsletters, they talk a lot about what it's like here, and how they've overcome their despondency and embraced hope. Well, some of us don't see that hope. But I continue to persevere.

Sometimes, it's all that matters.

from the Editor's Desk

Jeffery Rieber • October–December 2012

In looking forward to the coming holidays, and reflecting on the passing year, I am struck by the extreme contrast in our emotional state from the beginning part of 2012 to now, at its very end. The year began with two execution dates and the very real prospect of many more to follow. Such a thing is always terrible and emotionally debilitating, but one of those execution dates had the added aspect of being for a longtime Hope board member. As our supporters know, we had just recently lost a board member to execution, and the idea of losing yet another was almost more than we could take. That was the beginning of 2012.

I can't adequately express our joy that those two executions were not carried out. As a matter of fact, there have been NO executions by the state of Alabama in 2012 due to a legal challenge of the execution protocol. That good news, coupled with some other favorable court rulings for various men on the row, has turned what promised to be another execution-filled year into a year of thankful gratitude and wondrous moments spent with someone who was not expected to be alive for any of them. And even though we are painfully aware that next year may bring horrors untold, we must take each piece of good news to heart, use them to sustain us and recharge our abolitionist batteries.

So it is with these things in mind that I find myself, this week before Thanksgiving, paying closer attention to the "good news" in my life both organizationally and personally. I am grateful for all of you who have never even met us, yet continue to support us in this (let's face it) unpopular cause. I am grateful for the men and women I work with on a daily basis, who I glean comfort from and the will to continue tilting at windmills. Personally, I'm grateful to have connected and reconnected with friends and family. I am humbled by the care and affection shown to me by the few extraordinary friends I have been blessed with in the years I've been here.

They say hope springs eternal, and I really hope that's true. OOPs, there I go hoping. Maybe it IS true. I can say that today is good. I wish us all an unending supply of good todays. As ever, I ask that you all help us keep Hope alive.

Historic Event

de'Bruce • October–December 2012

I may have lost my right to vote, but I didn't lose my voice. With my voice, I told everyone I know to vote for Obama. I was so happy to be a part of history being made that I became emotional. As I sat and began to think of all of the things my parents and grandparents had to go through in a time when they weren't allowed to vote. They were even told, if your grandparents didn't have the right to vote, then you'll never have the right to vote. Hands that pick cotton could never pick presidents.

The idea of an African American becoming president was unthinkable. Now, not only is there an African American president, but he's a two-term president. I would like to thank all of the people who voted for president Obama and for keeping the dreams alive that so many people dreamt of. A time when the Jim Crow way of thinking would be a thing of the past. And as long as the person is the right person to lead America, it doesn't matter what the color is of that person's skin. Man or woman, it's about that person's ability to make America great. In my opinion, if America would end the death penalty and stop creating laws that are designed to hurt the minorities, such as the three strikes law and mandatory sentencing, America can then without any doubt be the country the song was talking about: my country tis of thee, sweet land of liberty, of thee I sing.

the Editor's Desk

Jeffery Rieber • January–March 2013

As we create this first newsletter of 2013, we have both happy and sad news. We have much hope for the future. The cycle continues as we persevere. Our determination is renewed and reinvigorated by you, the amazing people on the street who refuse to NOT see us as fellow human beings. To be sure, one must find one's own sense of value and worth, but it sure does help when others see it in you.

It is my sad duty to inform you that Clarence Simmons died on the row on January 6 of natural causes.

It brings me joy to announce that Bobby Tarver and Esau Jackson have both gotten off of death row.*

I wish I could bring you more definitive news on the status of the challenge to the lethal injection protocol (which is the reason there were no executions last year and none so far in 2013). The only thing we can say for sure is that there has been no court ruling resolving the issue.

We have great hope that the Senate Judiciary Committee hearings on Senator Sanders's death penalty bills will be scheduled and held, as promised, by Senator Cam Ward. Inside this issue of *On Wings of Hope*, you will find the excellent letter in support of this written by our development officer Brandon Fountain. We ask all Alabamians to follow Brandon's example by contacting your legislators and urging them to support these bills.

And finally, if this issue has reached you later than usual, it is a result of our being locked down due to construction taking place within the prison. Our board and groups have not been able to meet in almost three weeks but we are resilient and are finding ways to do what needs to be done. Things should be back to normal soon.

---

* Both men had their sentences commuted to life in prison.

I wish you all health and happiness, and ask that you help keep Hope alive.

A Christian Perspective

Ronald B. Smith • January–March 2013

Well it has been an interesting beginning to the New Year for me. I got turned down by the 11th Circuit Court of Appeals and an article was published in the *New York Times* by Adam Liptak, the US Supreme Court reporter for the *Times*, on the issue of ineffective assistance of counsel featuring my case.* Please keep me in your prayers.

The circumstances on death row rarely change but we are anxiously awaiting a new warden. It turns out that he is familiar to some of the ol' timers and we are of course hoping for the best. Please keep the administration of Holman in your prayers as well as the inmates. Trust me when I say that "stuff" rolls downhill.

With the recent lack of executions recently it would be easy for some to become complacent and apathetic. Thankfully, our friends at JAM and a few of our other affiliated organizations along with our own "Outmate" continue to keep lit the torch of awareness on capital punishment.† Brandon [Fountain]: your actions behind the scenes are not going without notice by those of us you seek to help. Thank you. Not only are you guys "staying in the game" but you are "keeping us in the game" as well.

How about that? I got through an entire editorial without mentioning food. Oops! Well, I was doing well while I lasted. Just keeping it positively real. Someone has got to do it. Keeping Hope Alive!

---

* Adam Liptak, "Lawyers Stumble, and Clients Take the Fall," *New York Times*, January 7, 2013, https://www.nytimes.com/2013/01/07/us/when-death-row-lawyers-stumble-clients-take-the-fall.html.

† Justice and Mercy (JAM) is affiliated with Mary's House, a Catholic Worker house in Birmingham, Alabama.

the Editor's Desk

Jeffery Rieber • July–September 2013

I am sad to report that, on July 25th, Alabama executed Andrew Lackey, a mentally ill man who tried to commit suicide and then asked the state to kill him. Of course, Alabama was happy to "help." I knew Drew. This was a young man who deserved to be in a medical facility, not a max prison on death row. Drew will be missed by all who knew him here. Rest in peace, Andrew.

Our thanks go to all of those who held and attended the prayer vigils throughout the state, and also to those who took the time to write to the governor asking him to stop the execution.

While I'm thanking people . . . Thank you, David Riley, for doing most of the typing for this issue. Our work in training the current and future leaders of this organization continues.

Looking to the future is, at times, a dismal prospect for those on the row, where most men live in the past, but members of Hope have the privilege of planning for the future of this organization, no matter what happens in our own lives. I see that as a gift.

Part of moving the organization forward includes growing our online presence. In order to further that goal, we ask each of our readers to "LIKE" our Facebook page at https://www.facebook.com/projecthopetoabolishthedeathpenalty.

As ever, thank you to our many supporters, who keep us inspired to continue. Please help keep Hope alive.

Season's Greetings

Carey Grayson • October-December 2013

Hello to all you in free world land! 'Tis I, Carey, here to once again speak to you from the editor's desk. Ignore the noise coming from the closet. Jeff's . . . um . . . doin' inventory . . . or something. Anyway, on with the show!!

It's been an interesting year for PHADP. Two men on the row got off and are no longer facing death. Very good news!

Esther and five others from NAACP had a sit down with the governor in February to discuss the death penalty, prison conditions, and other topics. The result was predictable, but getting him to the table was a feat in itself.

Our friend Sen. Hank Sanders once again introduced anti-death penalty bills. None of them made it out of committee, although that hasn't dulled his resolve. Keep swinging away, Hank!

On the flip, the Alabama senate voted to expand the death penalty to include those murdered under a protective court order.

There is also talk of a bill that will cut the appeals time in half by running certain appeals concurrently. Think they deserve a lil coal in the stocking, Big Red!

Ursula Malchau of Germany got the German Human Rights Commissioner Markus Leaning to write Sen. Cam Ward in support of Sen. Sanders's Bills. She also contacted Tom Koenig, chairperson of German Parliament Commission for Human Rights. Thank you, Ursula, for the proactive support.

For those of you who may not know, we had two deaths at Holman this year: Andrew Lackey was executed on July 25th, and at the first of the year Clarence Simmons died of natural causes. Two very sad days.

And finally, we the board are working twice as hard as you think and half as hard as you know! To all of those inside and out of the PHADP family, we wish you a most Merry Christmas and a very Happy New Year!!

the Editor's Desk

Jeffery Rieber • January–March 2014

Jesse Morrison, whose sentence was commuted to life in prison, died after a long illness on February 12, 2014, right around the time the so-called "Fair Justice Act" was first introduced in the Alabama legislature. Under this bill, those convicted of capital crimes would have to file a Rule 32 appeal, which reviews all aspects of the trial, at the same time as their direct appeal, which reviews only the written record. Critics including PHADP and the ACLU argued that the bill would result in an even greater number of wrongful executions due to the accelerated timeline it establishes.[*]

It is a hard time for the PHADP family right now. We recently lost a dear friend, family member and founder of PHADP, Mr. Jesse Morrison. A lot of the men on death row now didn't have the chance to know him because he got off the row years ago. He was the chairman of Hope when I got here in 1992, and it was Jesse's infectious strength of spirit, charisma, and boundless belief in our ability to effect social change that encouraged me to join in the struggle to fight the death penalty.

Jesse's fight did not stop once he got off the row. He affected people in a positive way wherever he went. This kind, soft-spoken leader truly made the most of his situation no matter what circumstances he found himself in. Jesse's legacy, Jesse's life, is the undeniable proof against the lie that death row prisoners are irredeemable and cannot offer anything positive to society. Bon voyage, Jesse.

In other news, the so-called "Fair Justice Act" to shorten death penalty appeals and other bills designed to make receiving a fair review more difficult will most likely be passed into law soon. We thank all those who tirelessly work to defeat these horrendous bills.

---

[*] ACLU, "ACLU of Alabama Challenges the Proposed Fair Justice Act," January 21, 2014, www.aclualabama.org/en/news/aclu-alabama-challenges-proposed-fair-justice-act.

As Jesse would say, "The work must continue," so, although many of us are devastated at his passing and would like nothing better than to curl up and feel sorry for ourselves, we will push onward instead. In his memory, with the knowledge that he would expect nothing less. Until next time, please help us keep Hope alive.

PHADP Lost a Good Man

Amigo • January–March 2014

His name was Jesse Morrison. I met him twenty-three years ago. It doesn't seem that long ago, but I've walked this journey because of a simple man who believed in me. From my very first meeting with PHADP, I received a warm welcome. I received encouraging words to address my struggle to write my very first article. He saw in me what I didn't see in myself. These are some of the reasons why I've walked this journey with him and PHADP for so long.

Using the tools to bring out the best in an uneducated man, as I was, seemed easy for Jesse. He knew what to say, and how to say it, for people to understand where he was coming from. He had a look, the encouraging kind, followed with a smile. He was a people person. He put Hope on his shoulders to walk this journey and fight for our lives. The very worth of being alive drove him. He knew many would die in the death houses across the US, but he never knew what "give up" was. He believed in us on death row. This journey has been long, but we've survived because of Jesse, a simple man with a gifted mind and a clear ability to organize a group of death row inmates to believe what we were doing was right. He knew the issues and how to attack them.

The states used emotional blackmail to fuel the vengeance and keep the death houses full. The very purpose the states used to kill motivated Jesse to speak out against it. This is the very reason we are here today, continuing that struggle he began so long ago.

The article he wrote, "Be the Other Voice," is a tool he shared with us.[*] The issues and points are still true today. How can we soften the hardest of hearts that fuel this vengeance? How can we get those who remain silent to speak out, as Jesse said? What energy will it take to see it through? Do we pack up and go home, give up, because the deck is stacked against us at every level of government? NO! We use our voice;

---

[*] See "Introduction," p. 4 of this volume.

we must be heard! How do we reach those main streets of America that he spoke about? Society has been on a journey too. I can only hope that one day the doors will close in the death houses and the visions Jesse saw will come true.

PHADP lost a good man, a man named Jesse. You are free now, my friend. The teachings will remain, I promise that PHADP will still fight that fight worth fighting, for we will not be silent, and we will help those who are silent to speak out, because Jesse knew and believed we could.

Untitled

Anthony Boyd • January-March 2014

Accomplice, co-conspirator, cohort, co-defendant. Words used by the highest court in the land (United States Supreme Court) to deem a person a criminal if they're not the actual culprits. Words they shouldn't be using to identify, label, or judge anyone. Here, such sayings as "the pot shouldn't call the kettle black," "people who live in glass houses shouldn't throw rocks," and "clean your own house before trying to tell someone how to clean theirs" would apply.

I say these things because the United States Supreme Court has sat on high and watched as the death penalty states have bent, broken, and eroded the Constitution to their will in order to continue their killing sprees, which makes them just as guilty as the actual culprits, i.e., accomplices and co-conspirators.

Wardens having prescriptions filled in their own names at the local drug stores in order to obtain drugs for executions. Meth users would be arrested for trying such methods to get high. Correctional officers meeting at state lines to exchange money for execution drugs. Any other time, that would be considered drug trafficking. Let me also add that the FDA was just letting such drugs pass through customs because they were what they called "just execution drugs" going to this state or that—drugs not on their approved list, but still allowed into this country. If some drug cartel, or everyday person, had known about this, they could have just shipped in drugs with the label "for executions only" on it, and it would've/could've passed right through customs. Still, the US Supreme Court sat on high, and did nothing.

More and more death penalty cases are revealing the lengths to which prosecutors are willing to go to get convictions and further their political aspirations. Jury tampering, threats, and intimidation. Then there are those who hide or destroy evidence—evidence that they know proves a person's innocence. This is, by any account, attempted murder, or even murder if the execution is carried out. The US Supreme Court is accomplice and co-conspirator as they wipe their dirty (blood-stained) hands clean with words such as "harmless error" and "procedurally barred."

Well, I have a few other words for them: "THE DEATH PENALTY IS UNCONSTITUTIONAL" and "IRREVOCABLY BROKEN AND CANNOT BE FIXED."

Words with substance!

the Editor's Desk

Jeffery Rieber • January-March 2015

Here we are in the first part of 2015, and some of the smart people we have elected to represent and govern us in the state of Alabama are trying to bring the electric chair back. Imagine that! I just can't see how they have convinced themselves that this is a step forward. Yet another questionable move by our legislature has Alabama about to shroud the entire death penalty machine in secrecy. Keep in mind that capital punishment is a government program just like health care and taxes. When you take away transparency, so too goes accountability. Do we really trust the government to kill its citizens in a fair and equitable manner while not trusting the very same government to see to our health care or take money from our paychecks without oversight?

This is the same governmental agency (ADOC) that was recently raided by the DEA, where illegal drugs were confiscated, illegal drugs the ADOC intended to kill people with. I ask again, do we really trust the government to kill its citizens in a fair manner? Or, as is much more likely, do we feel that no one we know and love will ever be in danger from this particular governmental program, so we allow it to slip through the cracks while we focus on matters we feel have a higher chance of impacting our own and our loved ones' lives? Are we going to allow the state to gut the very first amendment and kill with impunity based on a triage principle? Unfortunately, I fear we will.

In better news, both of the men who had scheduled execution dates received stays and are safe for now. The US Supreme Court will hear a case in April concerning the midazolam drug protocol with a ruling to come in June. Florida, upon whose protocol Alabama based theirs, has suspended any executions until the outcome of the Supreme Court (Oklahoma) case. Let us hope that Alabama has the same good sense! Until next time, please keep Hope alive.

A Christian Perspective

Ronald B. Smith • January–March 2015

Greetings and salutations! Well, the new year came with some surprises and a warning to those of us on Alabama's death row. The surprises—some good and some bad—gave hope and hardened the resolve of those of us fighting this cause. Execution dates were set for the first time in a while. Some of the guys here on the row haven't been here for an execution and weren't quite sure how to feel except scared. Thankfully, the support structures were in place and the attorneys for the two men were on their toes. A lot of heretofore uninterested parties here on the row turned their eyes on the men of PHADP and were welcomed back into the fold. And the core (board) rededicated itself as though it were a new day—and indeed it was.

The warning was given by the state itself. It was given in both subtle and overt statements made by various government representatives. The state is reenergizing itself to continue the battle. The lull we have been experiencing is over. The state wishes to make its protocol in secret and keep it secret.

Some good surprises: three guys on the row are going back for new trials, including Anthony Ray Hinton, who has been on death row for over twenty-five years. Thomas Crowe and Kevin Towles were both relative newcomers but there is never a bad time to get off the row. Good luck, gentlemen!

The Good Lord never gives us more than we can handle. Sometimes, we have to be tested. Sometimes, we need to prove to ourselves what we are made of. Sometimes, a family needs to struggle to strengthen itself for what is to come. Things are not going to get any easier until this fight is over. And it is not over.

We are not done yet. Just trying to keep it positively real. Thank you all for helping us to "Keep Hope Alive"!

Untitled

Jeffery Lee • January-March 2015

The state of Alabama has decided to expand its reach to all over the United States of America to come up with the perfect execution protocol. The state has decided to modify its protocol following the state of Florida.

Midazolam has been added to Alabama's execution protocol. Midazolam has an extensive history of causing malfunctions in executions from Oklahoma and Ohio. Recently in Oklahoma, the guy strapped to the gurney was heard yelling that his veins felt like they were on fire.* So midazolam has been just a mask over the face of the potential failure of execution protocols. The new combinations of drugs result in death but at the risk of excruciating pain. The appetite for revenge has started to outweigh the hope of justice in most death penalty cases.

Alabama is trying to go around federal law to execute two guys who have been issued stays. Tommy Arthur and William Kuenzel have been issued stays, but the state of Alabama has decided to continue to run their execution protocol as if the stays hadn't been issued at all. The state has decided to override the federal court ruling to allow gay people the right to marry in the state. Alabama has decided to allow county probate judges to override federal law and close their offices and not issue marriage licenses.

Our state has allowed for the risk of something to go wrong in executions by adding a lethal combination of drugs with the history of mistakes occurring during executions. The most perfect execution protocol is to have no death penalty at all.

---

* The botched execution of Clayton Lockett garnered national media attention.

Untitled

Greg Hunt • January–March 2015

After arriving on death row, execution was then by electric chair. High voltage electricity frying the body. You could smell the smoke and burning flesh, and then see the corpse driven off by the coroner. That Sunday, all involved in the execution went to church shouting, "Hallelujah, Jesus, he got what he deserved, bless us Lord!"

Today, the government wants to execute using a death cocktail, which is midazolam hydrochloride, rocuronium bromide, and potassium chloride. This potassium chloride fries every living cell in the body, resulting in a person having a heart attack. For that reason, the Supreme Court has said that if the first drug does not adequately sedate, then the effect of potassium chloride would violate the Eighth Amendment, which bars cruel and unusual punishment.

I learned while reading history in school, they used to set the condemned on fire. In the sixth century BC, there was the "Brazen Bull," a huge bull made of brass. The condemned were put inside, and a fire was lit underneath. The cry, the scream, the yelling of one being burnt alive made a noise coming out of the bull's nose and mouth. It made it sound as if the bull had come alive. In revelry, they all shouted to their god, "Hallelujah, he got what he deserved, bless us Lord!"

Almost all "professing" Christians, whether they realize it or not, go to church on Sunday, raise up their hands and shout, "Glory Hallelujah Jesus, we are sending another to hell, not only are we going to kill his body, but we are going to burn every living cell in his body, bless us Lord! Hallelujah!" Then they wonder why the world is not changing for the better.

the Editor's Desk

Ronald B. Smith • April–June 2015

Summer is upon us and so is the heat and humidity. Here at Holman, the board has undergone a changing of the guard. If this were Buckingham Palace, there would be fanfare and pageantry; but we're simple folk, so we sat around and discussed our options, took a few votes, and then called our Outmate [Esther Brown] and made her aware of the changes. Not as easy as that, but you get the gist. There are some new names on the board and a couple of old timers like myself. For those who don't know me, I am Ronald B. Smith Jr. and I have been voted chairman of the board of directors for PHADP. I have been here at Holman since October 7, 1995, and I worked my way from a group to the sub-board and then after being voted to the board I held several positions including assistant coordinator, coordinator, vice chairman, and editor of "A Christian Perspective."* I have been involved with the editing, typing, and formatting of the newsletters since about 1997. I have as of late been trying to write to everyone on our advisory board to introduce myself and thank each of them for their support. One thing I bring to the table (other than the requisite death sentence) is a long and productive relationship with our executive director. I truly see her as our Outmate. I promise you that I will do the best I know how. I've had the best mentors one can imagine and I will not let them down. It is a new day but there is still work to do, and with your continued support, we will get rid of the death penalty in Alabama. I truly believe we will.

---

* "A Christian Perspective" is an insert embedded within the *On Wings of Hope* quarterly newsletter.

Guerrilla Warfare

Anthony Boyd • April-June 2015

In the *Glossip* [*v. Oklahoma*] case, the justices were there to decide whether or not the drug midazolam, which has been used in numerous botched executions, has been/is violating the cruel and unusual amendment in the Constitution.[†] Instead of focusing on that, they decide to launch attacks on death penalty abolitionist groups. They evidently feel death penalty abolitionists don't have the right under the Constitution to speak up, speak out and challenge things they don't agree with! Go figure! The great protectors of the Constitution (for all) want to limit it when it suits them (for some).

They made statements that there would have been better drugs with which to execute (kill, murder) if drug manufacturers weren't under constant attack from abolitionist groups. They said that "what it amounts to is guerrilla warfare."[‡]

I wonder what those justices would have told our Civil Rights leaders when they were boycotting the buses and eateries. "Just be quiet and accept?" When police were beating them, turning hoses on them, would they have said, "Hold still—it's just a little water"?

Torture is cruel and unusual punishment.

---

† See Joel B. Zivot, Mark A. Edgar, and David A. Lubarsky, "Execution by Lethal Injection: Autopsy Findings of Pulmonary Edema," *medRxiv* (August 2022), doi: https://doi.org/10.1101/2022.08.24.22279183.

‡ Justice Alito asked, "Is it appropriate for the judiciary to countenance what amounts to a guerrilla war against the death penalty which consists of efforts to make it impossible for the states to obtain drugs that could be used to carry out capital punishment with little, if any, pain?" See Lyle Denniston, "Argument Analysis: Impatience with Death Penalty Resistance," *SCOTUSblog*, April 29, 2015, https://www.scotusblog.com/2015/04/argument-analysis-impatience-with-death-penalty-resistance.

Alabama Chooses Death

Internal Exiler 33 • April–June 2015

Anthony Ray Hinton was exonerated and released from Alabama's death row after spending thirty years in custody for crimes he did not commit. According to the Equal Justice Initiative, he is "among the longest serving condemned prisoners to be freed after presenting evidence of his innocence" because prosecutors refused to reexamine his case.* William Ziegler was released from custody upon pleading guilty to a lesser charge following the disclosure of prosecutorial misconduct in the case.

Is the state of Alabama violating human rights by forcing capital punishment on innocent and wrongfully convicted US citizens? You decide while the US Supreme Court juggles which method of poisons they will allow to be used to kill her next citizens.

Alabama condemned Anthony Ray Hinton to a death pit where over two hundred US citizens were executed by their death squads from 1927 until 2013. From 1983 until now, fifty-five men were murdered by the state of Alabama. Alabama bit down like a vicious king snake and held onto Mr. Hinton for thirty long, hard years. He was set free on April 3 with no apology from the governor or any elected officials. Alabama refuses to admit that capital punishment discriminates based on your race and indigent status.

Two weeks after Anthony Ray Hinton was set free, William Ziegler was freed from the same pythonic hold of Alabama's capital legal system. After spending seventeen years in the jaws of death, he was able to swim out to freedom's shore and tell the story of how Alabama attempted to murder him with diabolical poisons while the men he knew had their flesh fried out with a demonic beast called the "Yellow Mama."

Mr. Hinton is the 152nd person exonerated in the US.

It's one way in but two ways out. Alabama chooses death.

---

* "Anthony Ray Hinton," Equal Justice Initiative, https://eji.org/cases/ anthony-ray-hinton.

Supreme Ruse
The Botched Ruling
Castro • July–September 2015

In a narrow 5–4 decision, the Supreme Court ruled in Glossip v. Gross (2015) that lethal injections involving midazolam do not violate the Eighth Amendment. The ruling also established the threshold that people on death row must identify a "known and available viable alternative method" that involves less pain.

Midazolam is still on its feet after being knocked out and unconscious by several US Supreme Court justices. Midazolam was not physically in shape when it stepped into the legal ring, sweating evasively and walking on a cane of falsehood. Midazolam threw an empty punch at us by stating that it renders condemned humans unconscious before capital penalty states inject the paralytic and potassium chloride. Evidence reveals in several botched executions that midazolam isn't always reliable.

Dr. Evans, the state expert, helped midazolam to bob and weave in the court over and under the Eighth Amendment of the US Constitution, which prohibits cruel and unusual punishment by claiming, for example, that 500 milligrams are needed to render a human unconscious, and that it doesn't matter if the execution is speedy or if it is a two-hour torturous procedure with gasping and writhing convulsions.

It's bad enough that much of our country believes that capital punishment is constitutional, but it's much worse when the requirements vary from state to state. Some states require a unanimous (12–0) jury vote to sentence a convict to death. The standard becomes easier the further south we move. Alabama requires a 10–2 vote and Florida only requires a majority (7–5) vote. Does this sound like a country of united people and states?

PART V

Botched Rulings and Botched Executions

2016–2020

From the Editor's Desk

Ronald B. Smith • January–March 2016

On January 21, 2016, the state of Alabama ended a two year run sans executions by killing Chris Brooks. He is missed by a myriad of friends and family on the row and off. The state is reeling from the bad publicity it has received for its administering of law and order, from Dothan, where police officers planted drugs on people; Birmingham, where an unarmed Black teen was gunned down; and Gadsden and Huntsville, whose district attorneys began capital trials while the specter of a recent SCOTUS ruling in the *Hurst* case out of Florida could cause the cases to be overturned on appeal.

The Alabama Senate has decided to take on the issue of innocents in prison and on death row by introducing Senate Bill 237, which would create an Innocence Commission to review cases and file subsequent referrals to state courts for proper adjudication. Section 12 of this bill reads, "There shall be a moratorium on all executions in the state of Alabama until June 1, 2017." If this bill passes as is, we should have another year sans executions. Senate Bills 117, 152, 153, 154, and 155 also deal with death penalty issues and all were submitted by Senator Hank Sanders of Selma, Alabama.

There is reason for hope. A former chief justice of the Georgia Supreme Court noted recently that the death penalty will end in three to six years. Pope Francis spoke out against the death penalty again and will be holding an international forum on capital punishment in Rome. And we may get a Supreme Court justice who can sway the balance against state-sanctioned murder and its proponents for good. Now is not a time to give up. Now is a time to rally for Hope.

Untitled

Randy Lewis • January–March 2016

The refusal of Republicans in Congress to allow the Obama administration to appoint a replacement for Justice Scalia would set the tone for a contentious series of Supreme Court appointments over the next six years. People on death row rely on the federal courts for appeals as well as habeas corpus; the Supreme Court also has the authority to issue and lift stays prior to state-level executions.

In the wake of the death of United States Supreme Court justice Antonin Scalia, Congress vows to not even consider the president's nominee for his replacement.

According to the Constitution, the president is obligated to nominate someone he finds to be qualified to fill the vacancy of any federal justice seat.

According to the Constitution, Congress is obligated to hold a hearing and to consider the president's nominee.

Instead, Congress vows not to even consider the president's nominee. How could Congress reasonably expect the citizens of this nation to abide by the laws that they pass when they won't abide by them?

Alabama (Un)Just Being Alabama

Maximus Strong • January–March 2016

The Supreme Court ruled in Hurst v. Florida *(2016) that Florida's capital sentencing scheme was unconstitutional. Under the overturned statute, juries made recommendations to judges in an advisory capacity only, which the Court found to violate the Sixth Amendment's protection of the defendant's right to a trial by jury.*

There are three states in which a judge can override a jury's decision regarding capital punishment: Florida, Delaware, and Alabama. The Supreme Court has finally decided that such a scheme is unconstitutional. A jury's decision should not be a mere recommendation. However, one of these states is not like the others.

Two of the three states, following the *Hurst* ruling out of Florida, have begun reconstructions projects to "fix" their broken death penalty schemes, while one state remains in denial and as defiant as ever.

Alabama always seems to be first in all the wrong things.

Even after the *Hurst* ruling, they continue to press forward with capital cases, telling the public that the *Hurst* ruling does not apply to Alabama.

In a prior challenge to Alabama's death penalty, *Harris v. Alabama*, the Alabama Criminal Court of Appeals clearly states that "the Alabama death penalty scheme is based on Florida's sentencing scheme."

Three states were addressed in the *Hurst* ruling . . . Florida, Delaware, annnnd ALABAMA!!

A Christian Perspective

Anthony Tyson • April–June 2016

The US Supreme Court has spoken to the state of Alabama. SCOTUS remanded *Johnson v. Alabama* to the lower courts to re-examine Alabama's death penalty statute in relation to a recent ruling out of Florida.* Alabama and Florida's death penalty statutes are almost identical, with some of the same flaws, such as a judge taking over the Constitutional right that the Sixth Amendment guarantees: a fair trial by a jury of our peers. But I am in no delusion that this state will automatically do the right thing. We live in a very bloodthirsty place that thrives on revenge killing. We kill more than any other state per capita in the South.

A moratorium would have allowed Alabama to re-examine this statute as well.

---

* The plaintiff in *Johnson v. Alabama* was PHADP board member Bart Johnson.

Win, Lose, or Draw?

Castro • April–June 2016

Thanks to the recent *Hurst* case in Florida, hundreds of inmates are going to have their death sentences converted to life without the possibility of parole. This is a "win" we are hoping to see in the rest of the states that still have and/or practice this cruel and unusual punishment. But is there really a difference in spending twenty to thirty years on death row awaiting execution as opposed to spending twenty to thirty years, the average remaining lifespan of an inmate, in population? Either way, men and women are sentenced to die in prison. That doesn't sound like a win to me. A step in the right direction, maybe, but not a win.

We've won the fight, but not the war; the battle rages on.

the Editor's Desk

Ronald B. Smith • July–September 2016

A man I greatly respected died this summer. James "Bo" Cochran (fig. 29), a co-founder of PHADP and a friend to this board, died July 12 at the age of seventy-three. Bo lost more than nineteen years due to police and prosecutorial misconduct until he was set free in 1997.* Rest in peace, my friend.

We also lost Joseph Hooks on August 13 of natural causes here at Holman. Our prayers go out to their families.

The debate over the death penalty continues amongst the general public. Polls show that fewer Americans support the death penalty today than a few years ago. California and Nebraska voters will have their say this fall as both states are putting it before the voters. Thurgood Marshall, one of the most renowned US Supreme Court justices, said, "The American people are largely unaware of the information critical to a judgment on the morality of the death penalty . . . if they were better informed, they would consider it shocking, unjust, and unacceptable."† I believe the recent actions of the United States Supreme Court are opening peoples' eyes to the realities of the complex nature of capital punishment.

FIGURE 29. Bo Cochran, advocating with PHADP for a moratorium on capital punishment at the state capitol ca. 2008

Thank you to all who have shown support by mail, email, over the phone. Thank you for helping to "Keep Hope Alive."

---

* Bo Cochran spent twenty-one years on death row before he was finally exonerated. See "Alabama's Exonerated," Equal Justice Initiative, https://eji.org/alabama-exonerated/.

† From Marshall's dissenting opinion in *Gregg v. Georgia* (1976), 428 US 153.

Political Put-Away

Clayton Shanklin • July–September 2016

Judges in the US South are elected to their positions. Shanklin is Black; his victim was white.

I was sent to death row from Walker County by a jury override. Twelve jurors voted for life without parole; one elected judge sentenced me to death. Yeah—a political put-away, as it was an election year. The judge seized the perfect opportunity to send a powerful message to the community, especially since the nature of the case was Black on white. At first, I had a paid lawyer who was disbarred a month before my trial. Then the judge appointed me the same lawyer I had previously fired because he had never tried a capital case without calling me back to court to seal his election. Once I was convicted, the lawyer withdrew from my case claiming that it was a conflict of interest.

They are patiently willing to kill us, one by one. They want to strap us down and put a needle in our veins that causes us to suffocate while an audience gets to watch through glass until you take your last breath. But we are the monsters.

the Editor's Desk

Ronald B. Smith • October-December 2016

Executive director Esther Brown's greeting reads: "This Christmas edition of On Wings of Hope *is put together at the end of November and will be in the mail by December 8th—the day on which, if there is not a stay, there will be an execution in Alabama, the execution of our Chairman and my friend Ronald Smith."*

This year has been trying for me personally and a test of my faith. But I had the best teachers and mentors when it came to this situation. My family, on the other hand, had no practical experience and so I set my sights on being a comfort. My parents and I, and also my son and I, have been having some frank discussions—things that needed to be said. I recommend that you say the things that need to be said as soon as you can—you don't have to wait until you find yourself in dire straits.

For those wondering about the state of PHADP: well, to use a sports analogy, we are on the goal line but our opponents don't seem to realize it. Time is running out on them, not us.

A personal thank you to everyone who wrote the governor on my behalf. To my legal team: thank you for your diligence, professionalism, and for all of the time I posited theories to test the boundaries of the law and you kept from saying, "No, convict, that won't work." Although, Jon—you do have to admit that my belief about ineffective counsel post-conviction, the three facets of jury override claims, and the "suicidal burden" claim will all pan out. Just need the right court. I look forward to more philosophy in the new year.

See you next year.

the Editor's Desk

The United States Supreme Court

Ronald B. Smith • (2005; reprinted January–March 2016)

The botched execution of Ronald B. Smith was widely reported throughout the US. According to journalist Kent Faulk, who witnessed the execution, Smith "heaved and coughed for 13 minutes" while midazolam was being administered. *Smith had been part of the lawsuit initiated in 2012 challenging Alabama's execution protocol, including its use of midazolam. Executive Director Esther Brown's greeting in the January–March 2017 newsletter reads:*

> *The test for our organization came on December 8 with the botched murder/ execution of our chairman Ronald B. Smith. Ron was not our first chairman or board member to be executed and the question of how can one ever be prepared for this kind of test is a valid one. I mentioned the importance of preparation for tests and in our case the preparation consists of years of working together as a team or, as we like to say, as a family. That is crucial and keeps us from being broken by this ugly and devastating test. Instead we become even closer, putting aside all differences while doing our best to adjust to our new roles and new positions. The challenge is to make sure we don't drop the ball while supporting each other. And yes, we passed the test! What do you think? Could our country undergoing its own testing right now perhaps learn from us!*

The following article, which demonstrates Smith's prescient concern over the political makeup of the Supreme Court, was reprinted to commemorate his work.

---

* Kent Faulk, "Alabama Death Row Inmate Ronald Bert Smith Heaved, Coughed for 13 Minutes During Execution," AL.com, December 8, 2016, https://www.al.com/news/birmingham/2016/12/alabama_death_row_inmate_is_se.html.

Where can justice be found in the United States of America? Some would say that the highest court in the land presides over the vestiges of justice in the free world. However, how just are the judges of the US Supreme Court? Are they not tainted by the politics of the political parties and presidents who place them in office? Conservative judges are usually placed into office by conservative presidents, while liberal judges are placed into office by liberal presidents. Even now, Chief Justice Rehnquist of the Supreme Court says he will not retire until a Republican president is in office. Not only does this assure the placement of another conservative justice on the bench, but also helps to ensure that another conservative justice will represent the bench as chief justice.

Lately, the court's reputation has been marred by reports of infighting amongst the justices. Issues such as states' rights, school prayer, Miranda rights, and grandparents' rights have re-entered the US Supreme Court only to be passed by the narrowest of margins. And currently the court is being asked to step into the election results. They even handed down a clarification ruling in the midst of hearing an appeal on search and seizure laws. And after the presidential election has been decided, the next president will get to appoint at least two justices, including the chief justice. How will that have changed the current conservative climate within the US Supreme Court? How will that affect such issues as the death penalty and abortion, which are expected to once again be tested and heard before the high court? How will it affect the everyday lives of the citizens of the United States in the future?

The past has shown that rulings passed by liberal justices can be reheard and overturned by conservative judges, and vice versa. But considering the current climate of infighting and politically minded justices such as Chief Justice Rehnquist, how can the US Supreme Court be thought of as just? How can strife and political bias be said to inspire confidence in the highest court in the land? While not many questions can be answered without a full review of the court, many insiders think the court should be more insulated from political pressures and favors. In the end, the system only becomes more enmeshed and mired in the business that is politics.

Judicial Nominee Neil Gorsuch

New Shadow of Death for the US Supreme Court

Internal Exiler 33 • January–March 2017

Executions have found a supreme handshake in the highest court if he is approved. Trump's nominee doesn't shy away from violating the Eighth Amendment in recent rulings. Botched drug friends like midazolam will be glad to see their buddy Judge Neil from the Tenth Circuit.

Judge Gorsuch determined that badly botched executions were innocent misadventures or isolated mishaps and ruled that the states in which executions went horribly wrong were not "deliberately indifferent." With a new friend like Neil in the US Supreme Court, botched executions and cruel and unusual punishment will continue.

It Speaks for Itself

Castro • January–March 2017

During this presidential campaign and election process, I've had many negative thoughts. It's hard to find anything positive to say about this system, so I've remained silent. In these past two months, things have steadily declined as tension rises worldwide.

This is a tough time for opponents of the death penalty. Not only are right-wing Republicans marking their territory and staking new claims, such as the newest Supreme Court justice, or the new attorney general, but it appears that all of our efforts to save lives, fix a corrupt justice system, and restore our country are being erased by Trump's horse and pony show.*

While the newly elected president of the United States is busy lying to the citizens of America, Alabama has murdered a man who shouldn't have been on death row to begin with.

December 8, Ronald Smith was executed, although his jury could not return with enough votes to warrant a death sentence. In any other state in this country, that would have spared his life. In Alabama, the judge, one man, has the power to override the decision of the jury that this country's Constitution gives us the right to be tried by. Americans have the right to be tried by a jury of their peers. So why does the judge in Alabama have the authority to override the decision made by the jury that the US Constitution guarantees us?

---

* Neil Gorsuch was nominated to the US Supreme Court by President Donald Trump and confirmed on April 7, 2017; Jeff Sessions, who had served as United States senator from Alabama, was nominated by President Trump to the office of US attorney general and confirmed on February 8, 2017. He resigned on November 7, 2018.

Change Is Consistent

Bart Johnson • January–March 2017

There is certainly a lot of ground to cover for this newsletter. PHADP lost a dedicated member last December when the state executed Ron Smith. Even now I haven't fully come to terms with this loss. To say this is a unique situation would be an understatement, but he is in a better place, and he would certainly want us to continue in our mission. Ron would use a sports analogy, so I will, too: everyone loses at some point, but it's a long season, and we can still come out on top.

The board had to make some changes. Nick Smith and Sherman Collins have moved up to the sub-board. I believe we are well-situated to continue the work of our predecessors.

Both at the state and national level, there have been some changes with a potential new Supreme Court justice, Neil Gorsuch, and Jeff Sessions as the US attorney general. Governor Bentley appointed Luther Strange to fill Sessions's senate seat, and Steve Marshall to Alabama attorney general. While nothing signals anything other than business as usual for the death penalty in Alabama, it does at least bring the US Supreme Court back up to nine justices.

The proposed legislation to end jury override in Alabama is a step in the right direction, but it barely made it out of committee. Alabama continues to lag behind the rest of the country in how it treats juvenile and mentally disabled capital defendants. We are also keeping an eye on Washington and Montana as efforts to abolish the death penalty there progress.

A federal court has ruled the same three-drug protocol that botched Ron Smith's execution is unconstitutional.[†] And even though this

---

† In December 2016, an Ohio judge stayed three executions amid a challenge to the state law that shielded details about the drugs used during Ohio's execution protocol. The stays were overturned by a federal appeals court, which ruled in Ohio's favor. See Jeremy Pelzer, "Appeals Court Panel Upholds Secrecy Order for Ohio's Execution Drugs," cleveland.com, December 20, 2016, https://www.cleveland.com/politics/2016/12/appeals_court_panel_upholds_se.html.

happened in Ohio, we are hopeful that this barbaric practice can and will be outlawed here as well. Midazolam has never been an appropriate drug to use in executions, and one has to wonder how many times it must fail before it is abandoned. Florida has signaled that they are ready to move on, although with yet another untested anesthetic, etomidate. What's wrong with testing these drugs on the worst of the worst? That's the problem: they aren't. Ron Smith certainly wouldn't have been eligible for the death penalty outside of Alabama, and nearly one quarter of Florida's death row may be resentenced due to their unconstitutional sentencing scheme.[*]

Meanwhile, in Mississippi, they are bringing back the firing squad.[†] I encourage you to contact your representatives in Montgomery to let them know how you feel about the death penalty; otherwise, they might assume you support death at any cost . . .

---

[*] See *Hurst v. Florida* (2016), 577 US _.

[†] In 2015, Utah approved the use of firing squads as an alternative to lethal injection. Mississippi—after legalizing death by firing squad, electrocution, and gas in 2017—gave the Mississippi Department of Corrections the authority to choose the execution method for those on death row. See Death Penalty Information Center, "Mississippi Gives Department of Corrections Unprecedented Discretion over Execution Methods," (June 28, 2022), https://deathpenaltyinfo.org/news/mississippi-gives-department-of-corrections-unprecedented-discretion-over-execution-methods.

Lethal Injection

Have We Become the New Guinea Pigs?

Jeffery Lee • January–March 2017

First introduced as a common sedative for use before "minor dental and medical procedures," according to journalist Kent Faulk, midazolam—which is inexpensive and easy to procure—became a staple in Alabama's lethal injection cocktails as European pharmacies refuse to supply drugs for executions.[‡] In a 2012 lawsuit, people on Alabama's death row argued that the drug is not strong enough to mask the pain inflicted by the other drugs. In her dissenting opinion to the ruling in Glossip v. Gross *(2015), Justice Sonia Sotomayor likened the chemical process involving midazolam to "being burned at the stake."*

A federal court ruled in 2019 that Alabama must detail its execution protocol.[§] Midazolam hydrochloride is used as a sedative, followed by rocuronium bromide, a muscle relaxer. Potassium chloride, the final drug administered, causes cardiac arrest.

The new lethal injection protocols amount to states using human beings as guinea pigs. As more states scramble to come up with different ways to execute someone, the risk of pain and suffering continues to go up. Some states would have you believe that the lethal injection procedures are harmless and painless due to the fact that the human reaction to the lethal cocktail shows it, but the pain a person feels during these procedures is masked by the fact that they are paralyzed and can't respond. I believe it is time to put in place the best lethal injection protocol and

---

‡ Kent Faulk, "The Weak Sedative behind Botched Executions." AL.com, February 19, 2017, https://www.al.com/news/birmingham/2017/02/midazolam_from_colonoscopies_t.html.

§ The ruling was in response to a lawsuit from the Associated Press, *Montgomery Advertiser*, and Alabama Media Group following the failed execution of Doyle Lee Hamm, detailed in Maximus Strong's "Travesty of Justice" on p. 281 of this volume. For PHADP's letter to the Alabama Media Group, see p. 303 of this volume.

most efficient protocol, which is not to have a lethal injection protocol and abolish capital punishment.

Ron Smith as Remembered by Bart Johnson

April–June 2017

Ronald Bert Smith Jr. (Big Ron) was working as a trustee when I arrived at Holman in 2011. Those first few months are a rough transition, but he was one of the calming influences during that time: helping me to get settled in, giving me some books to read, showing me the ropes. The first ninety days on life row (we call it that) you are on single walk, a higher security status. But once I finally got off that I started seeing for myself the things he had been telling me.

At the time he was the vice chairman of PHADP. He was there at my orientation and taught me a lot about the history and purpose of PHADP. He also shared a lot about his personal story and about some of our supporters that he wrote. Eventually, I joined the sub-board, meeting with the board more often. I got to know him on a personal level. We watched a lot of the same TV programs, read the same books, and also had plenty to talk about.

Our spiritual journeys also paralleled in a lot of ways. I can't speak for him, but I learned a lot from him about relying on God to keep me strong, especially during this last year. It wasn't just me. I saw Rob lift up other brothers, too, as well as himself. During the months leading up to his execution, he stayed strong and firm in his faith. This was a good example for us.

Ron did a lot for life row, for PHADP over the years, and just like those who came before him, we are dedicated to the same purpose. We have already reprinted a very insightful piece that Ron shared some years ago about the Supreme Court. We will continue to remember Ron and use his memory as motivation and inspiration to reach our goal of abolishing the death penalty in Alabama.

Rush to Kill
Troubling Way to Die

Randy Lewis • April–June 2017

SB 187, the so-called "Fair Justice Act," was passed on May 16, 2017, despite opposition from legal advocates. Alabama death row exoneree Anthony Ray Hinton expressed his opposition in a guest editorial for AL.com titled "I Was Released from Death Row. Under the Fair Justice Act, I Would Be Dead."*

Alabama's legislature is pushing to pass a bill that will streamline capital cases on appeals. This will make it where direct appeals and collateral appeals will have to be filed at the same time. This bill has passed the senate. The bill then went to the house of representatives where it was passed with amendment. The amendment was: instead of paying attorneys $1,500 for capital murder cases, they will be paid $7,500.

If this bill is passed, it will cut years off of the appeal process for capital defendants who are found guilty after the enactment date of the bill. Defendants who are innocent will be at high risk of being executed. Alabama lawmakers are making this attempt despite the fact that Alabama faces opposition for the botched execution of the late Ronald B. Smith Jr. and also at a juncture where various states face challenges to the controversial execution drug midazolam. Arkansas attempted to murder eight death row inmates throughout the month of April. Three were botched and two received stays. Arkansas used midazolam in all three botched executions. Yet Alabama continues to seek execution dates and attempts to speed up death penalty appeals . . .

---

* Anthony Ray Hinton, "I Was Released from Death Row. Under the Fair Justice Act, I'd Be Dead," AL.com, April 27, 2017, https://www.al.com/opinion/2017/04/i_was_released_from_death_row.html.

Do You Remember Where the Line is S'pose to Go?

Jesse M. D. Y. Phillips • April–June 2017

The Hippocratic Oath requires physicians to vow that they will "do no harm." Consequently, prison staff—not medical professionals—perform lethal injections as part of an execution team.

Hello! I'm talking to you. / Who, me? I wasn't here last time. That's probably why it didn't go right. / Well, if you wasn't here then I'm not talking to you, am I. Matter of fact, why are you here now. Never mind—if you know, just tell me. / Look, it's not your job to know what line goes where. / I know it's not my job to know, but I want to know. Like you said, you wasn't here last time, but I was, and I don't want to see that again. If you had been here, you would understand. / Yo, I heard about that. Was it that bad? / Yes, it was that bad. If you ever see something like that, you will never forget it. / I heard they told them to continue like everything was going as planned. / Look: I don't want to talk about it. I don't see how you can do this to people you know. / Well, we really don't know them, plus it's good money. / Well for me it's not that easy. This is the second and last one for me. I don't need the money that bad. / And that's why they tell you not to get to know them, keep them at arm's length and you would be able to do your job. / This isn't my job. My job is to keep them from killing each other. Not kill them. I'm not that cold hearted. But you go right ahead. I'm good. Now will you show me how it's s'pose to go so we can get out of here please! / Yeah I'll show you.

Life Row

Justice Knight • April–June 2017

As I still frequently think to myself, "How did I end up on death row?" . . . I came here not knowing what to expect. Once I got here, I seen guys that showed compassion. Care for one another and welcome you with open arms. I thought for a second, this is too good to be true. You are not about to con me out of anything. But it was quite the contrary. There were no schemes or strings attached. I can't speak for what their charges are or what the courts found them allegedly guilty of, but I will speak of their character. From my own observation, this is not death row . . . this is LIFE ROW! There is an abundance of life shown through us. There is love. There is compassion. There is hope for a brighter day. But most of all, I see changed hearts, renewed minds, and loving spirits. We may have come to death row as the courts seen fit to put us to death. But we found life! And life more abundantly. To everyone, join the fight and help us abolish the death penalty once and for all . . .

The Arkansas Effect
Eight in Eleven

Jeffery Lee • April–June 2017

Due to a limited supply of midazolam, Arkansas governor Asa Hutchinson issued executive orders scheduling eight executions to take place over eleven days. This rapid schedule initiated a flurry of lawsuits; as a result, three men were issued stays, one was granted clemency, and four were executed.*

The great state of Arkansas in the month of April attempted to make the record books. Arkansas attempted to kill eight men in just eleven days. The 8 in 11 record was supposed to begin in April and end on May 1, when the drugs they were using were set to expire. Arkansas was trying to kill eight men in eleven days with drugs that were almost expired. The 8 in 11 record fell short and only four men were killed. Three men were issued stays on pending issues. The federal courts, pertaining to the state, used false pretenses to obtain a key drug stated to be used in the executions. The laws of the justice system should work for both the state and defendant, yet the states are allowed to bend and break the laws to benefit their agendas. Wake up, America, before the Arkansas 8 in 11 Effect becomes the norm!

---

* Hutchinson granted clemency to Jason McGehee and commuted his sentence to life without parole. "The 'Arkansas Eight' Update: Three Stays Remain in Place, One Granted Clemency," American Bar Association, December 1, 2017, https://www.americanbar.org/groups/committees/death_penalty_representation/project_press/2017/year-end/the-arkansas-eight-update-three-stays-remain-in-place.

the Editor's Desk

Anthony Tyson • July–September 2017

We are in the third quarter of the year, and a lot has transpired since our last letter to you all. Sadly, we lost two brothers to state-sanctioned murder. Tommy Arthur, who received eight stays and proclaimed his innocence, was executed in a very bizarre and crazy string of events.[*] They murdered him and started administering the drug minutes before the death warrant was to expire. We will miss him dearly. Tommy was a decorated veteran who fought and carried out top missions for this country—but that doesn't matter to this state or country. A famous rapper once said, this country eats its own. And on June 8, just two weeks later, they killed our brother Robert Melson.[†] Robert was loved by many here on life row. I've never met a man with a more humble spirit. They will be dearly missed. This state is not playing any more games with this killing machine. Just two weeks following Melson's execution, the state has already requested three more. Please visit our website or Facebook page for more information. We continue to get the word out and educate the public about this diabolical practice. We continue to join hands and pledge with our new ally, the Catholic Mobilizing Network. We recently signed a pledge along with other abolitionist organizations. We ask that you all hang in there with us and continue to keep the fight going. We appreciate you all.

---

[*] For more on Arthur's case, including "prosecutorial misconduct, the denial of adequate defense counsel, and questions of innocence," see "Alabama Executes Tommy Arthur," Equal Justice Initiative, May 26, 2017, https://eji.org/news/alabama-executes-75-year-old-tommy-arthur.

[†] For more on Melson's constitutional claims that went unreviewed by federal courts, see "Alabama Executes Robert Melson," Equal Justice Initiative, June 8, 2017, https://eji.org/news/alabama-executes-robert-melson.

War Against Hope

Internal Exiler 33 • July–September 2017

War against hope will not prevail.
The wings are impenetrable from a mortal blow from
ungodly thoughts below.
Leaning on the winds of hope shall get you through,
Keeping your eyes open for good news.
Winds are the sunrise of a feeling of
Expectation and desire for a certain thing to happen.
When you will it to happen
And expect to
The old and dingy washes away
To make room for the new.
Be more:
Set your hope on the wings,
And watch it soar.

Sight to the Blind

Castro • July-September 2017

Many years ago, there was a village set in a remote corner of the world. But despite its location, as in most societies, there were both rich and poor, the powerful and the weak, as well as the wise and not-so-wise.

The name of this village has long since been forgotten, but more importantly, the lessons and the knowledge contained within them have been lost as well. Until now . . .

In the forgotten village, on a day unlike any other, a man was leading his one-eyed mule to visit his friend, Mahatma Gandhi. And although his mule only had one eye, he was very mild mannered and reliable. But this is probably due to the man being the one who took his mule's eye in a fit of rage. Of course, that was many years ago, back when the mule was stubborn and not so mild mannered.

Some time during his trip, the man heard a nearby commotion and went to investigate. When he arrived he wasn't sure what to make of the scene. Two men were on their knees throwing dirt and rocks at each other like children. They were both crying, screaming, and spewing barely comprehensible profanities.

Normally, the man with the half blind mule wouldn't meddle in the affairs of others, but something seemed odd so he decided to separate the two men and find out if he could restore peace and order. And it was only after separating them that he realized who both of these men were. They were the two wealthiest men in the village, owning many, many acres of fertile land and much livestock. Then he noticed the reason for the cries of pain and hatred: both men's eyes had been gouged out.

Blood and dirt streaked down both men's faces. Now that things had calmed down considerably, he took advantage of the opportunity to question them. The reasons for the fight were trivial and forgotten over the years, but in response to the questions regarding the loss of their eyes, the first man admitted to taking the other man's eye in anger.

The second man claimed to have taken the first man's eye in retaliation. The first man took the other man's eye in revenge. And the second man took the first man's second eye because he was justified.

Now, the man with the half blind mule was astounded by the stupidity of their logic. Even though the first man admitted to his irrational decisions, and neither could dispute the justification of the second man's actions, he couldn't understand the extent they took things to. In frustration, the man with the mule began to point out the stupidity in retaliating when even an animal such as his mule could see the futility of their actions.

Deciding the wisest decision is to leave them to suffer the consequences of their actions, he began mumbling something about wealth not being able to buy wisdom as he departed, continuing his trip to his friend's home. Replaying the scene over and over in his head, he realized there was a strange coincidence that didn't dawn on him until now. Both of the rich men, who were so prideful and now left to crawl through the streets like beggars, shared the same name. They were both called Justice.

Last Words and Testament

Torrey McNabb,
as recorded by PHADP October 2017

---

*Torrey McNabb was executed October 19, 2017, for the killing of Anderson
Gordon, an African American Montgomery police officer. McNabb's final
curse, "I hate you," and his final act of defiance, two raised middle fingers—
all directed at the state of Alabama—were widely reported in the local news
media. McNabb was one of several people on Alabama's death row who were
challenging the state's use of midazolam under the Eighth Amendment. What
follows are the final words of McNabb as recorded by PHADP.*

A man who was to be murdered here two weeks before the day of
my execution survived his date. He should've. And I believe I should.
There's no difference in the claims that he and I are making in our
appeal to the same courts, the same judges. We're matched down to
having the same attorney representing both of us in our cases.

The only difference between that man and I is the amount of mel-
anin in our skins. I guess we'll get to see in real time how much it all
matters.

I know that I'm not alone in my anger when I see guilty cops being
acquitted of murdering us in the streets as though we're less than animals. Or when I watch a more fierce public outcry for the deaths of
Cecil the Lion and Harambe the Gorilla than I saw for the murder of
twelve-year-old Tamir Rice. I know that I can't be alone in my anger
when I hear that the city of Chicago had nearly eight hundred homicides in 2016, or when I know without having to be told that the race
of both shooter and victim are likely to be Black.

As African Americans, we like to say how strong and how proud
we are to be Black. But in my hometown of Montgomery and in cities
all over the country, we're killing one another at a record pace in petty
squabbles over crumbs. But like the slaves of old, we stand aside and
we watch as our enemies murder us at will and we do nothing. We get

angry, we march, and we scream about how someone else should do something. But we, especially those of us who claim to be about that life, do nothing. We treat each other as if our lives mean nothing to one another, but we act as though the lives of our enemies are sacred. It's shameful. I have zero regard for the heart that it takes to be violent inside our own communities. That's not gangster, brah. That's backward and self-defeating.

As sons and daughters of the same blood, we have to acknowledge and begin to live by a fact that we should all understand to be an absolute truth: the fact that we are not one another's enemies. We have a common foe, and common problems inside of our communities that only we're in a position to address. We gotta point the guns in another direction. Our lives have to matter to one another first because we're all we've got.

Given the opportunity, I've often wondered what I might say to any of you who loved or really knew Anderson Gordon: those who grew up with him, helped raise him, or who called him brother, cousin, son, father, or friend. What I would want you to know is that I understand what the loss of his life means to your family. I think I can understand because Anderson Gordon was a man who looked like me and whose family looks like mine.

I believe that Anderson Gordon was a good man who loved the people of his community so much that he was willing to wake up every day and put it on the line to help make the community around them a little bit of a better place to live. So I can understand that not only did the Gordon family suffer an irreplaceable loss, but that our community as a whole in west Montgomery was dealt a blow. For that I'm sorry. As a community we are in desperate need of more men like Anderson Gordon.

I understand some of what you've been through in the midst of this tragedy because who Anderson Gordon was and who I am at the core of my being are probably not all that different. Everything that Anderson Gordon was to you, I was and am to my family. So on behalf of my family and from the depths of who I am as a man and as a fellow African American, I want to apologize to the Gordon family and to the entire African American community nationwide. Anderson Gordon deserved better. His family deserved better. And the people in the community that he took pride in serving deserved better.

If these are my last words, I say: farewell cold, beautiful world. Let every witness tell you that the son of Africa stood on mine to the death. I know but one way to do it. To whatever's wise and powerful out in the universe: if this is my last day on earth, show me the way when I get there.

Travesty of Justice

Maximus Strong • January–March 2018

During his thirty years on Alabama's death row, Doyle Lee Hamm acquired lymphatic cancer and carcinoma. In lieu of surgery, the state set an execution date for Hamm, whose poor health had deteriorated his veins, making them very difficult to locate. On February 22, 2018, the state of Alabama tried for over two and a half hours to find a suitable vein for lethal injection. Hamm, who was strapped to a gurney, suffered eleven needle wounds in his legs, ankles, and groin. He also suffered substantial bleeding as his bladder and femoral artery were punctured. Following what his attorney described as "torture," Hamm fell unconscious just before his death warrant expired at midnight.* The state entered into a confidential settlement with Hamm that barred Alabama from seeking another execution date. Hamm would die of cancer on November 28, 2021.

What occurred last Thursday night in the minutes before the witching hour in Alabama can only be described as monstrous, torturous, and a flagrant travesty of justice.

Doyle Lee Hamm was scheduled to be executed by the state of Alabama on February 22, 2018. A man with terminal cancer, and yet Alabama still did every diabolical thing it could to bring about this man's demise before his illness could claim him. Alabama the beautiful, the murderous, would not be denied its pound of flesh, and the wheels were set toward Mr. Hamm's night of torture, both mental and physical.

In December 2016, Mr. Hamm was scheduled to have surgery to combat his illness, if only for a little while; instead, the surgery was canceled, and an execution date was requested and set. The federal courts for some time now have been allowing Alabama gratuitous leeway with its unconstitutional death penalty, and all the miscarriages of justice

---

* For more on Hamm's botched and failed lethal injection, see the accounts provided by his attorney, Bernard Harcourt in *Update: Doyle Lee Hamm v. Alabama* (blog), http://blogs.law.columbia.edu/update-hamm-v-alabama.

leading up to Thursday night's debacle only highlight the erosion of constitutional protection in order to preserve Alabama's death chamber.

The federal district judge that held the hearing after having Mr. Hamm examined actually discussed the findings on the phone with the doctor, came to a conclusion, and then proceeded to confer in the courtroom with Mr. Hamm's attorneys and the AG office representatives. After asking the state's attorneys to stipulate to only trying to find a vein below Mr. Hamm's waist, she then decided to let Mr. Hamm's attorneys know she would be turning over a copy of the medical report to them. Two things immediately wrong with that: first, Mr. Hamm's attorneys should have had a copy of the medical exam as soon as the exam concluded so that they could go over it and have their own expert go over it. How could they bring forth any challenges, had there been any, without seeing the report first hand. Second, in allowing the state to "stipulate" where it would "try" to find usable veins, she gave the state of Alabama permission to break the law by stepping outside of its set execution protocol.

Then Mr. Hamm's appeal moved to the Eleventh Circuit Court of Appeals. They should have, if worth even a bit of their weight in salt, seen Mr. Hamm's hearing in district court for the farce that it was and stepped in to intervene. Instead, they put forth some ridiculous "supposed" safeguards that had to be sworn to come by "fall guy" employees of the state. So damn ridiculous that the representatives for the AG's office in its response back to the court wrote, "Yeah, we'll do that."

Well, after the disrespect was complete and this part of the farce was over, Mr. Hamm's appeal moved to the United States Supreme Court, the biggest joke of them all. A bunch of judges who have a sense of justice but choose to ignore it in order to align with its conservative brotherhood. They granted Mr. Hamm a stay so they could "review" his case. Then, after their so-called review, the stay was lifted, and they moved aside to allow the culmination of Mr. Hamm's farce of justice to end.

That is when Mr. Hamm's mental and physical torture began. For three hours, Doyle Lee Hamm was poked and prodded by not one but two supposed medical professionals, as neither could find a vein.

Veins that the doctor who examined him and gave the report to the district judge said "were everywhere." Veins that two supposed medical professionals couldn't find after ten or more tries. An ordeal where they eventually tried to find a vein in Mr. Doyle's groin area. Their last resort. Determined to murder Mr. Hamm, the so-called medical professionals shoved the needle into his groin area and moved it around trying to hit a vein. To the extent that the covering on the murder table had to be changed twice because of the amount of blood spewing from Mr. Hamm. Finally, one of the two inept medical professionals left the room, then came back and stopped Mr. Hamm from being tortured further. Desperate to kill Mr. Hamm, one so-called medical professional was overheard to say, "I can get a vein, just give me one more try . . ."

And the federal courts allowed all of this to happen under their watch.

Untitled

Bart Johnson • January–March 2018

In Vernon v. Madison *(2019), the Supreme Court recognized that people with dementia cannot be executed under the Eighth Amendment.* *

It would appear that we've dodged the bullet(s) so far this year. With the courts intervening in Vernon Madison's case, and if you believe the ADOC commissioner, the clock intervening in Mr. Hamm's execution.

The truth is, we aren't out of the woods yet in either of these cases. The truth is, so long as Alabama is allowed to keep capital punishment as an option, Alabama will continue to pursue it regardless of factors that make it not only unconstitutional but unconscionable, as well.

There is a long track record here. Attempting to execute men who are actually innocent, men who are mentally disabled, men who are too sick to kill, men who were juveniles when they were sentenced to death. Nothing prevents Alabama from having its way except federal oversight.

I don't know about you, but I feel like the state shouldn't be allowed to continue a practice that it has proven it can't be trusted with.

When a human life hangs in the balance, it can't be left to the higher courts, who are obligated to defer to the lower court rulings. But it is.

Transparency breeds trust. An open process from start to finish would alleviate our mistrust in the judicial system. Exculpatory evidence shouldn't be withheld from defendants, and the execution protocol certainly shouldn't be kept secret. But it is.

It is our purpose to stop it.

---

* *Madison v. Alabama* (2019), 586 US __. For more on this case, see the Equal Justice Initiative's account, "Madison v. Alabama," https://eji.org/cases/madison-v-alabama.

From the Editor's Desk

Anthony Tyson • April–June 2018

2018 has been a fast track year. The state of Alabama started off the year by setting executions every month up until April. We lost two of our brothers, Walter Moody and Michael Eggers. Both will be truly missed and their family and friends will continue to be in our prayers. As this is an election year for two of the biggest names in the state concerning the death penalty, we were not shocked to see the dates and denials of clemency. But we continue seeking ways in which we can educate and motivate to vote.

May has marked our twenty-ninth year of operation. It has been a long journey since our first chairman, Jesse Morrison, told us to "Be the Other Voice." As a group, we have been taking a look back to our past to see from whence we came. It's been exciting to see the growth and maturity of PHADP today over the last twenty-nine years. We have sub-board members today that weren't even born when this organization was founded. The thing that has touched me the most was looking back at all I have personally learned. Darrell Grayson was my first chairman, and as he grew, he made sure those that followed him grew, as well. That is what PHADP is about. We don't just set out to educate the public: we educate each other, as well.

I would like to give a loud applause to Bryan Stevenson and the Equal Justice Initiative for their hard and dedicated work in establishing the Legacy Museum in Montgomery last month. We have read and heard great things about this historical event. Also, we would like to say congratulations to Anthony Ray Hinton for his book, *The Sun Does Shine*. It was a very interesting read, and we are sure it will sell widely.

We continue to see capital convictions throughout the state and this causes me to pause and wonder whether the purpose of the death penalty is really working, or are some of those too preoccupied with the president's tweets to see the error of the death penalty in deterring crime. We continue and we wish you all a great summer. Stay cool, stay blessed, and stay focused.

Editor's Desk

Anthony Tyson • July–September 2018

The 2012 challenge to Alabama's lethal injection protocol was dropped in a joint motion to dismiss the federal lawsuit in 2018 by the Federal Defenders of the Middle District. The lawsuit was rendered moot by the state's passage of a bill authorizing "nitrogen hypoxia": all eight surviving members of the suit opted into this new method. *

Our third quarter has been a pretty quiet one and the summer heat has been bearable. We had a few things going on that kept life interesting in our neck of the woods. Some kind of deal was made with the lawyers at the Federal Defenders Office concerning the future of executions in Alabama. I'm still not totally sure what has happened or what will happen, but I know that an olive branch was extended with the switching of the method of the state's execution. They are moving away from the barbaric method of lethal injection and will be looking to use nitrogen hypoxia, a gas formula that has yet to be determined in a protocol that is constitutional. June 30 was the deadline for those who wanted to opt in to this new method, which would have immediate impact on those who are out of appeals.[†]

We would like to thank all of our supporters who continue to stick with us through this fight. Your support means the world to us.

---

* "Alabama Prisoners End Lethal Injection Lawsuit," Death Penalty Information Center, July 12, 2018, https://deathpenaltyinfo.org/news/alabama-prisoners-end-execution-lawsuit-state-will-drop-lethal-injection-in-favor-of-nitrogen-gas.

† For more on this process and the decision-making behind it, see PHADP and Katie Owens-Murphy, "Choose Your Own Homicide: Tinkering with the Machinery of Death in Alabama," *Mississippi Quarterly* 74 no. 1 (2021): 125–42.

Evolving Standards
of Decency

Bart Johnson • July–September 2018

I want to talk about what that phrase means, its significance in juris-
prudence, and how it may be used by people on either side of the death
penalty debate to mean something other than what it is.

The phrase, the context, and the legal precedent are attributed to
Chief Justice Earl Warren in *Trop v. Dulles*, in trying to explain how
the court can figure out the meaning of cruel and unusual punishment,
which the Eighth Amendment prohibits. The court recognized that
an imprecise definition existed, and would need to exist to allow the
application of the Eighth Amendment to diverse issues. (Justice Warren
gave the basis for this fluid meaning of the Eighth Amendment as the
"evolving standards of decency that mark the progress of a maturing
society.")

Justice Warren also gave us this: "the basic concept underlying the
Eighth Amendment is nothing less than the dignity of man."

His idea was that in an enlightened democracy such as ours, there
should be rare cause to define what is cruel or unusual because our
government would not likely endeavor in these things. Unfortunately,
Texas, Florida, Georgia, Tennessee, Nebraska, Ohio, and Alabama have
shown that they want no part of an enlightened democracy by taking
the life and dignity of a man this year. Add Pennsylvania, Missouri,
Arkansas, Oklahoma, Arizona, California, Idaho, Nevada, and the federal government to that list if you consider that they all handed down
death sentences last year. Sixteen states and the federal government,
definitely the minority, and certainly centered in the South. All going
against the grain of a maturing society.

So, when you hear an abolitionist talk about "evolving standards,"
know that we are referring to the hope that one day these states will
catch up with the rest of the civilized world. We refer to the legal

doctrine set out over fifty years ago that should give the high court a framework for eliminating capital punishment from our enlightened democracy.

When you hear supporters of capital punishment using this phrase, they are always pushing against decency and human dignity. Wanting faster executions, opening the door for more innocent people to be killed at the hands of the state. Wanting more crimes punishable by death, with young offenders included, as well as the mentally disabled.

To me, the direction toward enlightenment is clear. No more killings.

Untitled

Anonymous • October-December 2018

As holiday traditions go, I think one of the worst is the flurry of court rulings that always seem to come down right before the holidays.

I've heard this viewed in different ways over the years. Someone said they were trying to "fly under the radar" and avoid attention while the world isn't watching, while the world isn't scrutinizing court decisions. But speaking as someone who has been on the receiving end of an unfavorable ruling in a capital appeal during the holidays, there isn't anything under the radar about it.

For us, it's a direct hit, when we are struggling to get through another Thanksgiving and Christmas away from our families and our lives.

Not a fan of this tradition.

A Divided People

Maximus Strong • January–March 2019

The state of Alabama denied Domineque Ray's request to have his imam pres-
ent during his execution. Ray argued that Alabama's practice of including a
Christian prison chaplain in the execution chamber while refusing to make
similar accommodations for his Muslim faith violated his First Amendment
rights. The Supreme Court vacated the stay it had issued, and Ray was exe-
cuted while his imam witnessed from an adjoining chamber.*

People around the globe are watching as the United States descends
into chaos and turmoil, on a path to self-implosion, not knowing the
true depths of this country's division. This country is not just divided
because of political party lines. It's not just a division of red states and
blue states. It's not just that the highest court in this country is no longer
rooted in the principles and integrity of equal justice for all and has
become a panel of political pawns. It's that there is no United in these
States. The United States is a very imaginative concoction, devised by
a handful of pranksters in a backroom, writing by candlelight.

A moral compass can only point you in the right direction; it can't
make you go there. When you have a constitution and laws rooted
in racism, division will always be there. No number of apologies will
change that. However, relations were getting a little better for a brief
period of time. Some states and people do not want relations to be
better. Those states and people thrive off of racism, chaos, and turmoil.

Yes, this country elected a racist narcissist to lead it, to be president.
A man-child who spends his late nights fighting Twitter wars with anyone who dares to speak out against his regime. In those states where
people are elected because of the color of their skin, and not on the
basis of their body of work, or the content of their character (thank you,

---

* See Lauren Gill, "Domineque Ray Is Executed in Alabama after Supreme Court Bid
Fails," ProPublica, February 8, 2019, https://www.propublica.org/article/domineque-
ray-is-executed-in-alabama-after-supreme-court-bid-fails.

Dr. King), sits the death penalty. Subjected to laws rooted in racism, judged by political motivation and murdered for the sake of revenge, sit the men and women of life row.

As more states move away from capital punishment, and are even putting forth legislation to do away with it altogether, some states (mostly southern states) continue to tinker with the machinery of death, are continuing to test their hands at playing God. When Alabama murdered Domineque Ray, they once again sparked a moral compass debate with their deplorable antics, showing how truly divided we are as a people. Are spiritual advisors at executions only allowed to be Christians? Are only Christians allowed to take part in executions? Have any Muslim or Jewish people volunteered to be on execution assassination squads, and have been turned down for not being Christian? The questions could go on and on, but you get the point . . . United States of Division!

Milk to Meat

Choose Meat

Willie B. Smith • January–March 2019

A good friend of mine asked me to reflect about Project Hope to Abolish the Death Penalty. I must admit, I was very reluctant to write this article. After twenty-seven years being here on Alabama's death row, my words are few, and that passion I once had is not what it used to be. If I had to define the way I feel right now, it would be simply, "tired." But for the benefit of PHADP, a sleeping giant now awakes.

My name is Willie B. Smith. Some of the fellows here have given me so many names. Butterbean, W. S. I. . . . and Money. Each of these names carries deep significant meanings. Butterbean makes me laugh the most because when I first got here I was skinnier than a toothpick. Now I look like a whale trying to make its way back to water. I say this to give the reader a clearer picture to make you smile, but more importantly, to let you know that death row is a family, and if giving me names provides even a little laughter, then I don't mind at all.

The ride here from Birmingham was a very long drive. There were times when the sheriffs stopped at a traffic light. I would duck down to keep from being stared at. When I was younger and my mom was driving, I would look to see who was in the back of police cars that stopped near us. I would wonder where they were going, but my biggest wonder was, What did they do? Now, instead of doing the staring, I was the one being stared at.

I arrived here at William C. Holman Correctional Facility and was placed in a holding cell that I later found out was "receiving." A white man processed me in, and this man had one of the kindest attitudes I had ever encountered. I was grateful for the humanity he showed me. He gave me a tray. I forget the contents of it. It didn't matter. I was extremely hungry after such a long drive.

After spending some time in receiving, I was awakened and given a piece of paper with my institutional number and cell number. The officers handcuffed me. Other inmates were in the hallway and the officer yelled at the top of his lungs, "Clear the hall! Death row inmates!!" They cleared the hall. I couldn't believe what I had just heard. I didn't know at the time that death row inmates couldn't be near population inmates.

I was brought to my cell and boy when that door slammed . . . it said something. It was more than a slam. It was reality. It was something I had been running from. Now I was trapped. I had to face it.

After returning back from the infirmary, I saw a care package on my bunk. It had what appeared to be a paper with *Wings of Hope* on it, some food, hygiene, and stationery. Reminded by the stories I was told in the county jail, my first thought was to find me something nice and sharp to defend whatever came my way. "No youngster, don't think like that," said an older man who passed out trays the next day. "That package is from a group called Project Hope to Abolish the Death Penalty. Their intentions are to help you, but most importantly to let you know that you are not alone." I said ok, but still kept my eyes open.

Every Wednesday, I heard an officer call for folks to get ready for the PHADP meeting.

In this place, you will be offered two different types of portions: milk or meat. I must admit that I chose milk for a very long time, but wisdom tells me we must crawl before we walk. I advise the ones who come after me to choose meat. Your life is at stake.

When drinking milk, you have these types of attitudes. You believe that, since you are in the early stages of your appeals, that you are safe—and, even worse, better than the next man. I had this type of thinking and wasn't aware of it.

PHADP goes far and beyond to get the word out to our families and friends to get involved. In our own foolishness, in choosing to drink milk, we ignore their pleas.

Sometimes I ask myself, how many men did I help the state to kill?

When you decide to eat meat, you will understand. I wrote the governor, I called the senator, I voted. Because now you realize that saving the next person with an execution date means also saving yourself.

One time, during visitation, my mother asked me about the man near our table who had an execution date scheduled. "Isn't that the guy I saw on the news who had a date?" she asked. "Yes, Mama, but stop staring," I said. If you truly pay attention to the questions your family and friends ask, they're really asking about you. They're seeking information. When you don't discuss the death penalty with them, you'd might as well help the state. If you stay here long enough, somebody else's mama might be asking about you.

When I began to eat meat, I understood the haters who put down PHADP. Sometimes, when you give up, your only cry is negativity, and anything positive hurts.

Some of those men have been executed. Before they died, PHADP held meetings and asked how they could help. They asked us to contact friends and family to help. I did. I stand, and will always stand, for PHADP. Now the sleeping giant will go back to sleep.

From the Editor's Desk

Anthony Boyd • April–June 2019

Being that this is my first time writing an editorial, and this being the thirtieth anniversary of Project Hope to Abolish the Death Penalty, I found myself under self-inflicted pressure to write something spectacular and profound, which in turn caused my mind and my pen to freeze up, and with the newsletter deadline fast approaching, that was not a good thing. So after a few deep breaths, and some mind clearing, it hit me. I don't have to write anything spectacular nor profound, as this organization is both spectacular and profound all on its very own merits.

Thirty years!! Wow!

Thirty years ago, a handful of men had a purpose thrust upon them, that soon turned into a mission, which they accepted, and so have the many like-minded men who followed. For thirty years and counting, PHADP has sought to inform and educate the public of the numerous injustices surrounding the death penalty with the goal of helping to bring about the abolition of such an archaic and barbaric tool of revenge that has no place in our modern society, and that mission continues.

On May 16th, the state of Alabama murdered Michael Brandon Samra, the day after its governor proclaimed that "ALL LIFE IS SACRED and PRECIOUS."* Our thoughts go out to both families.

Our work is not done! Thirty years and as you can see, we continue to be the other voice, and we continue asking all of you to join us!

---

* In a public statement following her signing of the Alabama Human Life Protection Act (HB 314), Governor Ivey stated that "every life is precious." See "Governor Ivey Issues Statement after Signing the Alabama Human Life Protection Act," Office of the Alabama Governor, May 15, 2019, https://governor.alabama.gov/newsroom/2019/05/governor-ivey-issues-statement-after-signing-the-alabama-human-life-protection-act.

Our Previous Chairman

Anthony Tyson

As we mark our thirtieth anniversary, I want to acknowledge some former members:

- Former and great chairman, Jeff Rieber, member of PHADP for over twenty-five years;
- Former coordinator and chief artist, Carey Grayson, member for over twenty years;
- Arthur Giles was mentored and brought up under the teaching of Jesse Morrison and a member for all thirty years;
- Kenny Smith, former board member and legal mind, member for many years and close friends with many of our board members;
- Nicholas Acklin, former secretary/treasurer and member for nearly twenty years.

These men and others that are here, such as James McWilliams, our in-house legal scholar; Larry Dunaway, former board member and close friend to many; Ulysses Snead; and Brent Martin. All of these men have played a vital part in the thirty years of building PHADP. We have too many outside supporters to name, but we have not forgotten about you and all you have done and will do in years to come. Thank you, and we celebrate you as well.

Greetings

Omar D. • April–June 2019

For almost two decades, I have resided on Alabama's death row. I became an active member of PHADP once I was on group walk. Within a year, I was voted onto the sub-board and, shortly thereafter, moved up to the board as an assistant coordinator.

Being part of PHADP brought about a great change in my life. The men of the board played a major role in my transformation, including those who are no longer with us: Gary Brown, Darrell B. Grayson, Leroy White, Ronald Smith Jr. and Derrick Moon, just to name a few.

To me, PHADP was not just about educating the general public about the biased, unjust, and barbaric practices of the death penalty. It was about togetherness, integrity, hope, peace, forgiveness, and being the best man that one can be despite what we are facing.

PHADP also taught me how to be a better leader through my actions. It's easy to "talk the talk," but walking it is not always so easy.

The men outside the board also played a key role. A brotherhood that's unbreakable was developed.

It saddened me deeply when I left for a new trial. I knew I would not be returning and couldn't bring my brothers with me. If society knew these men the way I do, there would be no death penalty in Alabama.

In closing, my fight is not over—nor are my hope and prayers for the eventual abolition of capital punishment. We must all continue to strive for justice. Happy thirtieth anniversary.

Fight or Flight

Jeffery Lee • April–June 2019

In times like these, the character of a man is revealed. The good in a man will be shown only in how he responds to the atmosphere around him. Fear is the fuel to flight. Faith will enable you to fight.

The ability to run away from our problems or situations has given us the opportunity not to face them. We called it fear. Fear has a way of enabling you to cower away from circumstances. Eventually, we become accustomed to fear; it becomes ingrained in the very fibers of our nature. We live with fear, we make room in our lives to be fearful. After we have downloaded fear into our minds, we begin to look for things to be afraid of. In our case, here at death row, some of the guys are afraid of death. So the fear of dying is felt every time one of us is executed or receives an execution date.

There are multiple ways to initiate a fight. Most of you are thinking of a physical brawl. Our strategy to fight is different from most. First, there are limits to what we can do here to engage the public about the battles we face each and every day. One strategy we have developed into a powerful weapon is the ability to voice our ideas and opinions about prison and about death row through writing articles. Also, we create and publish a newsletter called *On Wings of Hope* to get our voice out. The strategies we often use are essential to swaying the public opinion about the fairness of the death penalty. Yet over the years, a lot of guys in here have grown weary in the fight against the death penalty. Some have become complacent and others have become comfortable in this situation. Some have lost the hope needed to have the strength to see this fight against capital punishment through to the end. That is our ultimate goal: the end of capital punishment.

If anyone chooses not to stand and fight for what's important, you'd might as well give up. After almost nineteen years here on life row, I've had thoughts about throwing in the towel and giving up the fight that

I had waged alongside my brothers. When we're faced with adversity and injustice, we have to be the voices of hope and change. We need to put fear aside and continue the fight.

The Coming, Birth, and Longevity of Project Hope to Abolish the Death Penalty

Arthur Giles • April–June 2019

Giles would pass away from pneumonia on September 30, 2020, at age sixty-one. He was the longest-serving person on Alabama's death row, serving more than forty years in custody.

My name is Arthur Giles. I am a former board member. But our motto is "once a board member, always a member." Anthony Tyson asked me if I would write something for our upcoming special occasion. As this year marks the thirtieth anniversary of PHADP, and our involvement in the struggle in putting an end to state-sanctioned killings. This is my fortieth year on death row. I was nineteen years old when I arrived in 1979.

I was placed two cells down from Jesse Morrison, who was one of the first to befriend me. He took every opportunity he could to stress and instill in me the importance and value of education while inspiring brotherhood, hope, and unity among those around him.

How committed was Jesse to the things he believed in and stood for? Just before Henry Hays arrived, Jesse went around and asked everyone, Black and white, not to bother or try to harm Henry because he was in the same boat with us now.* That's how totally committed and brave he was, and he was respected by his peers.

In 1987, twenty-two of us—including myself—were transferred to Donaldson Correctional Facility, the ADOC's plan was to move and house death row inmates there, though after a few months the plan was halted. In 1995, Jesse was transferred there. I was elated to see my

---

* See "Killing the Scapegoat Won't Solve the Problem," p. 44 of this volume.

brother again. Several months after Jesse arrived at Donaldson, he started up a PHADP group and appointed me as co-leader and coordinated our efforts with the board members at Holman. In the fall of 1996, Jesse was resentenced to life without parole and asked if I would take over the group. I agreed and two weeks later, he was moved to another prison. After leading the group for about a year, I was abruptly sent back to Holman and voted back onto the PHADP board where I served for several years before passing the torch to the new generation.

I say this in closing: I pay homage to my brother Jesse who passed on February 12, 2014. Thanks for being a big brother and mentor to me. Also, thanks to the other brothers who created PHADP, which gave me an opportunity to be part of something good and meaningful for the first time in my life.

Alabama Media Group

Thank you for taking the time to read this letter and all the information included.

Please allow me to introduce myself. My name is Anthony Boyd and I am the chairman of Project Hope to Abolish the Death Penalty (PHADP). I have enclosed a brief biography of our organization. We are reaching out to you for two reasons: first, to congratulate you on the positive ruling in the lethal injection drug protocol lawsuit in the pursuit of state transparency concerning Alabama's death penalty.* Although it is still being appealed, the effort in the name of informing the people has to be acknowledged. That leads me to the other reason we are reaching out to you.

Alabama has never examined the cost or cost effectiveness of its death penalty. Other states have, and have concluded that it is far more expensive to execute people than to incarcerate them indefinitely. Just as the citizens of Alabama have a right to know the state's execution protocol, they also have a right to know how much of their tax money is being spent on the death penalty as a whole: money that could, and should, be put to better use benefitting the people of Alabama. As more and more states are moving away from the barbarism of the death penalty, numerous reasons are given for doing so, and the cost of the archaic process is very high on that list.

Why has Alabama never done a cost study of the death penalty?

As the group Conservatives Concerned about the Death Penalty pointed out in a recent news article, "cost and innocence" are major concerns with the death penalty. Note that cost came first in that statement.

---

* In 2019, a federal court ruled in favor of the Alabama Media Group, which requested that Alabama must make its execution protocol publicly available. See also "Lethal Injection," p. 267 of this volume.

In Pennsylvania, state rep Christopher Rabb, D-Philadelphia, listed reasons why the death penalty in Pennsylvania should be repealed, and at the top of that list was cost: one is the expense—the three most recent executions in Pennsylvania (in the nineties) cost taxpayers $816 million. It is estimated that death penalty cases cost $2 million more than non-death penalty cases. Although cost was at the top of the list, there are other points listed that require mentioning: the death penalty is not a deterrent (which everyone knows), homicide rates in states with the death penalty are about 18 percent higher than those without the death penalty, and the death penalty disproportionately hammers the poor.

In Florida, according to a survey on SupremeCourt.gov, enforcing the death penalty costs $51 million more than it would cost to punish all first-degree murders with life in prison without parole.

According to WTFX (Fox 4), the Florida Bar Association's website found that as of January 2018, Florida had about 390 people on death row, which represents about $9.36 billion in taxpayer spending.

We believe that the taxpayers of Alabama deserve to know how high the cost is to continue pursuing the ultimate punishment in their state.

We hope that you agree and can work to reveal the cost to them.

Surviving Death Row

Gary Drinkard, as told to Katie Owens-Murphy

October 2, 2019

Gary Drinkard is the ninety-third death row exoneree in the US.

It started with a warrant for marijuana possession.

My half sister had sold me ¼ oz of dried marijuana that was in my shed. It was stale; I believe the police had given it to her to sell to me. She was one of the only people who knew I kept it in my shed.

The police raided my house. They tore it up. They were looking for a pistol and ammunition related to a murder. They arrested me and my wife for marijuana possession and interrogated us separately. While I was interrogated for a capital murder, my wife was being told that I was a murderer; that I would kill her, too; and that if she did not cooperate with investigators, they would take our children away.

Several days later, my sister came over wearing a dress, which was unusual for her. She was wearing a wire on her leg. She brought up a newspaper article about the murder of a junk yard dealer in Decatur. Every time we said something that made it clear I knew nothing about the murder, she would rub her legs together. Later, they used this garbled tape to convict me: the lead investigator claimed he was listening on headphones and made up dialogue that was never spoken.

They went to the grand jury and got an indictment. In August of 1993, I was pulled over by the police. They jerked me out of the car and threw me to the pavement, scraping the left side of my body and bloodying my knees. They arrested me, brought me to jail, and took photos of my injuries, claiming that they occurred during the robbery-murder.

I sat in a county jail for two years awaiting my trial. During most of that two years, I was in regular population. The staff was abusive. Two police officers drug me out of my cell, threw my arms behind my back and over my head, and slammed my head against a wall, bruising my head, and threw me in a one-man cell. I filed an excessive force lawsuit in the county jail and won $5,000. Actually, I filed seventy total lawsuits for federal civil rights violations on behalf of myself as well as others. Judge Myron Thompson finally intervened in 2001 and ordered the county to build a new facility.

Meanwhile, my lawyers were doing very little for my case: they were not answering phone calls or coming to see me. On death row, we called these types of attorneys "cop-out lawyers." If you couldn't make bond or bail, they would leave you there indefinitely and tell you to plead guilty. My lawyers tried to convince me to plead guilty in exchange for life without parole due to mitigating evidence; I refused. From the way they were behaving, I knew I was in trouble.

I thought that alibis and testimony from witnesses who were with me while the crime was being committed would be enough. I was badly mistaken. The night of the murder, our neighbor was helping us to birth puppies. She was a professional dog breeder and she had the birth written on her calendar because I had to have the puppies

FIGURE 30. Gary Drinkard advocating for a moratorium on capital punishment at the state capitol ca. 2008

registered. The district attorney dismissed the alibi, claiming that she did not have corroborating evidence.

I later learned that the district attorney made a deal with my sister, who accused me of Mr. Pace's murder in exchange for his dropping cocaine charges against her.

The investigators did not explore any other leads, though the man who lived next door to the murder victim said he heard popping sounds and heard a car speed off. The lead investigator on my case later received a promotion.

No physical evidence linked me to the crime. In fact, the crime scene mysteriously burned about six months into my incarceration, so the case was built entirely from the evidence and testimony created by law enforcement. I was convicted and sentenced to death by electric chair.

Upon my arrival to Holman Prison in Atmore, Alabama, I felt a blanket of doom settle over my shoulders. I was terrified to go to death row with the "worst of the worst" as an innocent man. I didn't know what to expect while living among cold-blooded killers.

I was placed in a tiny five-by-eight one-man cell that was old, nasty, and smelled of fear and urine. (Perhaps the smell of fear was my own.) There was a hall runner who passed the phone from cell to cell, passed out food trays, and kept the tier clean. He came to my cell to ask if I smoked or drank coffee. Due to my experiences at the jail, I knew not to borrow anything unless I could pay it back quickly, and I didn't know when my money from the county jail would be mailed to me, so I said yes but I can't afford to borrow anything. He laughed and explained to me that they weren't like that on Alabama's death row—that nobody would want sexual favors if I couldn't pay back quickly. So I borrowed some roll-your-own tobacco and a bag of coffee.

When you first arrive on death row, you are on a single walk, meaning that when you get to go outside for fresh air and exercise, you are in a cage all by yourself for ninety days to make sure that you aren't suicidal or a troublemaker. After the ninety days are up, you can go to the law library in a group of ten or so, and you can go outside in groups of thirty to forty to play volleyball, basketball, or to just walk around the yard. We were locked down for twenty-three hours of every day.

After I got off single walk, I was approached by a member of Project Hope to Abolish the Death Penalty. He explained to me what the organization was, when it was founded, and by whom. He told me that they met in the law library once a week to discuss their business and to help new guys any way they could. I figured I would try a meeting if only to get out of that tiny cell for a little while. It was strange having an anti-death penalty organization on death row run by death row prisoners. (I will NOT call myself an inmate.)

I started going to the weekly meetings and showing interest and sharing ideas and, before long, I was elected to the board of directors, which made me feel proud. One man, a self-taught paralegal, helped us a lot with legal work and would teach us how to read and understand the law. Most of the men would admit their guilt; several professed innocence. This distinction mattered to me less and less; we were all sentenced there by the same unjust system. Everyone treated each other with respect and there were no fights—occasionally an argument, but never a fight. Everybody was working together for a larger purpose: to abolish the death penalty.

When my first appeal was denied, I found myself in a low, dark, ugly place that no one should go to. Not having much else to do, I wrote some silly little rhyming words about the depression I was in—and to my surprise, the depression eased. I continued writing, and my depression eventually went away.

I also began to write letters to everyone for whom I could find addresses: attorneys, journalism professors, ACLU, NAACP, EJI. I knew I had a good chance at winning an appeal, and I did not trust Morgan County to appoint a decent appeals attorney.

Five years later, I received word that I won my second appeal due to prosecutorial misconduct and would receive a new trial. Now I am really frantic to get a decent attorney. I had written to an attorney in Birmingham—Richard Jaffe—who had gotten two other men off of death row. To my surprise, he was one of the few who answered my letters. He said that he would take my case if I could come up with his fee or have him appointed to my case—both of which seemed impossible. I had given up hope. From the information I had supplied, however, Jaffe believed in my innocence. He spoke with another attorney in Decatur—John Mays—and had himself appointed to my case with Mr. Mays pro bono. Unaware of these developments, I had begged my appeals attorney, Randy Suskin, to find me a decent attorney. He spoke with Stephen Bright in Atlanta, GA, who was with the Southern Center for Human Rights. Bright secured for me an attorney named Chris Adams along with several paralegals and investigators. When I returned to the county jail, I was greeted by a newspaper article titled "Drinkard Has a Dream Team." When I found out who was working on my case, I was absolutely thrilled knowing that I could finally prove my innocence.

During my second trial, I was incarcerated at the county jail, where conditions had worsened: it had become horribly overcrowded and people were sleeping on floors and under bunks. Because everyone was on top of one another, violence and fighting erupted weekly. Third shift would wake everyone up intentionally at about midnight. The food became worse and worse as the sheriff pocketed money.* I spent ten months in this hell.

Finally, I won my trial, proving to the jury and journalists that I was NOT GUILTY—exonerated. It was the most joyful day of my life, but tempered by fear: if the police had lied about me once before, what would stop them from doing it again?

The first thing I did when I got out was to get some decent food—something that I hadn't had in almost eight years—barbecue!—while visiting with family and friends.

---

* Ambiguity in state law enabled sheriffs to pocket the money they did not spend on food in jails. In 2018, Governor Kay Ivey finally sent a memorandum to state comptrollers to end the practice, mandating that "leftover" food funds "no longer be made to the sheriffs personally." The money may still go to general funds, however. See Alan Blinder, "Alabama Moves to Limit Sheriffs from Pocketing Jail Food Money," New York Times, July 11, 2018, https://www.nytimes.com/2018/07/11/us/alabama-jail-food-money.html.

My mother had fixed a room for me in the country in Cullman County so I raced there to get away from Decatur and Morgan County.

The muscles in my legs had atrophied during my solitary confinement and it took me a year of walking the farm and through the woods before I was able to start working. I had to start making money because I couldn't stand the way my mother's husband was treating her and I had to get away from there. I saved most of the money I made so that I could buy a car. I couldn't do anything without a means of transportation.

My back was bothering me a lot and I knew that I couldn't continue to work construction, so I went to Wallace [Community College] to sign up for classes in respiratory therapy. I spoke with the teachers and explained to them what had happened. They assured me that I could get a job in respiratory therapy if I did well in class and clinicals. I did ok in my classes, but I excelled in my clinicals. I could feel the patients' fear and pain and could talk with them and get them to do what they needed to do to help them. Within six months of my graduation date, when hospitals were beginning to hire students from my cohort, I filled

FIGURE 31. Gary Drinkard (center), with Esther Brown (left) and fellow exoneree Bo Cochran (right), advocating for a moratorium on capital punishment at the state capitol ca. 2008

out several applications. I had to list any crime I had been charged with and explain. When I went for my interview, the human resources person laughed at me and told me that I would never get a job in a hospital because their insurance wouldn't cover me. I was so very disappointed. I still had to support myself so I turned to minor construction and digging in flower beds with little old ladies.

I was lonely for female companionship and dated a few times before I met a woman who I fell in love with. To me, she was beautiful, and country as corn bread.

Mother's relationship with her husband had deteriorated to the point where she was getting a divorce and wanted to purchase a home. She needed my income to bring hers up high enough. I said sure, I would move in with her and split the bills if she could find a house. To my surprise, she found a house and a loan company that loaned her $100,000 for thirty years—her being seventy years old!

We lived in the home together until Mother passed in 2014. The loan company wouldn't put my name on the loan and, to beat all, the probate judge demanded that I put up a $100,000 bond to become the executor, which made no sense to me whatsoever. I tried to go through a bonding company, but they would not help me. I suspect that my felony conviction played a role. After paying on the house for seven years, I lost the home again, resulting in the breakup of my current relationship. We remain friends and still love each other, but the strain of the situation with the house caused us to argue.

The reason why I continue to fight for the men and women on death row (fig. 31) is because some are actually innocent; some change, and would never harm another person again; and the death penalty is wrong. No one has the right to take a life except for God. The death penalty is political; it is not a deterrent. We are supposed to be one of the most civilized societies in the world, yet we can't find a way to punish someone without killing them.

I think every death row should have a PHADP. The organization gives people some semblance of hope and it gives the mind something to think about other than the fact that the state is going to kill you.

The death penalty is premeditated murder. The state is as guilty as the murderer being executed.

A number of my friends in PHADP were murdered by the state while I was at Holman. I believe that several, like me, were innocent of their charges. At times, when the wind was blowing in the right direction, you could smell their flesh burning.

I still have nightmares about being dragged to the chair myself. When I wake up, I can still smell burning flesh.

Season's Greetings
Christmas edition, October–December 2019

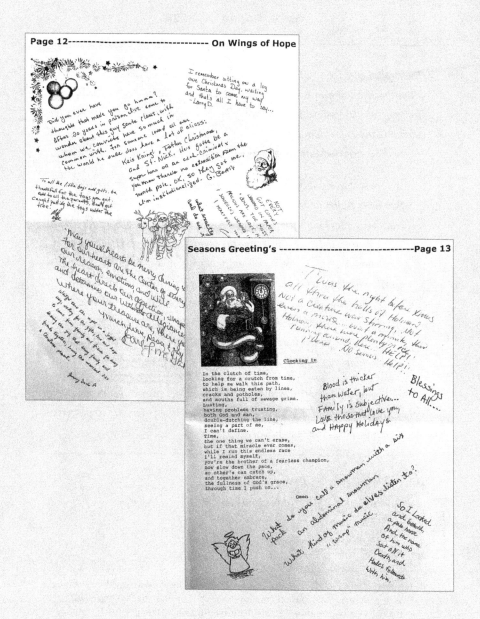

Page 12------------------------------------ **On Wings of Hope**

Did you ever have thought that make you Go humma? After 20 years in prison, live come to wonder about this guy Santa Claus, with whom we convicts have so much in common with. Jon someone loved all over the world he sure does have a lot ob aliass: Kris Kringl, Father Christmas, and St. Nick. He's gotta be a super hero or an ada-criminal x you know there's no extradition from the north pole. OK, so they got me, I'm institutionalized. G. Bear?

I remember sitting on a log one Christmas Day, waiting for Santa to come my way and that's all I have to say... —Larry D.

To all the little boys and girls, be thankful for the toys you get and to all the parents, don't get caught putting the toys under the tree.

"May your hearts be merry during For our hearts are the center of every our reason, emotions and will The heart directs our affection, shape and determines our utmost allegiance Where your treasure are, there you Munch Love, peace & joy

Seasons Greeting's ------------------------------------ **Page 13**

T'was the night before Xmas all throu the halls of Holman Not a creature war stirring, Not even a mouse...... want a minute, ther Holman, there more plenty pey, running around, there HELP!! Please ....NO Sorrie.....Help!!

Blessings to All....

Clocking In

In the clutch of times,
looking for a crutch from time,
to help me walk this path,
which is being eaten by lines,
cracks and potholes,
and mouths full of sewage grime.
Lusting,
having problems trusting,
both God and man,
double-dutching the line,
seeing a part of me,
I can't define.
Time,
the one thing we can't erase,
but if that miracle ever comes,
while I run this endless race
I'll remind myself,
you're the brother of a fearless champion,
now slow down the pace,
so other's can catch up,
and together embrace,
the fullness of God's grace,
through time I push on...

Blood is thicker than water, but Family is subjective... Love those that love you and HAPPY HOLIDAY's

What do you call a snowman with a six pack an abdominal snowman

What kind of music do elves listen to? "wrap" music

So I looked and beheld a pale horse And the name of him who Sat on it Death and Hades followed with him.

The Man He Killed

Nate Woods • 2020

The capital conviction of Nathaniel Woods was highly publicized, attracting attention from Shaun King, Martin Luther King, III, and Kim Kardashian.* Though Woods' co-defendant affirmed Woods' innocence, Governor Kay Ivey denied requests for clemency.

In the January–March 2020 newsletter, Esther Brown wrote the following:

> *We are still stunned by the event of March 5, 2020, when the powers that be in Alabama murdered an innocent man, Nathaniel Woods. Not that we had not seen this before—we had—but each time, the hurt, the loss, the grief is new and the question is always, How do we turn emotions into action to honor the man who was so ruthlessly and cruelly murdered by Alabama? What will you do to honor the memory of Nathaniel Woods and of all who were murdered by Alabama after the outrage and headlines have faded? We will continue to get the word out and work with other organizations and activists to fulfill our mandate to BE THE OTHER VOICE!*

The following poem, written by Nate Woods before his execution, was delivered to his sister, Pamela Woods, for publication. The poem also appeared on Shaun King's blog, The North Star.†

> *Had they and I but met*
> *At some old residence in Ensley*
> *Had they put their badges*
> *Before their criminal affiliations*

---

* For more about Woods' case, see "Nathaniel Woods Execution Reveals Disturbing Bias in Alabama," Equal Justice Initiative, March 5, 2020, https://eji.org/news/nathaniel-woods-execution-reveals-disturbing-bias-in-alabama.

† Shaun King, *The North Star* (blog), March 6, 2020, https://www.thenorthstar.com/p/the-man-he-killed-a-poem-by-nate-woods.

Claiming to be Law
Claiming to serve and protect
Didn't forget to call us niggers
White men's Mentality
Police Brutality
Bent on beating my colored life away.

And now, the kith and kin at once start preparing the funerals.
The cries and laments of the sympathizers are over and they
are calm now.
The enemies are jubilant.
The kinsmen are busy dividing the estate –
and as for the dead man, he lies entrapped by his own deeds.

Such is the reality of mortal life.
The cause of the death is severe indeed,
and, by and large, we fail to realize its gravity.
Involved as we are in our daily pursuits,
we seldom hint at death and even when we do, we just bring
it in as a piece of conversation.

This will not avail us.
Instead we ought to clear our hearts from the thought of all
other pursuits and think of death as if it were facing us.
This realization can be brought by recalling
how you prepared the funerals of your friends and relatives
and bore them on a cot, then interred them in the grave.

Imagine their faces,
their high stations in life;
and then reflect how earth would have disfigured the beauty
of their faces,
their bodies would have disintegrated into pieces,
how they departed leaving behind their children orphans,
their wives widows, and their relatives mourning.

Their goods, their properties, their apparels—all left behind,
and then let the realization dawn on you,
that one day you are inevitably going to meet this doom.

How those who lie dead and still today
used to raise laughter in the company of their friends!
How deeply were they engrossed in the pleasures of the world.
They lay in the dust today!
How remote the thought of "DEATH" was from their minds!
They have become its prey now.
They were intoxicated by the bubbling passions of their
youth!
Today their teeth lay scattered, the foot lays broken; the
worms are eating into their tongue; their bodies are infested
with mite!
How frank was their laugh! Today their teeth must have
fallen!

What plans had they conceived!
How they entertained the thought of making provisions for
years ahead!
And yet, death was hovering over their heads.
The final day of their lives had come,
but they knew not that tonight they would be no more.

Such is my own case.
I am busy planning my life today.
Little do I know what will happen to me tomorrow.

No living being knows the time of its end.
Man makes provisions for a hundred years,
yet, knows not that he might die the next minute.

Keeping Hope Alive

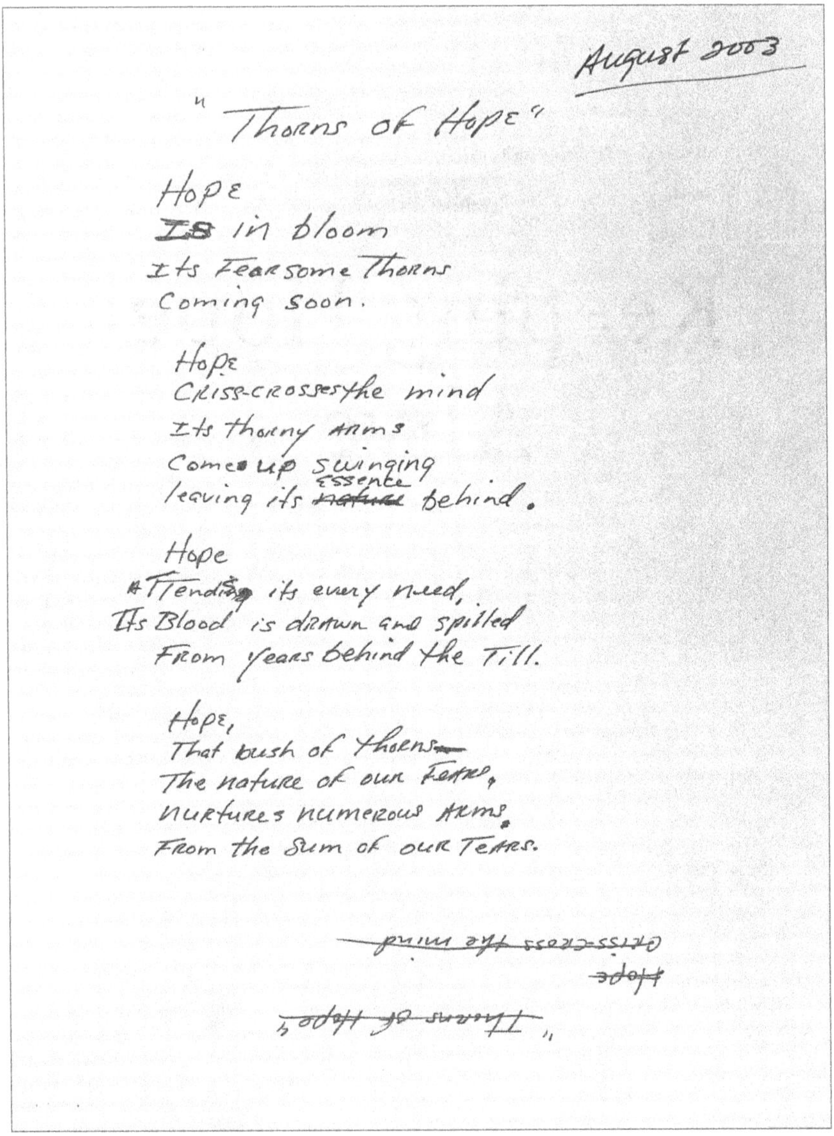
August 2003

"Thorns of Hope"

Hope
~~IS~~ in bloom
Its Fearsome Thorns
Coming soon.

Hope
Criss-crosses the mind
Its thorny arms
Comes up swinging
leaving its ~~nature~~ essence behind.

Hope
Attending its every need,
Its Blood is drawn and spilled
From years behind the Till.

Hope,
That bush of thorns
The nature of our fears,
nurtures numerous arms.
From the sum of our Tears.

FIGURE 31. Original handwritten manuscript of "Thorns of Hope," by Darrell B. Grayson

Thorns of Hope

Darrell B. Grayson • 2003

Hope
Is in bloom
Its fearsome thorns
Coming soon.

Hope
Criss-crosses the mind
Its thorny arms
Come up swinging
Leaving its essence behind.

Hope
Tends its every need,
Its blood is drawn and spilled
From years behind the till.

Hope,
That bush of thorns,
The nature of our fears,
Nurtures numerous arms
From the sum of our tears.

We Will Continue to Be the Other Voice

Project Hope to Abolish the Death Penalty
November 2021

Project Hope to Abolish the Death Penalty is an organization founded and operated by people facing capital punishment. We are the only such organization in the nation: all of our board members are on death row.

For years, this organization has faced obstacle after obstacle. We continue to persevere. The goals set forth by the founders of PHADP were not just to educate the public about the injustices surrounding the death penalty but also included educating ourselves. We also provide a voice for guys on the row and give them a vehicle for using that voice. This organization emerged out of a crisis and a collective feeling of hopelessness. From this sadness sprang forth a fight like never before seen on Alabama's death row, and a hopefulness where before there was none. The founders vowed never again to be without drive, without direction, or without a voice. They hit the ground running to better educate themselves on how to structure and operate an organization—not an easy feat for men with varied educational backgrounds, but nevertheless, a feat they achieved.

As this collection reveals, we stand on the shoulders of the founding fathers of PHADP as we illuminate the injustices of capital punishment. This organization has evolved through the years and has catapulted us to the world stage. None of this would have been possible without the hard work and years of dedication of executive director Esther Brown, the continued diligence of the board of directors, and the moral and financial support of our friends, family, and allies. The humble spirit of community and brotherhood still resonates in the heart of this group of board members. We fight the fight thrust upon all of us by Alabama's unjust criminal justice system for ourselves, for our brothers, and in honor of those who came before us. There are things of note that we have accomplished: the many people, organizations, and entities who joined us in signing onto a moratorium; politicians standing in the gap for us. There is work still yet to be done. The death penalty has yet to be abolished, though we commend the states that have seen fit to move away from the archaic, barbaric experiments of state-sanctioned murder.

We have learned to fight for ourselves. We fight, and will continue to fight, for abolition of the death penalty in Alabama, nationwide, and worldwide. We will continue to be the other voice.

FIGURE 32. Founding members of PHADP, 1990. Front row, left to right: James "Bo" Cochran, Gary Brown. Back row, left to right: Joe Duncan, Wallace Norrell Thomas, Daniel Siebert, Jesse Morrison. Photo courtesy of Tanya Connor

Printed in the USA
CPSIA information can be obtained
at www.ICGtesting.com
LVHW041207111023
760789LV00002B/84